ENDORS

"I've been married for twenty-eight years and thought I knew everything about relationships. While reading *STRONG*, I realized how wrong I was! Yes, I knew the basics—the need for communication and treating your partner with respect and daily kindness—but the author helps us understand relationships on a granular level and offers myriad strategies for improvement. Did you ever think you 'knew' football but then listened to an NFL coach break down the Xs and Os and you realized how much you *didn't* know? This book is kind of like that. It's also a fun and easy read."

— David Aretha, award-winning author

"Finally, a guidebook for men that gives us the tools to help us become not just the best partners we can be, but the best versions of ourselves. *STRONG* is a straightforward and easy-to-follow guide to healthy relationships for men that gives tangible, applicable information on becoming emotionally, mentally, and relationally STRONG. It is a must-read for any man invested in being a healthy person, loving partner, and present parent."

— Justin Baldoni, filmmaker and author

"Kristal DeSantis, M.A., LMFT, has written a book for men not because 'men are the problem,' but because, in our changing world, a resource to help men understand what a healthy relationship looks like for us is crucial. DeSantis, a Licensed Marriage and Family Therapist, offers men the basic tenets of a healthy, equal, modern relationship. Step one, understanding that a healthy marriage isn't about men "keeping our wives happy." It's about creating relationships in which all parties can thrive. This is a book for men by a woman who gets our challenges and offers concrete ways to help us grow. I strongly recommend it."

— Mark Greene, author of
The Little #MeToo Book for Men

"I truly enjoyed the journey through this book. The focus the author placed on six steps to a strong relationship was spot on and addressed all of the areas that we as men struggle with/in. Giving men access to such an informative and psychoeducational guide to creating and maintaining a STRONG and healthy relationship will save a lot of relationships. Thank you for taking the time to write this masterpiece."

— Ulysses Lee Moore, PhD, LPC, 1SG, retired
director of The Hope Project of Central Texas

"As our culture is quickly shifting to a desire for life-partner relationships to be centered on deeper connection, trust, and emotional awareness, men are struggling to find resources and information that help them navigate this new and unfamiliar path. In *STRONG: A Relationship Field Guide for the Modern Man*, Kristal DeSantis lays out a rich resource for men that is relatable, easy to understand, and deeply impactful for the *how* and *why* questions that must be understood for deeper and more fulfilling connections that can last a lifetime."

— Scott LePor, D.O., medical director of the
Texas Juvenile Justice Department

"What differentiates this book from many others is the emphasis on a strengths-based rather than a problem-focused approach. Men yearn for practical guidance on the green flags in life: what's good, what works, and what to aspire to. Men are tired of being labeled problematic. Instead, a message of compassion and non-judgment will help them realize life's untapped potential."

— Simon Niblock, M.A., LMFT, author of
Anxiety Workbook for Men

STRONG

STRONG

A RELATIONSHIP FIELD GUIDE
FOR THE MODERN MAN

KRISTAL DESANTIS, LMFT

MEDIA.COM

STRONG

Copyright © 2023 by Kristal DeSantis

www.strong.love
Instagram @atxtherapist

Published by
Illumify Media Global
www.IllumifyMedia.com
"Let's bring your book to life!"

Paperback ISBN: 978-1-959099-02-4

Typeset by Art Innovations (http://www.artinnovations.in/)
Cover design by Debbie Lewis

Printed in the United States of America

EPIGRAPH

"It is not the critic who counts;
not the man who points out how the strong man stumbles,
or where the doer of deeds could have done them better.
The credit belongs to the man who is actually in the arena,
whose face is marred by dust and sweat and blood; who strives valiantly;
who errs, who comes short again and again,
because there is no effort without error and shortcoming;
but who does actually strive to do the deeds;
who knows great enthusiasms, the great devotions;
who spends himself in a worthy cause;
who at the best knows in the end the triumph of high achievement,
and who at the worst, if he fails, at least fails while daring greatly,
so that his place shall never be with those
cold and timid souls who neither know
victory nor defeat."

– Theodore Roosevelt

CONTENTS

LIST OF ILLUSTRATIONS

THOUGHTS ON A THEME

"Everybody is busy empowering women. The worry is, who is preparing men for these empowered women?"

— LILLIAN ORWAH

I was scrolling through Twitter one day when I read that tweet by Lillian Orwah. It hit me like a ton of bricks. It so eloquently described what I had been feeling and seeing in my work as a Marriage and Family Therapist.

In my practice, I enjoy working with men of all kinds, but usually, the ones who find me (or are referred to me) tend to present as high performing, traditionally masculine men. My clients range in age from their twenties to their eighties, as do their partners.

Men who are: single, partnered, newly married, married for decades, divorced, separated, widowed, re-partnered with blended families, unfaithful, betrayed, grieving, recovering from past trauma, new fathers, and empty nesters have all sat on my office couch. Many of the men I work with are in therapy for the first time.

All the men I work with want better relationships in their lives.

The STRONG model is based on my clinical knowledge and experience as a therapist working with these men, their partners, and their families. This book is dedicated to all men and those who love them.

HAPPY WIFE, HAPPY LIFE?

In 2015, a study by the American Sociological Association revealed that women initiate nearly 70 percent of divorces.[1] There is no study showing the percentages of how many women initiate couples therapy vs. men, but I would be willing to bet that the numbers aren't that far off.

As a therapist who enjoys working with men and specializes in couples therapy, it is common for me to receive an email or phone call from a man coming into therapy with the threat of divorce hanging over his head.

Many men I saw in my office were of the mindset "happy wife, happy life," yet they seemed to be in this confusing place where the old ways of "making the wife happy" simply didn't cut it anymore. Married and partnered men were coming into therapy asking, "What do women want these days?" What I often saw as the significant issue was not the *willingness* of men to meet their partners' needs, but the inability to know *what it was that he was even supposed to do!*

For instance, a widespread complaint from women was, "I want to feel like he cares about me." This would often be met with incredulity from their male partners: "What do you mean I don't care about you? I pay our bills; I pick up the kids from school and ask you how your day was. What are you talking about?" And the women would turn to me and say, "I just feel like he doesn't get it. We're just not on the same page anymore." And often, the men would look at me with a shrug. "You're right. I don't get it. Nothing I do is good enough. She's never happy."

These situations would make both partners feel like there was no hope for change. She would walk away thinking either he didn't care or he was so far behind that it might not be worth waiting for him to catch up. On the other hand, he would walk away feeling blindsided or like the clichés are true—"Women really are way too complicated and impossible to please." What was he *not* doing that she was asking for, and where was the information on making the wife happy in this new way she needed?

What I found was that there was a significant gap between what these men wanted to provide and what they were actually capable of doing. And this is *not* because men are less emotional, or lack empathy, or are not "wired that way," but. . .

They didn't have the tools or guidance on how to do what their partners were asking them to do.

As a couples therapist, I know that one size does not fit all. Still, I wanted to find a guide map, a clear guide as to not what would make one particular woman or man happy in a relationship, but what are the basic tenets of a healthy, equal, modern relationship?

WHAT IT MEANS TO BE A MAN

So yeah, I have no idea. I am not a man, and this book is not me telling you how to be a man. One of my hesitations in writing this book was my fear that this would be the response: "Oh, here we go, a book written by a woman on how to be a man-fantastic!" I get it. I can't do that. I am not male. I have never been male. I am a cisgender female who will never know what it is like to inhabit the masculine experience or live in this world as a man.

So, what do I think I can contribute here if I am not a man and can never speak to that experience? Well, one thing I do know is relationships. I have studied them, gotten my master's degree in Marriage and Family Therapy, and over the years have seen hundreds of couples, families, and individuals for relationship counseling. I know healthy relationships, and I definitely know unhealthy ones.

With that said, I want to be clear that the reason this book is for men is not because "men are the whole problem" or that the use of male pronouns in this book means that women in relationships are off the hook. Absolutely not. A STRONG man needs a STRONG partner by his side to build a healthy relationship. One person cannot do all the work in a relationship—no matter how hard they try.

However, one of the things I noticed in my work is there are a lot of resources already directed toward women. There are hundreds of books, articles, websites, channels, and support groups that speak to women and help women understand her experiences in relationships—with herself, her loved ones, and her partners. I did not find the same wealth of resources available for men. Often, if I was working with a couple, the number of resources I was able to offer to the female vs. the male partner was almost 3:1. So that's why this book is directed to men. To level the field a bit.

This book is a guide map for finding your way back to (or building from scratch) fulfilling STRONG relationships in your life.

Think of this book as the CliffsNotes, TL;DR version of the existing research on healthy relationships.

With that said, there is no "right way" to absorb the information in this book. Read it back to front, pick a random chapter that interests you, only read the client stories, whatever—you do you! However you choose to read this book, at the end of the day, if you find one single idea that sticks with you, one single exercise that leaves you feeling a little more empowered in your life and relationships than you are right now, congratulations!

You're one step closer to being a STRONG man with the tools to build a healthy, STRONG relationship.

"Luck is what happens when preparation meets opportunity."

– SENECA

DISCLAIMER

Throughout this book, I will be using some characters to illustrate the concepts and techniques of the principles. These characters are not actual clients in and of themselves but rather a blend of many clients and many personal and professional experiences.

If you find yourself reading this book and thinking, "That sounds like me and my relationship. . . did I see her at some point?" No, probably not (but I mean, if so, hi!). However, rest assured that these stories are not any one client's personal story. Any similarities to any person's individual experience are simply because the struggles of creating a healthy relationship are universal.

Also, although the principles of a healthy relationship are universal, this book is written with gender binary language to reflect the audience I am writing to, and to speak to and reflect some of the common dynamics I see in heterosexual relationships. This does not mean that the only healthy or valid relationships are between a man and a woman—or that those are the only two gender options.

This book is your guide to building a healthy relationship, but it does not replace individual or couples therapy. If you find you would like some extra support, there is a list of resources at the end of this book.

WHERE HAVE ALL THE COWBOYS GONE?

Change is the law of life, and those who look only to the past and present are certain to miss the future.

— JOHN F. KENNEDY

Relationships are tricky these days, especially for men! The dating landscape and interactions between men and women in relationships have shifted significantly in the past few decades. Relational norms have gone from "courting" to "swiping" all in the relative blink of an eye. The rules of relationships that were rigidly enforced in the previous generations—no premarital sex, no cohabitation, no divorce, the expectation of parenthood—are all optional in the current one.

However, with more freedom comes more responsibility. If there are no explicit rules for relationships, where is the guide for navigating the new landscape safely? Many men these days express being lonely, disconnected, and are struggling in relationships. Often the message they get is "try harder" or "do better," but where is the guide on what that actually means or looks like in practice?

As one of my clients put it,
"I know how to not be a red flag, but what are the green flags?"

I often hear that men are unsure what the current rules are these days for dating and relationships. And without a clear guide on how to "do better," I tend to see a few types of responses: Some men are giving up and shutting down because the consequences of getting it wrong in the dating world are too high. Others, undiscouraged, are simply throwing themselves into the wasteland of online dating again and again, hoping they will magically get lucky and find love. This seems, honestly, incredibly painful and inefficient—two things I am not a fan of. There has got to be a better way!

Alternatively, some men have already gotten hitched, but rather than having a clear guide to having a successful long-term relationship, their strategy is simply "hoping for the best." This leads them into relationships in which their partner takes the lead in the relational space, and the men end up becoming followers, simply waiting for direction from their wives and girlfriends to determine what the next move is.

This dynamic leads to complacency in men and brings a lot of women into my office with the complaint that they feel like they are their husband's teacher or mother—and that they didn't sign up for that! It's lose-lose on both sides of the equation. So what should men do?

THE OLD STRONG MAN

For his book *Manhood in the Making*, anthropologist David D. Gilmore studied men in hundreds of cultures and societies worldwide. He found that there were three primary ways in which men inhabited their masculinity in relationships. For the majority of history, men were celebrated for excelling in these three categories. Brett McKay, founder of the Art of Manliness, summarizes these three masculine identity traits as "the 3 P's."[2]

1: The Protector – Physically being able to protect your family was crucial for survival, and men were praised and celebrated for this quality. Physically strong men were able to protect and keep their families safe, which meant that their families would be able to survive into the next generation. If you were a man who was capable of protecting your family, your community, and your country against raging beasts, marauders, and hostile forces, you were a man of high value.

2: The Provider – Going back to the hunting and gathering days of evolution, a man who was able to "bring home the bacon" was highly desired. Even up to relatively recent times, the bulk of responsibility of providing financial support for a family rested squarely on a man's shoulders. The status and value of a man were often reflected by his ability to provide a robust and financially stable foundation and a "good life" for his wife and children.

3: The Procreator – And finally, masculinity, as defined by the ability to procreate and continue your family line and maintain the family legacy, was another aspect of male achievement that was celebrated and endorsed. The sexual prowess of a man, his sexual performance, and his virility were all markers of masculinity that were endorsed as central to the identity of a "real man."

THE MODERN MAN'S DILEMMA

These 3 P's of masculinity have defined the male experience in relationships for generations of men. However, the dynamics between men and women have changed over the decades, and limiting expectations of men to the 3 P elements has become challenging in today's world.

Do we still need men to protect us women? From who? From "bad men"? First of all, let's focus on helping men not be "bad men" if that's a concern, but also when it comes to physical protection, women can protect themselves too, you know.

"Preliminary data from Harvard's School of Public Health suggest that women accounted for about half of all gun purchases between 2019 and 2021 and that new gun owners are more likely to be female."[3]

What else? Well, you need men to provide financially, right? Hmm, families in which the female partner is either the primary earner or the sole breadwinner make up over 50 percent of American households.[4] This represents a long-running trend that indicates women's earnings and economic contributions to their families are of growing importance. According to a 2020 report by the National Women's Business Council, 40 percent of all businesses in the US are now women-owned.[5]

And the importance of procreation in a modern relationship? A study by researchers at Michigan State University found that

"In childfree women under 40, deciding to live childfree was particularly common, with 30 percent of women of childbearing age identifying as such (rather than being undecided or ambivalent about having kids)."[6]

Okay, how about we take the procreation part out and just use the explicit *P*: the penis? Well, judging by how well d*ck pics are received by the modern woman (hint: they are NOT), men simply relying on that *P* to be their calling card for entry into a relationship is precarious at best and criminal at worst.

Additionally, not that many heterosexual women are getting *pleasure* from that penis. Studies by the *Archives of Sexual Behavior*, *The Journal of Sex Research*, and *The American Sociological Review* found that

> "Only 65 percent of straight women always have an orgasm during sex [with a male partner], and that number goes even lower when looking at the statistics of casual hookups – on a first time hookup… only 40 percent of women [reach orgasm].[7] This was compared to lesbians (85 percent orgasm rate) or women who had sex with both men and women (66 percent)." [8]

So what now? Are masculine men obsolete? Is there room for men to inhabit these traditionally masculine ideals in the modern relationship? Or is it true that we need to either a) send women back to the kitchen so men can "be real men again" or b) resign ourselves to the new reality that "it's a woman's world" and men who want to embody these ideals are going to be pink-slipped due to redundancy at some point?

THE NEW STRONG MAN

In my experience as a clinician, a researcher, and as a woman, I know that there is still a desire for masculine men. However, the traditional 3 P's are not the high-value items that many women are looking for anymore. Those ways of "being a man" rely on a woman playing a complementary role that not all women want.

However, if we are saying that the traditional ways in which men have shown up to protect, provide, and please their partners are no longer doing the trick, then it is *imperative* that we give men other options. Rather than lamenting "where have all the good men gone?" we have to acknowledge the fact that the traditional ways we have encouraged men to show up in relationships have led to depression, anger, loss of a sense of healthy identity, and even suicide when they cannot fulfill those roles.[9]

So much conflict in relationships happens when there is a struggle between men trying to "be men" in the ways they have been taught are valuable and women who are *actively* resisting the rigid return to traditional confines of femininity. But you can't have one without the other. As Jennifer Wright observed in her *New York Post* article on the expectations of millennial men, "Women aren't going to go backward. If men want relationships to last, they'll have to go forward into the twenty-first century."[10] Women have changed; it's time for men to.

Of course, there are still women who want that stereotypical "knight in shining armor, white horse" business. To each their own, but more and more women don't want to play the "helpless damsel in distress." And let's be honest, for men, being constantly shoehorned into that traditional "savior" role doesn't leave a lot of room to be a human being.

Overall, more and more people seeking long-term romantic relationships are beginning to realize that these strict gendered norms reduce them to a role they are often no longer willing or want to play.

Many people these days are choosing to stay single rather than enter or stay in unhealthy or unfulfilling romantic partnerships.

The new high-value partner for those seeking a healthy relationship is not necessarily the guy with the biggest paycheck or the woman with the most beautiful body. Healthy people want to be more than objects fulfilling a function in a relationship. The healthy modern woman is not looking to be sought out as a romantic partner solely for her looks, childbearing, or housekeeping abilities, and men deserve more than being reduced to objectified roles in a few pictures or stats on a bio: "6 figure salary, 6 feet tall, 6 inches-plus."

We need to change and shift what it means to allow men to be men in a relationship. The modern man cannot exist according to the old rules, and a modern healthy relationship cannot be designed to the same metrics we have used in the past. Just as women are more than uteruses and pretty faces, men are more than a fist, a wallet, and a penis. Healthy relationships are not based on objectification of either gender. Challenging men to be healthy whole men in relationships will also challenge how we need to show up and support them as equal partners.

Men can still be strong in a relationship, you can still inhabit your protector, your provider, and your procreator, but let's refine those skills to be applicable to a modern relationship and attractive to the modern woman. A term that gets used a lot on the internet is the "high-value man." Many men still take that to mean the traditional tall, rich, handsome guy that can take care of a woman's needs financially and sexually.

Of course, there will always be people who prefer the traditional model of marriage with clearly defined and gendered roles. However, the egalitarian relationship is one I am describing as the modern reality in this economy, and the ideal for most millennials.[11] Most modern men and women want a partner who is emotionally available and has the skills to build and maintain a strong, healthy relationship.[12]

> **"The new High Value Man is the person who has the skills to be an equal and present partner in building a healthy relationship."**

THE STRONG RELATIONSHIP

There are *lots* of ways to have an unhealthy relationship, but the qualities that make for a healthy relationship are simple: Safety, Trust, Respect, Openness, Nurturing, and Generosity. And lucky for me, they come in a conveniently masculine acronym: STRONG. The STRONG model is a guide to help you be a big shining green flag in your relationships.

My goal in writing this book is to help men have a few more tools and resources to help them navigate this new egalitarian relationship playing field and come out feeling successful—or at least more hopeful. This guide is my offering to you and all men who want to be successful in creating and maintaining better relationships.

In this book, I will lay out six building blocks of a STRONG relationship with a chapter dedicated to each one. In each chapter, you will find an explanation of the principle, why it is essential, a client story as an illustrative example, and tools to implement these building blocks in your life to build healthy, long-lasting relationships. At the end of each chapter, you will find some highlights to reflect on.

This basic field guide of the green flags to being a STRONG man capable of building and maintaining a healthy relationship won't cover every red flag. It won't go super in-depth on every topic, but hey, maybe it will be enough to get you started.

It is my hope that this book and the resources contained within will help you understand what you need to be a big green flag as a STRONG man in a modern relationship. I also hope it will help you understand what a healthy relationship *is*, so you can recognize when a relationship is unhealthy for you. And when you do find love, it can be a map for you and your partner to build a healthy, STRONG relationship together.

TL; DR: PREGAME

1) A STRONG relationship is made up of Safety, Trust, Respect, Openness, Nurturing, and Generosity.

2) A STRONG man has all of these character qualities.

3) A high-value man is defined as the man women find most desirable.

4) For generations, that man was the man who excelled in the 3 P's: Protection, Provision, and Procreation.

5) But for the modern relationship, the new high-value man is someone who can be an equal and present partner.

6) STRONG is healthy relationship material.

CHAPTER ONE

SAFETY

*"Being able to feel safe with other people is probably
the single most important aspect of mental health;
safe connections are fundamental to
meaningful and satisfying lives."*

— BESSEL VAN DER KOLK

GREEN FLAG #1

The first big green flag in a healthy relationship is Safety. Safety is our foundation in a relationship and as human beings. Without safety, we have nothing.

Being SAFE is the first green flag of a STRONG man.

Most people would agree that safety is a crucial part of life, but what is safety in a relationship—and how is it defined? If I were to ask people on the street, I might get answers like "Safety in a relationship is no yelling at each other," "Safety is no physical violence," or "Emotional safety means you can be yourself in a relationship."

And yes, safety is all of the above—and then some! In this first chapter, you will learn about these different parts of safety and why each one is different but equally important. These are the most fundamental skills needed in any healthy relationship.

WHY SAFETY MATTERS

One of the biggest hurdles that men face in the dating and relationship realm is the reality that most women think about their safety needs far more than men do.[1] There is a biological component to this as well as a social reality. Men, on average, are physically larger and possess more body strength than women. Women are also more likely to be targets of sexual harassment and violence.

Of course, men are also victims of violence and can be targets of sexual assault and harassment, but on average, women tend to feel less safe than men do.[2] This puts women in a vulnerable position, and many have developed heightened responses to this reality. A Pew research study found that twice as many women as men cited "increased risk" as a reason why dating is harder these days.[3]

Safety violations are generally the big red flags women pay attention to in a relationship. If you can be a safe man in an unsafe world, you will be ahead of the game in working toward building a healthy relationship. One of the most common obstacles I see with men struggling to build a healthy relationship is when they themselves are a threat to the safety of the relationship. If your partner does not feel safe with you, she will never be able to trust you, you will never gain her respect, and you will not have the basic ingredients for a healthy relationship, no matter what else you bring to the table.

Often when I bring up Safety as the first step in a STRONG relationship, I hear responses like, "Of course I am a safe guy! I'm not an asshole." But when I ask follow-up questions like "Do you know how to regulate your body when you are fighting with your partner?" or "Are there any emotions or feelings that you don't feel comfortable with?" or "Can you articulate why you chose your partner?" or even, "What are markers of safety in a relationship?" the answers get a little vague.

But unless you know the answers to those questions, you cannot even begin to build a healthy, long-lasting relationship for yourself and your partner. Each of those above questions correlates to a specific aspect of Safety that is an essential skill in a healthy relationship: Stability, Self-Regulation, Self-Expression, and Self-Awareness. These four skills are the new way you can provide security and protect your relationship from danger. I promise you that you will save a ton of time, money, energy, and pain for yourself if you get these skills of Safety under your belt before you get into your next relationship.

I would say that 90 percent of people who come into therapy with their relationship in a crisis are struggling with these 4 S's of Safety. Most individual and couples therapy work centers on helping people build and practice these skills. If you read this chapter and realize that you need more help skill building for Safety, get thee to a therapist!

And safety goes both ways. You also need to know what safety feels like in a relationship because knowing what unsafe behavior in a partner looks like will empower you to take steps to address your own safety needs. Looking for the markers of Safety in a new partner is the easiest way to spot the red flags so you can protect yourself in a relationship even before you begin. You also deserve to be safe in your relationship.

THE FOUR S'S OF SAFETY

Safety starts with

1) SELF-AWARENESS – This is the skill of being intentional about what you want and need in a relationship and understanding your impact on your partnership.

2) STABILITY – This skill focuses on creating a stable environment to begin to build a healthy relationship.

3) SELF-REGULATION – This skill will teach you the importance of calming your body during a conflict.

4) SELF-EXPRESSION –These are the skills for accepting and connecting with your own emotions so you can communicate them to a partner.

SAFETY SKILL ONE: SELF-AWARENESS

"In our personal lives, if we do not develop our own self-awareness and become responsible. . . we empower other people and circumstances to shape our lives by default."

— STEPHEN COVEY

Before picking up a guide to any journey, it's essential to ask yourself why you are going on that journey in the first place. The next 3 S's of Safety are the essential skills people need to have healthy relationships in general. Being stable will help you keep your house and your job. Being able to self-regulate will help you be less stressed. Being able to self-express will help you to have difficult conversations more competently. These are generally good life skills and will translate to any relationship—with friends, family, coworkers, etc. However, romantic relationships are on a whole other level.

Long-term romantic relationships are long-term work. Not everyone is ready for or wants to put in the work of building a STRONG long-term relationship. That's okay, but part of self-awareness is about understanding what you want, accepting where your skills do not match the challenge, and deciding to either learn new skills or pick a different challenge.

So, before you get into the rest of the book, let's go to the first Skill of Safety in a STRONG relationship: Self-Awareness.

FINDING YOUR WHY

Why be in a committed romantic relationship in the first place? This might seem like a weird question coming from a marriage therapist in a book about relationships, but really. We all know the statistics on marriage,[4] and if you listen to people's experiences in relationships, it often seems like a giant exercise in pain and heartbreak, so why do it? What's the point?

People who lack self-awareness often can't articulate why they are in or want to be in a relationship in the first place. This can lead to a lack of security and safety in the relationship. If you're unsure why you're here, what's to stop you from chasing the next best thing that comes along? Being in a relationship these days is not a given. It is an option. Why are you choosing this one?

When you have purpose and clarity in your relationship, dedication comes easy. When you are unsure of your "why" in your relationship, your commitment to the relationship will come into question when times get tough. And this goes both ways. If your partner threatens divorce or separation every time you fight, it will prevent you from feeling secure or safe in the relationship. If the relationship is that easy to walk away from, why put in any work at all? And if there is no commitment to put in the work, eventually there will be no more relationship.

Another part of self-awareness is understanding the role you play in your relationships. If you do not know your relationship pattern, you may repeatedly end up in the same relationship every time, just with a different partner. Repeating a toxic cycle in relationships without self-awareness can make people feel like their "picker is broken" or that they somehow just "end up" in relationships that never work out.

People who lack self-awareness struggle to see how they are impacting their interpersonal and relational dynamics. If you are unaware of your part in the cycle, it's tough to be empowered to change anything. You must know what you can do differently to make a difference in your relationship. And if you don't have any power to do anything in the relationship, it's probably not a healthy relationship.

FUNCTION OR CONNECTION?

Until recent generations, the "why" of committed romantic partnerships was almost entirely based on mutual need. Marriages were either explicit business arrangements based on the needs of the bride and groom's families or based on a societal contract that people were expected to follow. The expectation was that most people would get married and have children eventually. Traditional marriage rarely had to do with the personal connection of the two people within the relationship. Finding a match, getting married, and having children was all part and parcel of the expectations of the larger community and society. Relationships had a larger function and purpose to fulfill. The individual's personal fulfillment or emotional connection within the marriage was considered a bonus, not a feature of the role. Marriage and relationships were a means to an end.

As Stephanie Coontz, author of *Marriage, a History: How Love Conquered Marriage*, notes, "Marriage was not fundamentally about love. It was too vital an economic and political institution to be entered into solely on the basis of something as irrational as love."[5] For thousands of years the theme song for most weddings could have been "What's Love Got to Do with It?" The love and connection needs of the people in the couple was a secondary consideration—if it was considered at all. Business trumped pleasure every time.

Also, once you got married, the security of your relationship was based on the idea of marriage as a lifelong contract. Divorce was not something that was accepted in most communities up until as recently as the 1970s.[6] Even then, many people stayed married for the sake of their families or because they thought it was the "right thing to do." Function was at the foundation of most relationships. It brought people together, and it kept them together.

In the function-based relationship model, men were often told that their value in the dating market was directly correlated to their ability to provide financial stability. The higher the paycheck, the higher the man's value in the marriage market. Conversely, a woman's value was her fertility, beauty, and domesticity. Women needed men for financial security, and men needed women to have sex, babies, and a clean home.

However practical that approach was, most people now want personal connection and emotional fulfillment in their romantic pairings. For most modern men and women, getting into a relationship is an option, not an obligation. We are moving away from function-based relationships to connection being at the core of a marriage or romantic commitment. We want to be loved, chosen, and committed to for who we are, not just because we fulfill some kind of checklist or perform a function for our partner.

**We want to be WANTED, not just NEEDED
by our romantic partners.**

THE FRAGILITY OF FUNCTION-BASED RELATIONSHIPS

Function-based or transactional relationships are valid and generally make up the majority of human interactions. But these relationships always have a limited shelf life. When the function ends, the relationship tends to fizzle out too. Think of former coworkers, classmates, teachers, etc. These may have been people you interacted with a lot at one point in your life. Still, over time, if there is no genuine connection to the person, the relationship ends when the function does.

Romantic relationships that are function-based can be very vulnerable to outside threats, because functions are replaceable. This can lead to insecurity and suspicion in relationships because sure, you might have been the best option for fulfilling the need for a "provider" or "hottie" at one time, but what if you lose your job? What if someone more attractive comes along? Will your partner trade up? If you do not know why you are wanted, you will always wonder if you are safe in the relationship and may struggle to feel secure in your partner's love.

The lack of relational safety in a function-based relationship occurs because there is always the fear that your partner does not actually love you for *who you are*, but for *what you do* for them. When I meet people in function-based relationships, I often hear about how well they work together to handle the logistics of their life, but not much else. Function-based relationships work well in theory, but the people living in them often feel unfulfilled and lonely.

Function-based relationships have their place in the world for sure. But they are a lot less work when the function-based nature of it is clear. If your partner wants you for your function, let's say they just always wanted to marry a doctor, have a certain lifestyle, or want someone to raise their children, well, then you can decide if this is a contract you want to enter into. What are you getting out of it? What might you be giving up to be in it?

Both function-based and connection-based relationships are valid choices, but you better make sure you know which one you are signing up for. If you are looking for a connection in a relationship, but all your partner wants is your function, you are setting yourselves up for a lot of hurt feelings, conflict, resentment, and dissatisfaction. If you or your partner are not getting your emotional connection needs met in your romantic relationship, you will be looking for it elsewhere. As humans, we seek to connect, and if we don't feel that sense of connection with our romantic partner, we will look for it in other people.

So, this piece of self-awareness is asking yourself what you are looking for in a relationship. Are you going into your relationship looking at your partner as a whole person, or are you just seeking someone to fulfill a function? Apply the same filter when looking at a potential partner as well: are they looking at you for what you can provide them, or are they invested in forming a connection with who you are as a person? Can they articulate what they like about *you*, not just what they like about what you have or what you do for them?

THE SAFETY OF CONNECTION-BASED RELATIONSHIPS

The opposite of a function-based relationship is a relationship based on connection. As social animals, forming safe interpersonal connections is a core need that hearkens back to our most ancient roots. We want to be seen, known, and accepted for who we are. Connection-based relationships are the ones we naturally gravitate toward. These relationships provide relational safety because their basis is not "I need you for what you *do for* me" but "I want you based on *who you are* to me." Connection-based relationships create a safe space to genuinely connect as human beings.

Awareness of who you are and what it is you are looking for in a relationship is the first step of creating this essential piece of relational safety. When you know yourself, you can share yourself with your partner authentically. This creates a foundation for a STRONG relationship that is based on true connection between two people and is not simply a reliance on a shared function.

Now, I want to add a semantic caveat here that all healthy long-term relationships need to be function-*al*. Here is a little gradient to see how functionality and connection work together.

- Transactional – High Function/Low Connection. This relationship is function-based. The two individuals are not emotionally connected and instead rely on their shared function to maintain a relationship.

- 404 – Low Function/Low Connection. This is a strangers on a train scenario. There is no shared function or personal connection. There is mutual inhabiting of space, but no actual relationship.

- Troubled – High Connection/Low Function. These relationships can last for a moment—a connection with a stranger on the street where you share a moment of laughter; or can last a lifetime—a couple that keeps

breaking up and making up. However, to paraphrase
Esther Perel, not every love story is a life story. When
people love each other, but cannot function well
together, the end result is usually temporary, troubled,
or toxic.

- #Goals – High Function/High Connection. This
  relationship functions well together *and* the people in it
  are deeply emotionally connected.

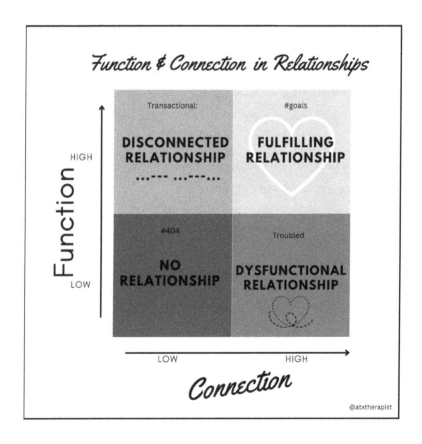

Functionality is part of any healthy relationship, but in order to have a romantic relationship be STRONG and lifelong, you will have to commit to creating a deeper connection with your partner.

And connection-based relationships are a Whole. Lot. Of. Work. Keeping the connection alive is the challenge of any long-term relationship, because connection needs to be continually nurtured. Otherwise, function tends to take over.

MARK and CHRISTINA

WHEN CONNECTION FADES TO FUNCTION

Mark and Christina met in college. They connected over their love of music and travel—and found each other incredibly attractive. They also shared values around marriage and starting a family. After college, Mark proposed on their two-year anniversary, and Christina happily accepted.

Seven years and three kids later, most of their interactions center around the needs of their home, their jobs, or their children. Mark and Christina notice that they don't really have the same types of conversations they used to have, but they both agree that they are just too busy to do the things they used to. They are starting to feel a little less like romantic partners and a little more like co-parents and roommates, which neither of them want. They try to reconnect sexually with a vague hope that will help them to connect again on a deeper level.

On their fifteen-year anniversary, they attend their college reunion. This trip highlights the ways in which they have grown apart. Their sex life never got back on track, and they never learned to rekindle their emotional connection. They spend most of the trip fighting and cut the trip short to come home early. The fights on this trip are ugly enough that they reach out to a counselor, but after so many years of no emotional connection, the work of reconnection feels overwhelming. They stop attending couples therapy after four sessions. Over the next few months, they consider divorce, but both agree they are excellent co-parents and don't want to put their children through a disruption of their home.

Six years later Mark and Christina are empty nesters. They realize that without their children at home, they really have nothing in common. The agreement to stay together for their children is no longer necessary, and so with the function fulfilled and the personal connection lacking, Mark and Christina file for divorce.

When people come into therapy saying that they feel disconnected, it's often because there was a mismatch of expectation from the beginning: one person wanted a function-based relationship, while the other was hoping for a genuine connection. Or there was a genuine connection on both sides in the beginning, but they neglected it and relied on their function to get by. Now they feel unfulfilled in their relationship because the connection has dwindled.

Function will become the norm if you aren't vigilant. Being a protector in your relationship today means keeping watch, not for the wolves at the door, but for function and logistics taking over the space that used to be filled with connection. We'll cover what this looks like more in the chapter on Nurturing, but for now, in self-awareness: when you know what type of relationship you are looking for, you can set your intention, choose a partner who wants the same, and be empowered to create your purpose for the relationship together.

CREATING YOUR OWN SCRIPT

There tends to be an overarching idea that there is a rule book somewhere for marriage and relationships where there is a list of *thou shalts* and *thou shalt nots*. These unspoken *shoulds* and *shouldn'ts* are usually based on stigmas, assumptions, or traditions and don't actually work for many modern couples. Heck, they probably didn't work for many couples in general.

Well, there is no one-size-fits-all that applies to all relationships. There isn't! There is no universal rule book of how your marriage or relationship "should be." Now, this might be the phrase that makes you want to throw this book across the room while yelling: "THERE ARE *SO* RULES!"

Hopefully, this line catches your eye as you are rearing that arm back because I have a point here that you might like. Freedom. When there are no shoulds, you have the freedom to create a relationship that actually works for you. Don't let what you think your relationship "should be" get in the way of what it could be. The modern relationship can be a bespoke relationship curated to fit your specific needs.

When you throw away the "should," it allows you to look for the "could," and the "want to." I mean, if you're going to be in a relationship, don't you owe it to yourself to make sure that the relationship is one you genuinely want?

For the modern man or woman, marriage and relationships are choices, not obligations. Make empowered and honest choices.

Self-awareness and autonomy allow for increased intentionality and personal agency in creating your personalized relationship script. Your path to a successful marriage or any long-term relationship has to be custom-created to suit your and your partner's needs. Your relationship is unique and needs its own carefully laid plan. In order to write a successful script, you have to know what you want your story to say.

There is no script for a successful relationship, life, or career *for you* besides the one you create to suit your needs. Your script may not work for anyone else, but guess what? Good news. It doesn't have to. *Your* relationship needs to be custom-made for you and your partner. But you can't create something custom if you're not honest about what you want.

A MAN WITH A PLAN

Imagine this, your favorite football team has hired a new head coach. The team hasn't seen much success the last few seasons, so you're hopeful this new guy will come in and help turn things around. Maybe he'll help get you to the playoffs this year. You sit in front of the TV to watch his first interview.

The guy looks confident as he strides up to the podium and introduces himself. "Hey, all, I'm Coach Wander, but uh, you can call me Coach Winner." The room breaks into a laugh and applause. *Nice. This guy seems legit,* you think. *Heck, the team could go all the way with the right leadership.* You turn up the volume a bit to make sure you catch what the coach has to say.

The first question comes. "So, what's your plan for the team this year?" a reporter asks. "Uhhhh. Whoa there," the coach says nervously. "Man, that's a pretty intense question for my first day, don't you think?" There is an awkward pause as the coach drinks a gulp of water. "Why don't we just enjoy the moment?" he says with a smile.

The camera pans back to the reporter and you see the look on their face: confusion. Exactly what you're feeling at this moment. "Ummm, okay," the reporter tries again, "where do you see the team headed this season?" The coach looks visibly uncomfortable. "Yeah, you know, I'm more of a go-with-the-flow kinda guy," he finally says. "But hey, I'm real happy to be here." And he walks off stage. Now, how confident are you feeling about your team's chances with this guy's leadership?

We can't trust leaders who don't have a vision. Why the heck would we follow someone who doesn't know where they're going? They don't give us a sense of security. If you cannot articulate why you want to be in a relationship other than "I thought that's what I was supposed to do," you will not be setting yourself or your relationship up for success. Many men get into relationships, and when the time comes to have the "what are we" or "where do you see this going" talk, they pull a Coach Wander. They take a backseat to their own life plans.

Instead, this is where women often end up taking the lead in relationships. "Oh, you don't have a vision? Don't worry, I do." This leads to men being the followers in their relationships, which, I gotta tell you, never works out in the long run. A STRONG relationship is an equal partnership. You both have to be able to talk about your hopes, dreams, and vision for the future, because in the long run, you must have a shared vision to feel safe and secure in the relationship.

So, what are you looking for in a partner? In a marriage? In life? If you don't know what you're looking for or where you're going, you cannot make a plan of action. And without a plan, you will not be successful. Take the bull by the horns and start by deciding what you are looking for before going into a relationship. Then you can be a man who has confidence engaging in the important conversations.

When you are a man with a plan, you will attract partners who want what you want. When you are confident in your direction, you will provide a sense of safety for your partner. When you have a clear vision for your relationship, you and your partner can work toward it together as a team. When you have a shared dream, you can work on making it come true together. A well-laid, clearly articulated plan is a key ingredient for establishing a sense of safety and security in a healthy STRONG relationship.

PERSONHOOD OR PERFORMANCE?

The flip side of "what are you looking for in another" is taking a closer look at what you are bringing to the table. This part of self-awareness is looking at how you are presenting yourself as a potential partner. Are you leading with your personhood or your performance? Do you expect connection from a partner, but are only bringing function to the table?

Brené Brown talks about the difference between fitting in and belonging.[7] Relying on a function to "fit into a role" or fulfill a need in a relationship might get you in the door, but it won't fulfill the need for true connection and real belonging. Self-awareness as the first S of safety in a STRONG relationship is also about the importance of understanding why you are lovable for who you are.

Many people are raised in homes that explicitly or implicitly teach them that their value is based on their function and love is earned based on achievement. Something I hear from men frequently is that they never knew what it was to feel truly wanted, so instead, they learned how to be needed. They grew up feeling like love was conditional and had to be earned through performance or perfection. This pressure to perform in a specific way can lead to a lot of insecurity in a relationship for men.

Children raised in "conditional love" homes often become hyper-focused on performance to earn the love they so desperately crave. These children then become adults who think their only lovable quality is their functionality and performance. Compounding the issue is that in many ways, our society reinforces the view of people as assets, as human capital.

When a child is raised in an environment of conditional love, it can prevent them from developing their core, defining their personhood, and discovering what makes them uniquely lovable in their own way. Because if love is conditional, then it can be lost if the conditions are not met. Unconditional love is based on your intrinsic value as a human being. It is not a reward for your function or utility.

To truly trust the connection of a relationship and establish relational safety, you have to know what makes you uniquely, intrinsically valuable as a human *being*, not just a human *doing*. Safety and security in a healthy relationship comes from knowing you are *wanted* as a person, not just *needed* because you're useful.

**If you don't know why you are wanted,
you will find where you are needed.**

If this was how you were raised or what you experienced in previous relationships, you might not know how to respond when someone does not "need" you. If you are not sure why someone would want you, you won't trust that that's the basis of your connection. If you do not know what you have to offer to another person in a relationship besides your function, you will default to being in a function-based relationship.

Often, I see this fear at the core of so many men's workaholism. Their drive to provide financially is because they think that is all their families want from them. And there are a lot of men who have consistently been told their value was in their performance, not their personhood. We tend to seek the type of love we think we deserve. If you are unsure of why you are worthy of love just as you are as a person, you will continue to try to earn love by leading with your performance.

Many men I have met describe themselves as an "open book," but sometimes I see that they are open only to a certain page. All the other pages are sealed shut. And it makes sense as a survival mechanism. If you lead with your performance, you can hide the parts of yourself that might be harder to look at. However, if your sense of worthiness for love or relationships is tied to your function, it will be hard to feel securely connected in a relationship. To have an honest and authentic connection with another person, you first need to have a healthy connection with yourself. You cannot connect to another person's humanity when you are disconnected from your own.

JAKE

PERSONHOOD OR PERFORMANCE?

Jake came to see me for individual counseling. Recently engaged, he had been with his fiancée Lisa for three years, but as he described it: "We've had the worst fights of our relationship in the last few months since getting engaged." He was understandably concerned and decided to come to counseling to address the issue before moving forward with the wedding.

"It makes no sense," he said. "We both make really good salaries, and money is not an issue, but I find myself getting irritated as hell every time she wants to talk about the wedding costs, and we end up fighting about something stupid." The last argument he described was a raging argument about a $500 personalized centerpiece which, he added, "actually turned out really nice and was totally worth it." He paused before continuing. "You would have thought that $500 was $50,000 the way I felt about it. I'm worried I'm picking these fights because I don't really want to get married."

As I explored his individual family history and his history of past relationships, a pattern began to emerge: I noticed that whenever Jake described himself he only spoke in terms of achievement or failure. The next time he did that, I pointed it out to him and asked where he learned to describe himself in that way.

He thought for a moment and then said, "My mother was a perfectionist, and my father was a football coach. My whole life I have been told that my value was in my performance."

As we continued to work together it became clear that this was at the core of all the fights they had been having. Jake was worried that Lisa's love was conditional and based on his function as a provider. He wanted to be loved for who he was but didn't know how to initiate that conversation so he ended up picking a fight about finances.

Once we uncovered that, Jake spent the next few sessions exploring what he had to offer as a person, outside of his performance. After a few months of working together, with Jake feeling more confident about his worthiness of being loved for who he is, and with the wedding getting closer, I wondered if Jake was ready to have a difficult conversation. "Jake, what if you asked Lisa why she is marrying you?" I asked one day.

He balked a bit at the suggestion. "Damn, why am I afraid to know the answer?" he wondered.

"I don't know, Jake, what do you think she's gonna say?" I asked. We sat in silence for a few minutes until he spoke again.

"Hmm," he finally admitted. "I guess I'm kind of worried that she's gonna confirm my fear. That she's gonna say something about how much money I make or how I promised she could take off work after we have kids if she wanted to, or that she's gonna say something like 'Well, you proposed with that big freaking ring, how could I say no?'"

"And?" I prompted.

"And then I will realize that she's just with me for my function and I will have to call off the wedding."

"What does that tell you, Jake?"

"That tells me that I don't want to settle for a marriage in which I am only used for my function. I want to be in a relationship where I can be sure that my partner wants a connection with me. For me. And I want to know that she wants the same thing. Not my stuff or the life I can give her."

"Okay, so this is going to be a hard conversation for you, but it sounds like it may give you the clarity you need on whether or not you want to go through with this marriage," I reflected.

The next session, Jake was all smiles.

"What did you learn from your homework, Jake?" I asked him.

"A lot," Jake responded. "Lisa told me things that she loved about me that I didn't even know she knew. She saw me. All of me. She told me all about what she loved about me as a person that. . ." He choked up a bit. "I've always been secretly worried that all of my girlfriends were only with me for the lifestyle I could provide them. Maybe some of them were, in the past, and maybe I only saw function in some of them too, but after having that conversation with Lisa, I feel very confident that this marriage is happening for the right reasons. I feel loved. Truly. We are on the same page about what we want out of our life together. We want a connection-based relationship, and we'll fight for that moving forward. Not about centerpieces."

If you are not sure why anyone would want to be with you without your performance as your calling card, if there are no relationships in your past in which you have felt truly valued as a person, then there may be some important self-exploration you can do on this topic. Going to individual therapy can be a great first step in figuring this out. Don't wait until your next relationship is on the rocks to go to therapy. Self-awareness and knowing why you are worthy of love are gifts you give yourself.

The dictum "go to therapy" is one that gets thrown around a lot these days, so I want to make it super clear what the point is. Therapy is not just where you go into a room and a therapist waves a wand or does some kind of woo-woo magic and suddenly "Thanks, I'm cured." I mean I tell my clients all the time that I *wish* I was magic, but that's not how it goes. No, it is a process of getting to know yourself more deeply with the help of an objective, trained observer. When you know yourself more deeply, you are empowered to change your own life by making new choices.

The Johari Window[8] is a concept used to illustrate the idea of how therapy helps with self-awareness.

Johari Window

OPEN

Things I know about me
and what others know about me

Here I am confident in knowing who I am
and understand how I present to others.

ONE WAY MIRROR

Things others know about me
that I don't know about myself.

This is my blind spot.

The goal of self-awareness is to increase the area of openness

CLOSED

Things I know about me
that I do not share with others

This is my hidden area.
I use a mask to protect this information

UNKNOWN

Things I don't know about myself
and that others don't know about me.

I don't know what I don't know

@atxtherapist

Adapted from Joe Luft and Harry Ingham. "The Johari window, a graphic model of interpersonal awareness,"
Proceedings of the Western Training Laboratory in Group Development. Los Angeles: UCLA, 1995

The goal is to lessen your blind spots and the areas of unconscious awareness so you can have more agency and understanding of how you show up in the world and impact others in your life and relationships. You can't change what you aren't aware of. A therapist can help you by showing you your blind spots and helping you explore the parts of yourself you keep hidden so you can have more confidence in putting your masks aside and showing up authentically in your life and relationships.

Therapy can help you understand how your patterns of choosing others for their function or leading with your performance have impacted your past relationships. When you become aware of your impact on others, you are then empowered to make changes that enhance your ability to connect with them in the way you want to.

When you can start to look at the painful chapters of your life with understanding and self-compassion, you can then be empowered to choose new types of partners, relationships, and behaviors. Then you can begin to change the trajectory of your future relationships. Your history does not have to be your destiny.

TL; DR: STEPS TO SELF-AWARENESS

1) OPTIONAL – Romantic relationships are not a requirement. They are totally optional *and* they take a ton of work, so before you sign up, do some self-reflection. Why do you want to do the work of being in a relationship? Get clear on your reason before jumping in. Intention sets the tone.

2) OPTIONS – There are two types of relationships: those based on function ("I need you") and those based on connection ("I want you.") Both are valid, but they are two totally different ways of being in a relationship. Many relationships fail because the partners are looking for two different things out of the same relationship. Which type are you looking for?

3) CUSTOM – Once you get clear on what you want out of a relationship, you can begin to design your relationship to fit your unique needs. Everyone is different and everyone has different needs in a relationship. There is no one-size-fits-all. Treat designing a custom relationship with the level of care you would give to anything you intend to last for a long time.

4) VALUE – What do you have to offer a relationship? Why are you valuable? Why are you lovable? When you don't know why you are wanted, you will default to finding ways to be needed. Everyone wants to be loved and valued for who they are, but some of us don't know why we deserve that kind of unconditional love and belonging. Doing self-discovery work leads to more self-awareness of your patterns of seeking love and acceptance.

SAFETY SKILL TWO: STABILITY

"Everything else will improve when you develop your stability. . . You gotta have stability underneath if you're gonna have true strength."

— JEFF CAVALIERE

Another basic skill you will need to help a healthy relationship survive is stability. Being a STRONG man in a healthy relationship means being a stable man. Lacking basic stability is a factor that can derail a healthy relationship from starting or throw an existing relationship into a tailspin.

What does it mean to be "stable" in a healthy relationship? Well, if you are reading this and thinking that it means you must have a six-figure income, own your own home, and be perfect in every way to have a healthy relationship, and you're thinking, *What the heck, didn't we just cover this in the last section?* Good news, that's not what we're talking about. Stability is about getting yourself solid and settled before getting into a relationship. You can't contribute to creating a stable relationship if you can't stand on your own two feet.

When evaluating your stability, the question to ask is:

What chaotic or unstable factors in my life are within my power to change?

I want to be clear that lacking stability doesn't mean that you or anyone else doesn't deserve love. Being a person who deserves love is a given. Everyone deserves love. However, sorry to be unromantic here, but love is not enough to have a healthy relationship.

Going back to the grid of function vs. connection in relationships, connection without having basic functionality will create chaos and dysfunction in any relationship. Loving someone and having the skills to build and maintain a healthy relationship are two totally different things. A healthy relationship takes work. Stability is the solid ground that helps make building a STRONG relationship easier. Lacking stability makes having healthy relationships harder.

> "Stability is more important than ecstasy. If ecstasy comes before stability, you are heading for a crash."
> — SADHGURU

STABILITY IN SELF

The factors that I have seen bring the most chaos and conflict into relationships are actively destabilizing things like:

- Untreated mental health issues
- Untreated physical health issues
- Impulsive or violent behaviors
- Out of control alcohol or substance use
- Financial instability
- Ongoing active affairs or other betrayals
- Other ongoing, unmanaged external stressors

I call these environmental safety violations as they actively create an unsafe environment for you and your partner. When these factors are present, it is significantly more challenging to build a healthy relationship. It's not impossible, but it's like trying to begin an exercise program at the gym when you are actively bleeding from the head. It's a bit of a cart before horse situation. You must handle any active and ongoing threats to your own stability and safety before further work begins. Stabilization and crisis management must be done before any skill-building work will be effective.

<u>KEVIN</u>

I had just finished my first session on a Monday morning when I glanced at my phone to see four missed calls from the same number. There was a voicemail, but the muffled message was impossible to decipher.

I decided to give the number a call. If they didn't pick up, I would try again at my next break. But after only about a ring and a half, the phone picked up.

"Hello?"

"Hello!" I responded. "I am returning a call from this number."

"Oh. Yes, are you the couples counselor?" asked the muffled voice on the other end.

When I affirmed that I was, he identified himself as Kevin and explained the reason for his call.

"I think I need help to save my relationship."

I asked him what was going on, and he explained, "I have a girl, Casey, who I've been seeing on and off for like three months. She thinks I have bipolar because sometimes I get like real mad, and I guess it kinda scares her and stuff. It's also why I lost my job last month."

I paused him to clarify. "I'm sorry to hear that. Have you been assessed or diagnosed?"

"Um, no. But I have real bad anger issues. I had a freakout at work and I got fired. I mean it happens sometimes, like it's real hard for me to keep a job and stuff I guess, so I've been living on my friend's couch for now, I guess. Anyway, my girl Casey. She's been coming over and we chill, but last night I was having a bad night. I was drinking and we got in a big fight. I don't remember much but ended up I think I threatened suicide, so she called the cops on me. Now she's staying with her sister and is saying she doesn't want to see me anymore unless I quit drinking or like take medication or go to therapy or something. I really like her, and I want this to work, but I don't know how to fix this."

Kevin is an example of someone in a state of crisis in his relationship due to a lack of personal stability. No matter how much he wanted to be a good partner, Kevin's untreated mental health issues and alcohol use made it hard for him to maintain a stable job or home environment. This instability and the resulting chaos in the relationship made it difficult for Casey to feel safe with him.

Kevin had the best intentions, but the relationship had no ground to stand on because he lacked stability. He needed to work on finding stability in himself before he could be a healthy partner. Once his issues were managed and stabilized, he could move on to the next steps. I referred Kevin to a psychiatrist and an individual counselor who led him to some community resources, and eighteen months later, a healthy, stable Kevin (and Casey) came in for couples counseling—with excellent results.

Stability is a state of being, not a moral judgment. You can be a good person and lack the skills needed to be stable. Your partner can be a good person who is not stable enough to maintain a healthy relationship at this point in their life. It is what it is. Timing is everything. My motto for focusing on stability is this:

If someone is drowning, the first thing you do is throw them a life preserver, *not teach them to swim*.

If you want to set your relationship up for safety and success, pay attention to the things that will make a difference when it comes to the basic stability of your life. This skill will help you evaluate if you are stable partner material right now, or if you need to take care of your own mental health or other basic stability needs first before diving into a relationship. Paying attention to stability will also give you things to be on the lookout for when choosing a partner for yourself.

STABILITY IN A PARTNER

This book is not only targeted toward helping you be a safe man but also how to recognize unsafe behavior in a partner. You also deserve to be in a safe environment that lets you feel calm, settled, and secure. Safety in a relationship is co-created. Evaluate whether your partner is exhibiting any of the environmental safety violations that I asked you to look at in yourself:

- Untreated mental health issues
- Untreated physical health issues
- Impulsive or violent behaviors
- Out of control alcohol or substance use
- Financial instability
- Ongoing active affairs or other betrayals
- Other ongoing, unmanaged external stressors

If they are, they may not be capable of being a healthy partner at this point. Again, exhibiting any of these behaviors does not make you or your partner a bad person. But, if you or your partner are actively in the midst of, or are the source of, chaos in your environment, you're defeating yourself in your goal of trying to have a successful, stable relationship before you even start.

JAMES

I got an email request one morning from a man named James. Here is what his email said:

"I recently found out that my wife of seven years has been having an affair with a coworker of hers. It has wrecked me. I am not sleeping, I am not eating. I'm drinking more. We have been fighting every day since the discovery last weekend. We need help."

I made an appointment to speak with James on the phone and asked him to ensure that his wife would also be on the line. On the day of our consultation, we spoke.

"Hi, this is James."

"Hi, James, is your wife on the line as well?"

"Yes, hi, this is Ashley."

"Hi, Ashley and James. Tell me, what is going on?"

James began, "I found out about an affair that Ashley has been having with her coworker. It looks like it has been going on for months, if not years. We are in a really bad place and I would like to make an appointment to come in for couples therapy."

"Ashley, do you have anything to add?" I asked.

"Yes, actually," Ashley said. "So, I am not actually sure that I want to come to couples therapy. I admit I had an affair, but our marriage hasn't been good for a while, so I think I need more time."

"More time?" I echoed

James chimed in, "She hasn't stopped seeing him."

"Ashley, is the affair still going on?" I asked

"Well, I actually don't want to answer that," Ashley said tersely.

"But you want more time to decide if you want to continue the relationship with this other person or repair your marriage?" I clarified.

"I guess when you put it like that, yes," Ashley responded.

A STRONG relationship is an equal partnership. You cannot do it alone. You and your partner need to work together to avoid behaviors that will actively destabilize the foundation of your relationship. Although James was desperate to save his marriage, Ashley was not ready to be an equal partner in that work with him.

My recommendation for James was to come in for individual therapy to regain his stability after being rocked by this painful discovery. After doing his own work for a few months, James regained some stability in his life. Even though Ashley did end up going to couples therapy with him after ending her affair, he eventually found the strength to file for divorce.

Perhaps, after reading this, you realize you and your partner are incapable of sharing the load of a healthy relationship because one or both of you lack the stability you need. In that case, you may need to pause and reevaluate what needs to be addressed so you can both be equal contributors to the safety and stability of your relationship.

**"Stability doesn't require a relationship,
but a healthy relationship requires two stable people!"**

– UNKNOWN

MENTAL HEALTH AND STABILITY

Mental health issues can be due to chemical imbalances in the brain, brain injury, trauma from childhood or past relationships, experiencing traumatic events, or any number of other reasons. No one chooses to have mental health issues; however, your mental health *will* affect how you show up in the world and your relationships.

People aren't perfect, and you don't need to be perfect in order to have a healthy relationship. But if you are unhealthy and unstable in your own life, you will bring that into your relationship. You can't bring stability to an environment or protect a relationship if you are the chaotic or unsafe factor. If mental health issues are not adequately addressed and treated, they can wreak a lot of havoc on the person who has them and can contribute to chaotic and unstable relationships.

I want to be super clear that having mental health issues or lacking stability in your life does not mean that you don't deserve a healthy relationship. Everyone deserves love and belonging. However, trying to create a healthy relationship when these destabilizing factors are unaddressed or unmanaged is working against yourself.

When people are under chronic stress, it is difficult for them to be their best selves in a relationship. If you are not stable or your basic needs are not being met, your mental energy will go there first, no matter how much you want to show up for your relationship. This will not leave much left over to be the best version of yourself in your relationship—and your relationship will show the strain of trying to survive on the scraps.

You cannot build a stable house on shifting sands. Stabilization comes first before building a STRONG relationship.

If a healthy relationship is your goal, start with your own self-assessment. When you look at the list of "environmental safety violations" and examine your own life, are you a safe and stabilizing influence on your environment, or are you an instigator of chaos (wittingly or unwittingly due to untreated issues)? What would you need to do to begin addressing any unaddressed or untreated issues in your own life before beginning a new relationship? What do you need to feel solid and stable in yourself?

Unfortunately, if you do not have stability in yourself, you may search for a partner to be that stability for you. This dynamic sets relationships up for failure because it immediately places an unbalanced load on your partner. Also, as James found, you cannot be in a healthy relationship with a partner who is an active threat to the stability of the relationship.

I like to say that a STRONG relationship is not addition, as if you are half a person looking for your lost soul mate, a.k.a. your other half, so you can say, "you complete me." Instead, think of it as multiplication, as in "one healthy person × one healthy person = one healthy relationship."

Start with creating safety and stability in yourself by getting the help you need to address any issues that are blocking your ability to create a stable and healthy connection. If you realize you have been overly reliant on your partner to be the stability while you've been bringing the chaos, it doesn't mean your relationship is doomed, but it does mean some foundational work needs to be addressed so you can be a stable partner. Once you are both stable, you can work together as equal partners to create a stable base from which to build a STRONG relationship.

"She is not your rehab. She is not your mother. She is not your savior. She is not your quick fix. She can support you, but she can never do more for you than you are prepared to do for yourself."

– MATT BROWN

STABILIZING THE SCENE: BASIC LIFE SKILLS

Another of the biggest stressors on a relationship is when people lack the basic skills to maintain a household. Practical life skills sometimes go underappreciated, but they contribute a lot of stability to a relationship. Maintaining a stable home environment contributes to and supports your relational stability.

LIAM

Liam was a twenty-seven-year-old man who came into my office wanting some help with his relationship. This was his dilemma.

Liam: "My girlfriend Emma and I have been together three years. She was in a bad relationship when we met, and we started as friends. After her breakup, she needed a place to stay, so I let her move in with me. One thing led to another, and we started dating."

Me: "What brings you in here today?"

Liam: "Well, she had been with her ex since high school. She went straight from living with her parents to living with him, and she's never had the experience of living on her own. I had been living on my own for a couple years when Emma first moved in, so I was able to show her a couple of things that she didn't know how to do. I thought it was pretty cute that she didn't know how to work the laundry machine at first. But now, it's been three years and I know she wants us to take our relationship to the next level—she's talking about rings and stuff, but I am really hesitant."

Me: "What's the hesitation?"

Liam: "I mean, I love her and all, and I feel really bad for saying this, but I don't think I want to marry her. I have a vision of my future family, and I just don't know if she is going to be a good partner."

Me: "Can you tell me more?"

Liam: "Ugh, this is so hard because I really do love her and I feel terrible about this, but she is such a mess. I mean, she has figured out the laundry at this point, but I feel like I'm constantly picking up after her. We got a dog because she saw a rescue who needed a home and I was on board with that, but I'm the one who ends up having to walk him and take him to the vet and all that. Sometimes I'll come home, and he's gone to the bathroom in the house. Even though she works from home, she forgets to walk him unless I remind her, which is frustrating. She also is really bad with money. I've tried to help her set a budget, but she just doesn't really get it. We keep our money separate right now so it's not that big a deal, but that would probably change if we get married. Emma's talking about wanting kids and moving to a bigger house, but honestly that makes me really concerned. I want to see a future with her, but I just don't know if she is someone I can do life with in the long-term if she doesn't get better at some of these things. Am I wrong for thinking that way?"

Building a healthy relationship is hard work, but it is even more challenging when coupled with trying to maintain a home with someone who doesn't have the basic skills for living as an adult. If you know what you need to maintain stability for yourself and set a standard of living that feels good for you, you will find it much easier to notice when someone shares or doesn't share those standards.

This might be where you want to evaluate your adult life skills. Do you know how to balance your finances? Are you able to do your own laundry? Shop for, plan, and prepare healthy meals? Keep your house clean? Like Emma, maybe you never learned how to do these things. Perhaps you lived in a home with parents who never taught you how to eat healthily, keep the house clean, or manage your finances.

If that's the case, you're definitely not alone. There are hundreds of YouTube, Instagram, and TikTok channels dedicated to helping people learn these skills. One of my favorites is the YouTube channel called "Dad, How Do I" where author Rob Kenney teaches what he calls "practical dadvice for everyday tasks." However you choose to learn, it would help to ensure that some basic life skills are under your belt before you enter your next relationship. When you are capable of the practical skills of everyday life, you improve your ability to provide stability in your environment.

ONGOING STABILITY

You may be surprised to know that many couples who are experiencing marital or relational distress are being hugely impacted by disruptions in their environment, and they don't even realize it! When there is job loss, a move, a new baby, an illness, anything that is threatening physiological needs or the stability of the environment, the couple will be taking a hit.

Even if the change is a wanted one, like a baby, or a new job, any shift in the environment will have repercussions on the couple. But the good news is that when you expect the impact, you can prepare for it and address it together. Why is this important to know? There's a saying in therapy, "under stress, we regress." When we are stressed, we become a less great version of ourselves. We sometimes go back to acting like angry, tired, frustrated toddlers rather than adults. This makes maintaining a healthy adult relationship difficult.

Being stable in a healthy relationship means creating and maintaining a non-chaotic environment. Many things can cause stress, but when you notice that you and your partner are getting snippy with each other, start by checking the environment! Did you recently move in together? Is it the holidays? Are one or both of you sick? Are your in-laws visiting? Is the house a disaster? What is the new stressor in the environment that you are adjusting to? What is the chaos that has awakened your danger sensors? And what can you do to help stabilize and address it as a couple rather than letting it become an issue between you?

Our environment is the first place we show signs of stability or chaos. Having a stable and calm home will help contribute to the overall feeling of stability and calm in your relationship. If you notice that your home is a source of stress or disruption, ask yourself what you can do to help protect your peace, your relationship, and your family from chaos.

Let's get real here for a minute. Looking at environmental disruptions on a macro scale is essential, but so is looking at the disruptions in your microenvironment. So, I'm going to ask you to look at your environment. Right now. Look around you. What is the level of chaos? Is there laundry on the floor? Dishes piled in the sink? Toys or shoes all over the floor? If your home is a disaster, your relationship is probably suffering from added external stress that it doesn't need to be. What can you do in five minutes to help stabilize your environment?

Now, you might be thinking, "This is a trick to get me to clean my house and help out with chores!" Well, no and yes. No, no trick. Yes, get up and stabilize your environment. If that includes cleaning up some chaos or fixing something unsafe for yourself, your partner, or your kids, do it! Removing unnecessary external stressors to yourself, your partner, and the home environment is part of creating stability in a healthy relationship.

And just FYI, everyone hates chores. Dr. John Gottman, marriage researcher extraordinaire, found that two of the most common things that couples fight over are house management related: chores and finances.[9] Other studies have found that married women's mental health, stress levels, satisfaction with the relationship, the amount of conflict in a couple, and likelihood of divorce can be directly correlated to the amount of chores and housework they are responsible for in comparison to their partners.[10]

STABILITY IS SEXY

One of the most common blocks to a sexual connection that women express is having a chaotic home environment.[11] You may have heard of the studies that found that women found men who do house chores extra sexually appealing,[12] and why not? A fellow clinician, Tiffany Berry, introduced me to the term "choreplay," which is a great way to think about this.

According to the polyvagal theory by Stephen Porges, our nervous systems only switch into "play" mode (which includes sexual play) when we feel safe and calm[13]. When we are anxious, dysregulated, or in a state of activation due to a disruptive or chaotic environment, our internal defenses prevent us from becoming vulnerable or receptive.

A calm environment that is safe and clear of chaos allows a person's nervous system to relax so we can move into the subsequent phase: seeking intimacy and connection.

If your partner is worried that your kid is going to fall in the pool that hasn't been fenced, you stub your toe every two minutes with all the crap on the floor, and dishes in the sink are starting to become a silent standoff between you and your partner, why not get rid of some chaos and see if that makes a difference? When you can help stabilize your home environment by reducing chaos and calming stress, you allow room for other experiences. If you can remove any unnecessary blocks to intimacy by helping stabilize your environment, why not do it?

Let's go back to the man in the protector role. Can you protect your family from an unanticipated external threat or stressor? Maybe, sometimes. Can you help protect your family from added stress by eliminating needless chaos in yourself and/or the immediate environment? Probably most of the time.

TL; DR STEPS TO CREATING STABILITY

1) STABILIZE YOURSELF – When you are in chaos, you will bring chaos into your relationship. If you have untreated mental or physical health issues, out of control substance use, are lacking basic needs, or are leaving major stressors unaddressed, you will not be able to bring the needed stability to have a healthy relationship. Get yourself stable and healthy first.

2) CHOOSE WISELY – It is not your job to be the only source of stability in your relationship. You deserve to be in a safe

relationship with a stable partner. If your prospective partner is in active chaos in their life, you're not going to have an equal partner in the work of building a healthy relationship, which means you're going to be working against yourselves. Like Abraham Lincoln said, "A house divided cannot stand." If you recognize that you are in an unsafe relationship or have suffered intimate partner violence, there is help.

3) GET SKILLED – There are some basic life skills that you will need to maintain stability. If your environment is chaotic, it is probably activating unnecessary chaos in your relationship. Get active in learning the skills needed to create a stable home environment and see how that stabilizing effect multiplies in other areas of your life and relationship.

4) RESTABILIZE OFTEN – Ongoing changes in life will continue to challenge the stability of any couple. Anticipate, plan for, and learn new skills for any upcoming changes you will face in your life and relationship. Don't get thrown off by life's challenges. Rise to meet them head on.

5) GET SEXY – Being in a calm, non-chaotic environment allows your nervous system to switch to a state of relaxation and play. When our bodies are in "relax and play mode," we are more receptive to intimacy and connection. Take a moment to examine your immediate environment. Are there things within your power that you can do to bring your domain back to a sense of stability, calm, and/or safety?

6) GET CLEAR – Establishing environmental safety and creating stability begins with removing any unnecessary

external blocks to a healthy and intimate connection. When you start with finding stability in yourself, a partner who values the same, and stabilizing your environment, you are clearing the way for a healthy relationship to thrive.

SAFETY SKILL THREE:
SELF-REGULATION

"Peace. It does not mean to be in a place where there is no noise, trouble, or hard work. It means to be in the midst of those things and still be calm in your heart."

— UNKNOWN

The third skill for creating safety in a relationship is having the ability to self-regulate in a healthy way. What does this mean? Well, one of the most common reasons people seek couples therapy is for "conflict and communication" issues. Often people seek out therapy thinking that if they can just learn the right combination of conflict and communication skills, they will be able to navigate their relationship issues smoothly.

When I first started hearing "conflict and communication" issues over and over as the reason most of my clients were coming in for therapy, I really got curious. Most of the people I met were highly functioning, working at skilled jobs, and communicating effectively with their coworkers, friends, neighbors, and others already. What was the issue that suddenly made them unable to communicate clearly with their partner?

Well, what I found was, when people talk about things or topics important to them, they often get activated and passionate. Sometimes things get heated. And sometimes things get ugly. Has this ever happened to you? Maybe you're in a conversation that suddenly turned into a conflict? You don't even know how you got there, so you definitely don't know how to get out of it. This cycle can be pretty hard on a relationship. Sometimes I say that most of what I do as a couples therapist is: "Help people have high-stakes conversations in a safe way."

Our brains are highly evolved, but sometimes they struggle to differentiate imagined danger from real danger.[14] In the interests of safety, our brain tells our bodies to treat all threats the same. A real "better safe than sorry" approach. Self-regulation helps your body differentiate between real danger—a speeding car coming at you—vs. imagined danger—my partner and I have a difference of opinion.

And high-stakes conversations happen often in intimate relationships.

Although learning tools on how to communicate effectively and negotiate conflict are important, what will help to make a change immediately is understanding what happens to you when you become dysregulated. Self-regulation is the third Skill of Safety in a relationship.

REGULATION AND COMMUNICATION

We tend to exist in our modern world from the neck up. We often ignore our body's signals until we are in pain or need something crucial to survival, like food, water, or sleep. However, a ton of information comes from our body's experience in the world that we need to pay attention to, especially concerning communication and conflict.

There are two ways we communicate: verbally and nonverbally. When you and your partner interact, you are not only paying attention to the words coming out of their mouth. You are also subconsciously paying attention to the signals their body is sending you. Asking your partner "How was your day?" and hearing "It was fine" from a smiling partner who has an open and relaxed body posture hits different from hearing "It was *fine*" from a partner with a clipped tone and tight neck muscles who then proceeds to slam the front door.

Often, couples who struggle with conflicts that seem to escalate out of nowhere or those who end up in an endless cycle of conflict are hearing one message verbally while another conflicting message is being sent nonverbally. Your brain picks up on the disconnect: "Hmmm, something suspicious is happening here" and flags the whole conversation as suspect. This activates your danger sensors. And when you are in a state of activation, your body has switched from being in calm mode to dysregulated mode.

Dysregulation is a sign of distress or danger, and as herd animals, dysregulation is contagious. We have these cool things in our brains called mirror neurons. These help us mirror the people around us. Don't believe me? Think about yawning when you see another person yawn. Heck, you might even be yawning right now reading this. These mirror neurons help us stay connected to the people around us because they might have important information for our survival.

Reacting quickly to herd agitation is an evolutionary adaptation that helped us survive. Think about seeing one person running. "Okay," your brain might think, "maybe bro is out for a jog." But you see three, four, or five people suddenly start running in the same direction? Your danger sensors will start picking up that something might be wrong, and you will probably get up and run as well.

This quick reaction by paying attention to the distress of others around us is an excellent survival skill. Our bodies *want* to react to the people around us, so unless we take active steps to remain regulated, one person's dysregulation can often trigger dysregulation in another. Sometimes that's all it takes to send a couple into a spiral of conflict. Like the saying goes, "If you're not having a good day, ain't no one having a good day."

Generally, we don't like being around dysregulated people because it activates our own dysregulation system. Being dysregulated is stressful for your body and your mind. It's like having the gas pedal pressed on your nervous system. This is why we especially don't like being around people who can't be soothed. Think about being on a plane with someone trying to soothe their crying baby and having no luck. Maybe it's been thirty minutes, and there is no sign of stopping the child's distress.

Your whole body might be reacting to that scenario right now, and yeah, that's exactly it. Your brain might think, *The baby might be tired, or their ears are probably hurting.* But regardless of all that logical information, your body is probably feeling anxious, agitated, and sending the message, "Ughhhhh! Make it *stop~!* This is so uncomfortable."

If you do not learn to self-regulate in a healthy way, your body will either a) stay in a high-stress state of activation, which is very damaging to your physical health (see: effects of chronic stress[15]), or b) you will find unhealthy ways to regulate.

Here are some common (unhealthy) ways that people self-regulate:

- Drinking
- Drug use
- Zoning out – mindless scrolling or TV/video games
- Porn use
- Overeating
- Overwork
- Overexercise
- Violence – physical or verbal to self or others

Unfortunately, all unhealthy ways to deal with stress don't actually teach you healthy self-regulation skills in the long-term. All they do is disconnect you from your distress by distracting you or numbing you out. It might help you get through the stressful moment, but it just kicks that can down the road. As you can see, many unhealthy coping habits will bring you right back to step one—the stability of your home and life is now compromised.

THE WINDOW OF TOLERANCE

Since we live in a world that is not perfectly safe all the time, each of us has developed a "window of tolerance"[16] for threats. Inside our window of tolerance, we can respond appropriately to danger, navigate through our days using reason, and make decisions appropriately. When we are in our window, we are regulated.

But, when we perceive a threat that pushes us outside our window, we become dysregulated (you can call it getting triggered, activated, etc.). Our bodies react quickly to >activate danger mode<, and that's when things get a little reactive in relationships. When we

sense a threat or danger, we go into one of the five stages of response
to the threat:

Flight/Fight (active responses: yelling, leaving, throwing
things)

Flop/Freeze (passive responses: shutting down, tuning out,
falling asleep)

Fawn (appeasing response: people-pleasing, submission,
acquiescence)

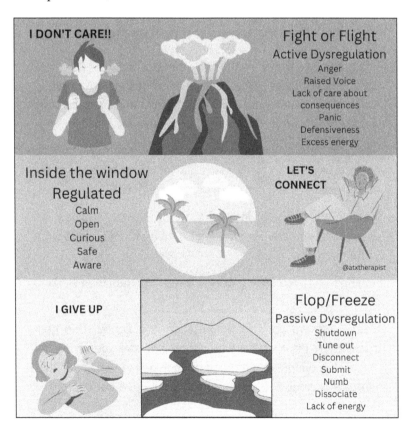

One thing I want to highlight here is that you can be dysregulated internally and not show signs externally. This is part of the disconnect that drives a conflict cycle. Sometimes people who look externally calm are significantly dysregulated on the inside. Not everyone has a red face and steam coming out of their ears when triggered. Sometimes, getting activated looks like flopping, freezing, fleeing, or fawning.[17] However, all these responses are signs of dysregulation and can perpetuate the cycle of conflict in a relationship.

FOUR PEOPLE, FOUR RESPONSES

MATT AND AMANDA: FLOP AND FIGHT

Matt and Amanda came to therapy for conflict and communication help. After we discussed the four ways in which our bodies tend to seek safety, Matt and Amanda were quickly able to identify what their problem was:

Amanda: "Matt is a flopper. When we're in a conversation, he shuts down and actually starts getting sleepy. He even fell asleep right in the middle of an argument once!"

Matt: "Our fights last for hours, which is why I usually fall asleep! I mean, the last one ended at like 4 a.m.! I have work in the morning."

Amanda: "Are you saying work is more important than working on us?"

Matt: "Here we go. Clearly, Amanda is a fighter. She gets triggered by the most random things, and she goes into fight mode. She brings up more and more things to talk about, and she gets angrier and angrier. I just don't have the energy for that."

PETE AND LUNA: FLIGHT AND FREEZE

Another couple I worked with also had conflict and communication issues, but they presented very differently from the high-conflict cycle of Matt and Amanda. When looking into how Pete and Luna handled emotional conversations, it became apparent that they had a lot of difficulties having high-stakes discussions because of their patterns of activation.

For instance, Pete would ask Luna, "Hey, should we talk about having kids this year?" and she would immediately freeze.

She described the feeling to me. "It's not that I'm scared of having kids. I just. . . in those moments, I lose all my words. Especially when he springs it on me like that. I mean there's a lot wrapped up in the conversation about pregnancy these days. I guess I never thought about the topic itself as unsafe, but yeah, I feel like I'm frozen and don't know what to say, so I just say nothing."

Pete said, "Yes, and then I get this sick feeling because I'm like. . . I thought we were going to have kids, but now I'm stressed because she won't talk to me, so I want to just go somewhere else to calm down. I usually go to this bar that I like and chill with the bartender."

Something that happens when our danger sensors are activated, as Amanda demonstrated, is that our brain goes 100 miles an hour. Our rational thinking brain goes off-line, and we kick into survival mode, a.k.a. "lizard brain." This survival skill helps us anticipate and plan for the worst-case scenario as quickly as possible. However, jumping to the worst-case scenario in relationship conflicts often escalates a dispute to a point where it doesn't need to go.

Although all the people in the previous example had different reactions, you can see how they each triggered their partners' danger systems. Even though none of them were physically in danger from their partners, their brains tagged these "high-stakes conversations" as potentially scary and threatening, which triggered both partners' individual bodily safety-seeking responses. Because these couples lacked a way to have difficult conversations safely, they continued to escalate and be stuck in their conflict cycles of unproductive or unresolved discussions.

When dysregulated, our goal is no longer problem-solving or collaboration. It is: Make. The. Problem. Stop. This is where couples get into fights that feel like there is only a win-or-lose situation. And no one wants to be a loser, so they fight on! Or flop, or flee, or freeze. Stopping the cycle of conflict in a relationship starts with recognizing when dysregulation is playing a role.

Unless we understand this safety-seeking cycle, we cannot begin to address managing conflict constructively. When you can understand what it feels like to be outside your window of tolerance, you can pay attention to when you are too dysregulated to have a productive conversation with your partner. When you are dysregulated in conflict, you are probably making it worse by triggering your partner's dysregulation as well.

The bad news is that you will continue to trigger each other's danger responses until you get to know your body and its responses to threats and your partner understands theirs. If your physical reactions are left unaddressed, it creates an escalating cycle of conflict where couples' fights go nowhere, stay unresolved, or end in a worse place than they began.

The good news is that once you understand how your body responds when it is outside the window of tolerance, you can start to cultivate exercises to get back into your safety zone. Once you are in your safety zone, your neocortex: your "rational brain," comes back online, and you can then connect safely and calmly with your partner. Practicing self-regulation will help you have healthier discussions and avoid heated or unproductive conflicts.

FAWN: A TRAUMA RESPONSE[18]

A caveat about the Fawn response that I mentioned earlier as one of the five responses to threat: fawning can often look like people-pleasing and can be mistaken for codependence in a relationship. However, it is actually a fear and trauma response triggered by lack of safety when faced with an abusive partner. Because a person with this response has learned their partner is abusive when upset, they will try to appease and pacify their partner by any means possible. Their subconscious need for safety overrides any other conscious need they may have. This is an adaptive response to trauma or abuse, but it is detrimental to your mental health in the long run. If you notice yourself fawning in a relationship, this may be a sign there is either abusive behavior occurring in your current relationship, or that you experienced previous relational trauma. Both can be addressed through individual trauma-informed therapy.

RECOGNIZING DYSREGULATION

If you do not know your triggers or know how to self-regulate when your body is agitated, you present yourself as an unsafe partner.

The ability to regulate yourself when you are upset is a key skill in maintaining a sense of safety in a healthy and thriving relationship. People who struggle with self-regulation skills tend to experience higher conflict in their social and intimate relationships. If you are a powder keg ready to blow at any moment because you do not know how to regulate when upset, you are setting a tone of anxiety in your home. Repeated activation and chronic stress harm your body and damage your relationships.[19]

TOM and MARIA

When Tom and Maria made a request to meet with me, they said they were on the brink of divorce. However, they seemed very calm and connected when they walked into my office. He held the door for her and handed her an extra couch pillow when she got situated. They sat comfortably together on the couch in silence until I asked them to share with me what brought them to see me.

Tom: "Maria, do you want to start?"

Maria: "Sure. Yes, um. It's his temper. We have a great marriage most of the time, but I cannot deal with his anger anymore."

Me: "Tom, will you tell me what your temper looks like?"

Tom: "Oh, I don't know. I've always had a short fuse, I guess. I know she doesn't like it when I flip people off and cuss them out while I'm driving. I know she doesn't like our kids hearing that."

Maria: "No, Tom. This was not just flipping people off." She turned back to me. "This is why we're here. After this last time,

I told him I want to move out with the kids. I just can't do it anymore."

Me: "Will you tell me what happened?"

Maria: "We were driving home with the kids from soccer and this guy cut us off. He was kinda rude about it and flipped off Tom through the window. Tom lost it. He started cussing and chased the car through traffic yelling out the window—speeding the whole time—and then the other car pulled over, and Tom got out of the truck to yell at him. Then the guy got out of his car with a bat, so Tom came back to get the gun we keep in the truck for safety. The kids were screaming and crying. I was terrified and begged him to stop. I thought we were going to die or watch Tom kill somebody."

Tom cut in, "I didn't get the gun though, did I?"

Maria: "That's only because the cops showed up before you could grab it! I can't even think of what would have happened if they showed up and you had the gun in your hand. Your children would have watched you die!" Maria broke into sobs. "I cannot do this anymore. You're always yelling and so angry all the time. It's not just driving. You get mad at the contractor. You threw a beer bottle at the dog yesterday. I'm scared!"

Tom: "Babe, you know I would never hurt you, right? I was yelling at the contractor because he was supposed to have that security system installed last week, and I thought the dog was chasing one of the kids. I'm trying to keep you guys safe."

Maria: "I know you try to protect us, but what would make me feel safe is not being worried about your temper. I want to know the kids are safe when driving with you. I want to feel calm in my home."

Tom: "When things are good, you feel safe with me, right?"

Maria: "I do, but in the back of my mind I always wonder how long things will stay good. And I don't want to have all this stress about when you are going to explode again. It's too much."

Living with someone who is in a constant state of stress and activation is stressful! No matter how much they love you, eventually, your partner's and children's bodies will learn that yours is unsafe for them to be around. They will start to protect themselves from the distress they feel around you by avoiding you. If you are a walking stick of dynamite, ready to explode at any sign of distress, your family will begin to walk on eggshells around you. Their self-protective instinct will kick in and say, *Avoid the activated guy because being around him makes us feel unsafe.* This will lead to fewer opportunities for connection and bonding. No one wants to connect with chaos.

And vice versa, if you don't know how to stay regulated, you will not be able to manage or soothe anyone else's distress. Have you ever tried to calm a crying baby when you were mad? Yeah, it doesn't work. You must be regulated within yourself to soothe or regulate anyone else. When you can be relaxed and regulated, you will set the tone of safety and calm your home. Once again, you cannot bring safety if you are the chaotic and unsafe factor. Being safe and regulated is a fundamental human need and a nonnegotiable in a STRONG, healthy relationship.

So, let's start with recognizing what happens to your body when you become dysregulated. You could get triggered by an argument, a look, a word, or an action. We will look at identifying triggers in a moment, but for now, think of a time when you felt dysregulated. Some common physical symptoms are:

1) Shallow breathing

2) Rapid heart rate

3) Heat in the face, neck, or chest

4) Clamminess or cold sweat

5) Tightness in the throat or gut

6) Narrowing of vision

7) Selective hearing

8) Feeling tired or shut down

Get to know your signs of activation to understand when you need to take a moment to take a break to self-regulate. A man aware of his bodily signs of activation can proactively take steps to address anything that can escalate to a place that would be threatening or unsafe for himself or a partner. You cannot control anyone else, but you can take control of yourself if you are becoming dysregulated.

If you do not understand what you need to feel safe, you will not be able to tell your partner what they are doing that activates your bodily sense of danger and sends you into a state of dysregulation. When you don't know your partner's triggers, and they don't know yours, chances are high that you are both walking into them all over the place. When you become aware of your and your partner's trauma triggers, that is when you can become empowered to start dealing with them safely.

> "It's hard to keep a conversation in a safe zone
> when you're filled with so much pain."
>
> **– JOHN WILSON**

UNDERSTANDING THE ROLE OF TRAUMA

Some people just don't like the term *trauma* and resist the idea that they have ever experienced trauma. And maybe they haven't— maybe you haven't—but when I am meeting with someone, and they are trying to understand if they have ever experienced trauma in their life, I ask them this question:

> **"Have you ever had an experience that made you feel pain
> (physical or emotional) coupled with a sense of helplessness?"**

There are a lot of ways people talk about trauma, but this to me is the simplest explanation. Trauma occurs at the intersection of pain and helplessness. Humans do not like pain, and we really don't like feeling scared and helpless. When you experience those things together, whether or not you like the term *trauma*, your brain and body has probably experienced that as a traumatic event.

The ACEs (adverse childhood experiences) study by Kaiser and the CDC[20] looked at the link between adverse childhood experiences and the impact on one's health later in life. The experiences they looked at were childhood sexual abuse; physical or emotional abuse or neglect; growing up in a home with household dysfunction: having an incarcerated parent; having a parent with mental illness or substance abuse issues; and experiencing divorce or domestic violence in the home before the age of eighteen. These experiences tend to combine the feeling of pain, either physical or emotional, and the feeling of helplessness. As children, we don't usually have the resources to leave scary or dangerous situations, so we are stuck in that intersection of pain and helplessness.

The study found that the more ACEs one experienced, the higher the number of negative mental, behavioral, and physical health conditions a person would have as an adult including smoking, substance use, depression, strokes, alcoholism, heart disease, and suicide attempts.

Experiencing trauma will impact your life, health, and relationships, whether or not you choose to acknowledge the effects. However, in the words of psychiatrist Nabil Kotbi in the documentary film *Cracked Up*, which chronicles *Saturday Night Live* star Darrell Hammond's journey of healing from childhood trauma, trauma is *mental injury, not mental illness*. If you experienced trauma as a child, there are ways to address and heal those old wounds. However, ignoring them or denying that you have experienced trauma will not allow you to access the tools you need to begin to heal.

RECOGNIZING YOUR TRIGGERS

Our bodies are incredibly sensitive to unsafe people and situations. If you have ever been bullied, you may remember the feeling of your body bracing for impact as you walked through the hallways of school and saw your bully walking toward you. If you grew up with an abusive parent, hearing their car pulling into the driveway may have given you a sick feeling in your gut.

If you have been in a car accident or experienced any form of physical trauma, you know that even years after the most obvious injuries are healed, there may still be points of pain that you are left with. Emotional trauma works the same way. If you have old wounds from childhood or past relationships, they may not be outwardly obvious to a new partner, but they still cause pain.

Our brains' and bodies' jobs are to protect us from pain, so if your partner bumps into an old pain point of yours—even if it's by accident—it will trigger you to protect yourself. Unfortunately, your self-protective behavior might be to snap at or push them away. This reaction to protect yourself when triggered can lead to a constant cycle of conflict in your relationship unless you can get to know your pain points and let your partner know what triggers them.

One of my most often used phrases in therapy is this:

"You can't tell your partner what you don't know or acknowledge about yourself."

When you can let them know where your emotional bruises are, "Hey, this is a painful topic for me," it lets your partner know to be gentle and cautious when they want to approach that area. So, sit down and think of the most common things that "push your buttons." What gets your blood boiling? What makes you disconnect and shut down? What are some behaviors, words, or phrases that really get under your skin? Where are your emotional pain points?

After identifying those pain points, start thinking about why this might be a trigger for you. Is there a previous trauma or painful memory connected to this trigger, i.e., "Being yelled at brings back what it felt like when my dad used to yell at me"; "Being ignored by my partner reminds me of what it felt like to be ignored by my friends in school." Triggers tell us about old wounds, and they are adaptations to protect us from being hurt again.

When you have information about your triggers, you will know when to regulate your body back to safety before beginning or continuing a high-stakes conversation. When you know your partner's triggers, you can gently approach high-stakes topics by going into discussions regulated and prepared to take breaks as needed.

As a trauma-informed therapist, I see safety-seeking and pain avoidance as the primary issue of any dysfunctional communication and conflict dynamic. It's just trauma bumping up against trauma. When we have experienced trauma or are under a chronic state of stress, our window of tolerance gets smaller. We get triggered or activated more quickly because we have less bandwidth to deal with distress.

When you can identify and address your own past trauma you can be aware of when your safety-seeking and pain avoidant behaviors become controlling or abusive. Many controlling behaviors I see in relationships come from someone's lack of awareness of how their own trauma has affected their internal sense of safety. They are simply reacting to their bodily sense of "Danger! Pain incoming!" For example, you're sitting with your partner on the couch and her phone pings. She looks at it and smiles. Your internal monologue goes:

She has her phone turned away, and she's smiling. My body is starting to react. I don't like this feeling. I will control the threat by taking her phone from her by force.

When you recognize that your sense of bodily safety is something you are in charge of, and *no one else*, you can then take steps to regulate your body. Instead, when you are more aware, your thought process might go like this:

I glance over and see my girlfriend smiling at a text. I notice my body starting to react. My face is getting hot and my heart is pounding. I'm feeling triggered. Why? Oh, right—this is my old trauma wound from being cheated on by a previous partner coming up. That was a really painful experience, and my body is trying to protect me from a repeat of that pain. But I need to remind myself that this is a different relationship. Before reacting, I can take a moment to regulate myself by taking some deep breaths. And then, once I am calm and feel safe in my body again, I can ask my partner if she's willing to share the joke with me.

You cannot rely on controlling your environment or your partner to control your triggers. All you can do is understand what you need to feel safe in triggering situations. Studies have shown that people who lack internal control tend to try harder to control others around them.[21] When you can learn to manage and regulate your own bodily responses, you will rely less on trying to control others in order to feel safe and calm. Attempts to control your partner or children in a relationship often leads to escalation of unsafe behavior that can become abusive.[22]

When you take the time to look at your triggers and responses you will most likely find a pattern that goes back a long way. We repeat what we know until we learn new skills to do something different! This might be a time to seek out the help of an individual therapist if you feel stuck. When you can learn to self-regulate, you will be able to show up as a safe person in a relationship. Additionally, when you can share your pain points with your partner, they can learn to be aware of how they can show up safely for you. It is not your job to heal your partner's trauma. But it is your job to address your own.

USE YOUR TIME-OUTS

First things first. When you become dysregulated, take a time-out. Remove yourself from the situation if possible. If you are in a discussion with your partner, make sure that you let them know that you are dysregulated and need some time for yourself to figure out how to continue the discussion calmly. Taking a time-out is a good first step to give yourself some space to practice your self-regulation skills.

If you are the one to take a time-out, you need to be the one to set the time-in. Taking a time-out is not an excuse to avoid having a hard conversation. Avoidance might trigger an old trauma wound in your partner of feeling abandoned. Make sure the time-out is clearly defined (I recommend between fifteen minutes to two hours). Don't go longer than twenty-four hours before circling back.

Often, I see people "take a time-out," but they use that time to ruminate on their arguments in their heads. That's not self-regulating. That's keeping the frustration fire burning. The goal of a self-regulation break is to bring yourself back into your window of tolerance so you can concentrate calmly on the topic at hand. If you can't revisit the topic calmly after twenty-four hours, you may need the help of a third party.

It might take a while to get to know your signs of dysregulation and practice taking time-outs, but once you do, you can start looking at ways to self-regulate.

PRACTICE SELF-REGULATION SKILLS

Self-regulation or grounding skills usually rely on connecting you back to your body, your five senses, and your breathing. These are some skills you can use:

- Box Breathing – Used by the US Navy to help SEALs regulate their breathing in high-stakes situations. Dysregulated SEALs make more mistakes that can hurt themselves or others, so they use the process of tactical breathing in four counts to help calm the nervous system. It goes like this: breathe in through your nose for four seconds. Hold that breath for four seconds. Exhale through your mouth for four seconds. Hold for four seconds.

- Bilateral Stimulation – Developed to help with self-regulation in extremely stressful situations. Place your palms on your chest with your thumbs interlaced. Your right fingers should be pointing toward your left collarbone, and your left should be pointing to your right collarbone. Next, alternate the movement of your hands, so you pat yourself on the chest with one hand and then the other. Bilateral stimulation activates both sides of the brain and gets the brain back online as one integrated unit.

- Progressive Muscle Relaxation – Have you heard the saying "Don't go to bed angry"? Well, sometimes, it is healthier to stop an argument and go to bed if you are too dysregulated to have the conversation productively. However, it is important to go to bed regulated. PMR is the process of activating and relaxing your muscles intentionally to relieve pent up tension. You can do this lying down or sitting in a comfortable position. Beginning from your toes all the way up your body to your forehead, squeeze one muscle group for five seconds, and then release it before moving on to the next muscle group. It usually takes about fifteen minutes to complete the PMR process through your entire body.

- Physical Movement – Resets your nervous system, and exercise can help discharge excess adrenaline buildup. Take a walk around the block or hit the gym for a bit.

- Co-regulation – Call a levelheaded friend for support. Connecting with a safe person is the very first way we learn how to soothe ourselves when we are young. Accessing another, regulated person for support is a way we can mirror their nervous system to help calm our own.

- Self-soothing – When we are feeling stressed, it can help to do something to let your body know it is safe—drink something warm, take a warm shower, cuddle a furry pet, sing, play guitar, or do something that feels kind to your mind and body.

- Rhythm – This might be a random one, but do you remember the chest pounding and humming scene by Matthew McConaughey's character in *The Wolf of Wall Street*? That is actually not a bad way to ground yourself! (Just skip the drugs and alcohol part.) Steady rhythmic beats have been shown to help with regulation, and humming helps you control your breathing and lowers your blood pressure as well.

- And finally, self-affirmation phrases you can say to yourself can help you get your focus back. One of my favorite mantras is "Even though my body is dysregulated, I am safe, I am okay, and I am learning to handle my distress. I am doing the best I can to take care of myself right now."

Anything that connects you to a sense of calm and greater safety is key to getting from dysregulation back to regulation. Start by practicing these skills when you are calm so you will feel confident in using them when you are triggered. I sometimes compare learning self-regulation skills to learning to swim. You can read about it all day, but you're not going to become a good swimmer by reading a book.

Also, if you practice swimming when you're *not* drowning, you will be more confident if you get into a situation where you are. The same is true for these self-regulation skills.

TL; DR STEPS TO SELF-REGULATION

1) SENSE – Get to know what your body feels like when you are outside your window of tolerance. When you are in a conflict situation, can you notice when your heart starts beating faster? Do you notice if your palms get sweaty? Do you notice when you are no longer listening clearly or when you are getting tongue tied? What are your body cues of activation?

2) STOP ACTION – When your body is unsafe, your thinking brain is off-line. You cannot make thoughtful, reasoned decisions when your body thinks it's under threat. If you continue to have a high-stakes conversation with your partner, it will probably go badly if either of you are outside your window of tolerance.

3) SIT WITH IT – Get to know your triggers so you can be aware of them in the future. Do you not like being surprised? Do you not like to be compared to your father? Is there a different way your partner could bring up a sensitive topic? Is there a time limit you can put on high-stakes conversations, or can you build in breaks as needed? Figure out what you need so you can let your partner know for next time.

4) SELF-REGULATE – Begin practicing getting yourself back in your window of tolerance by using one of the healthy self-regulation tools. Remember, practice makes perfect. The more you can train your brain to reach for a healthy rather than unhealthy tool, the easier it will be. Habits get stronger with use.

SAFETY SKILL FOUR:
SELF-EXPRESSION

*"Self-expression is the dominant necessity
of human nature."*

— WILLIAM WINTER

Being able to communicate clearly and articulately with your boss, coworker, or anyone else is one of the most important skills you can master in any relationship. All communication fosters connection. Emotional communication fosters intimate connections.

This fourth skill of creating Safety is not only about expressing yourself more openly, it is also about getting to know yourself more deeply. If you cannot access your emotions, you cannot talk about them. If there was only one thing I could tell men about relationships it would be this:

**The ability to connect emotionally is *essential*
to a successful intimate relationship.**

When you cannot express yourself emotionally, your ability to form an intimate relationship is severely hindered. Any relationship that has the potential for more than a surface level of connection:

friendships, parent-child relationships, and definitely romantic connections, will require you at some point to connect with and express your emotions. If you cannot connect to your own emotions safely, you will not be able to provide emotional safety in your relationship.

Now, some of you might be tempted to skip this part of the chapter because you think, *I'm not an emotional person.* Well, sorry to break it to you, but news flash! All humans are emotional beings. Men are often encouraged not to *talk* about their emotions. But it doesn't mean you don't have them. It just means you don't have the tools for self-expression that more emotionally expressive people do. There is a difference.

THE MYTH OF THE NON-EMOTIONAL MAN

Many men proudly describe themselves as "unemotional." There is a perception, especially among men, that logic is somehow "better" than emotion and that if you just deny you have feelings long enough, you will somehow erase them to become pure logic. But that's just not true—and it's actually terribly unhealthy.[23] All humans experience emotions. We have an entire limbic system in our brains dedicated to the production and processing of emotions.

If you are reading this right now and thinking *No, she's wrong. I am a being of pure logic,* then I would ask you, what's your favorite food? What movie or book genre do you enjoy? Why did you choose the car you drive, your career field, or the partner you have? Those are all decisions you have made with the help of your emotions.[24]

There are statistics and data for all of those categories: i.e., the optimum number of calories for a person of your age/size/activity level; the highest paying jobs in your area, etc. However, you don't walk into a restaurant and say, "Give me 600 calories of whatever." You might say that most of your decisions are based on logic, sure, but the tipping of the scale always goes to emotion when there is no pure logical outcome. As an engineer client of mine once put it, "Ah, emotions are the weighted variables." Correct! There are studies that show that when a person's emotional center of the brain is damaged, they are incapable of making a decision when there is no clear "logical" choice.[25] Most of life's choices are going to be based on preference and subjective experiences—the emotional variables.

Most of the conflicts in relationships boil down to a fundamental difference in the subjective experience of the two people in the relationship, which—umm, yeah! You're two different people so of course you're going to have your own opinions and preferences. But framing your preferences as "logical" and your partner's as "emotional" is presenting a false dichotomy. Ignoring your partner's subjective experience by trying to claim yours is the only logical one is in itself illogical if your goal is harmony and collaboration in a relationship.

Many men have overdeveloped their logical skills, but the flip side of that is that they have atrophied emotional and relational skills. There is context to this adaptation though. Our society has not always encouraged men to access their emotional and relational selves, so it makes sense that those muscles are a little underused and underdeveloped. If you haven't been given the chance or encouragement to develop your emotional self, it makes sense that you would over-rely on your logical self.

It is a human tendency to avoid doing things we're not good at and to overcompensate with things we are good at. However, this can lead to a situation where a man continuously struggles in relationships because he is using logic when emotion is called for. Emotions and logic come from two separate parts of the brain and serve different purposes. Comparing logic to emotion is comparing apples to oranges. They are both necessary and useful in their own way. But using logic when emotion is called for is like using an orange to make an apple pie. It's all wrong.

When you close the door on emotion you lose opportunities to experiences of love, longing, belonging, vulnerability, joy, connection, and intimacy. Sure, you might protect yourself from some more "difficult emotions," but you lose access to parts of yourself and you miss out on the full experience of being human. The more you can accept that you have emotions, the better you can get at articulating those emotions honestly, and the more successful your relationships will be.

WHY EMOTIONS?

At their core, emotions are simply the data sent by our brain saying, "This is what you are subjectively experiencing right now." Both emotions and sensations are data sent by the body to the brain that tells us what we are experiencing as we go about our day being human. They are what inform our subjective experience in the world. Subjective experiences are what makes us unique as individuals.

Experiencing an emotion or a sensation is data, information about your state of being. An easy way to remember this is to think of it like this: sensation words like hot, cold, painful, comfortable, etc., are how we talk about experiences that happen to our body, (external experiences) and emotion words like lonely, sad, excited, proud, etc., are how we talk about experiences that happen in our soul (internal experiences).

Emotions, like sensations, are just information. They have no value judgment attached to them besides the assessment we give them. They are just the facts. They don't go away or change just because we choose to ignore them. For instance, if you walk outside in -20 degree weather with a t-shirt and shorts on, you will experience the sensation of being cold. Facts. You may deny it verbally—"Nah, it feels great out here"—but the fact that you're cold will be evidenced by goosebumps on your arms and legs, your body shivering, and your fingers and toes beginning to go numb. You can choose not to *acknowledge* the cold, but that doesn't change the fact that physiologically what you are experiencing is: cold.

Emotions are trackable in the brain by measurable brain activity. Different regions of the brain become activated when a person is experiencing emotions. Emotions, like sensations, give you options: connect to your experience (accept that it's happening) so you can do something about it—get a jacket or go back inside—or disconnect from your experience (deny that it's happening), which doesn't help— or change—the situation at all and is just keeping you in harm's way.

This is why it doesn't work to simply say, "I don't have emotions" because you do, and they are affecting you and your relationship whether you like it or not. You cannot "control them" in the same way that you cannot control whether or not you get cold when you are in below freezing weather.

**What you can control is how you express and deal
with your emotions.**

When I hear people say they don't feel emotion, it tells me that they have trained themselves not to acknowledge that they are experiencing emotion. They have gone numb emotionally. But either way, like anything else in the world, denying something doesn't mean it's not there. Like Neil deGrasse Tyson tweeted, "The good thing about science is that it's true whether or not you believe in it."

The ability to see emotions as simply another form of data can help you change conversations with your partner from "this is illogical" to "this is a form of information that is telling me about a subjective experience happening to me or someone I love." A well-rounded STRONG man is able to use both the muscles of emotion and rationality as the situation requires. Like the saying goes in the gym, "Don't skip leg day." When you deny emotionality, you sacrifice a lot of what it means to be human. Don't neglect your emotional skills.

ALPHAS AND EMOTIONAL INTELLIGENCE

Google defines emotional intelligence (or EQ) as "our capacity to be aware of, to control, and to express emotions." Interestingly, being emotionally intelligent correlates with "alpha male" behavior in our closest evolutionary relatives. The original idea of the "alpha male" was supposedly supported by a study on wolves in which the pack's most aggressive, physically dominant wolf was the "alpha." However, this study has since been debunked—by its original author, I might add.

More recent studies of chimpanzees—which are closer to humans in the evolutionary chain than wolves anyway—show that the "alpha male" is not the one who is necessarily the strongest or most physically dominant but the one who is the most successful at maintaining connections. Relationships are what help these alpha males maintain their status and position at the top. Travis Bradberry, author of *Emotional Intelligence 2.0*, says, "Decades of research now point to emotional intelligence as the critical factor that sets star performers apart from the rest of the pack."[26]

Of course, "bully alphas" occur (those who bully their way to the top by brute force), but their tenure tends to be less stable and more conflict-filled. They are ones to whom the "live by the sword, die by the sword" adage applies. If they fight their way to the top, they must keep fighting to keep their spot. The minute there is a younger, stronger, more robust ape in town, their reign is over.

One of the essential roles of a high-ranking male requires providing emotional support and stability in crisis. It also requires the ability to calm conflicts between lower-ranking males and among females. As Frans De Waal, the researcher behind the study, noted in his 2018 TED talk, "Males who are good at these two [skills]—keeping the peace and providing comfort—become extremely popular leaders."[27] The alphas that got to the top supported by the relationships they made retained their position beyond the point they could physically defend their position as alpha.

The same is true for human leaders. After decades of research into the importance of EQ vs. IQ in business success, the results show that emotional intelligence is one of the core skills of effective leadership. It was also the top trait of high performing teams and successful entrepreneurs.[28]

The ability to be emotionally self-expressive is essential to forming bonds and strengthening long-term connections that we can rely on when times get tough. We increase our survival chances when our connections to others are based on fondness, not just skill. If resources are scarce, Jeff and Jim can both build a fire, but Jeff is a friendly and connected tribe member, and Jim is a bully who has no connections in the tribe; which one do you think will get voted off the island? Being emotionally open gives us an edge regarding connection, which is often a key to survival, even today!

Evolution is adaptive. Everything developed to help us survive. And evolution decided that we have significantly better chances of surviving when we form a tribe. Evolution has hardwired us for connection because we need connected, intimate relationships with others to thrive. When bonds are tenuous or broken, we struggle. The skill of self-expression helps us share our experiences and allows others to get to know us. Emotions are how we can form deep connections based on knowing and understanding others personally, not just needing others practically.

EMOTIONAL SCARS

In my work, if somebody tells me, "I don't feel sensations. I never feel hungry, hot, or cold," I would start by evaluating if there is some deeper underlying issue, perhaps a neurobiological or medical condition that needs serious and immediate attention.

In the same way, when somebody tells me, "I don't have emotions. I never feel angry, happy, sad, or scared," I take that same approach. We have to rule out any biological or medical issues that might be contributing to that condition first. But often, the real question that needs to be asked is:

"What has happened to you in your life that made you feel you had to disconnect from owning and expressing your emotions?"

There are many reasons men do not feel safe expressing their emotions honestly. Maybe you grew up in a home where no one cared about your feelings. Perhaps you were shamed for talking about your feelings and have gotten good at hiding them. Maybe you were bullied for being a "crybaby" in school, so you taught yourself not to cry in front of others. Maybe you grew up in a home with an emotionally distant father who modeled a type of stoic masculinity that allowed no room for emotion.

Or perhaps you were honest about your feelings in a previous relationship and were taken advantage of. Now, you may feel less vulnerable in a relationship when you hide your emotions or deny that you are being affected emotionally. If you experienced emotional neglect, denial, or betrayal in your life, it may help explain why you learned to manage, hide, or deny your feelings and disconnect from your emotions.

Many men are raised with the ethos that to deny your emotion is a good thing and that to show emotion is a bad thing. I cannot tell you how many men have apologized to me for showing emotion in therapy. More than one man in my office has even tried to explain his emotionality as "something I get from my mom," as if it was a hereditary defect and not a natural response to what he was experiencing. This says a lot about how they have been taught to view their own emotions as unmasculine, wrong, or something to apologize for. There is still a lot of shame directed at men for being "emotional."

We need to change this narrative that emotions are shameful, weak, or unmasculine. Emotions are not the problem. The stigma and shame around emotions is.

Emotions are essential for forming connections! Without the ability to communicate your feelings in a relationship, there will be no emotional intimacy. And disregarding your feelings doesn't make them go away. It just leads to internalized pain, shame, and a lack of emotional skill. Denying and repressing emotions doesn't allow you to get good at understanding and processing them. You cannot get better at talking about something you are ignoring.

Also, let's be honest, humans are actually pretty terrible at hiding their emotions. Your partner, your children, and your friends will know that something is wrong, something hurts, something is being hidden, but without your insight or ability to express what you are feeling, they will not know what you need from them to feel loved and cared for. This disconnect will erode your connection with your partner and your children. You cannot have genuine, intimate connections without being able to talk about your emotions.

Emotional conversations can be hard, but they are even harder when you don't have the tools and skills to have the conversation successfully. Most people's inadequate language and communication skills to talk about their emotions is what leads to emotional conversations feeling scary or unproductive.

But suppressing your emotions also has significant repercussions on mental and physical health. Emotionally repressed individuals have reduced executive functioning, more chronic pain, higher instances of gastrointestinal distress and heart disease compared to those who express their emotions regularly.[29] Studies have shown that people with higher levels of emotional suppression have weakened immune responses and are at higher risk for early death.[30]

The lack of ability to express emotions safely and openly has harmed many individuals and stunted many relationships. In his book *When the Body Says No*, Dr. Gabor Maté writes, "Emotional competence is what we need to develop if we are to protect ourselves from the hidden stresses that create a risk to health."[31] When you start to develop your skills for self-understanding, self-acceptance, and self-expression, you gain the emotional resilience needed to protect your physical, mental, and relational health.

UNDERSTANDING OLD PATTERNS

There are two ways that we can approach emotion. One—the healthy choice—is *connective*. We can connect with our emotions and use them as information to connect with others, or two—the unhealthy choice—is *disconnective*. We can disconnect from our emotions, which will also require us to disconnect from others when we/they are experiencing emotions.

Identifying and talking about emotions is a skill learned through practice. Unfortunately, many of us were not taught healthy and safe ways of expressing our emotions while growing up. Maybe you, like many people, grew up in a home that tended toward unhealthy emotional styles of expression that led to disconnection rather than connection.

Here are some common unhealthy and disconnective ways of managing feelings and emotion you may have seen in your home growing up. You may have heard these messages explicitly, or seen them in the way your parents managed their own emotions:

- Denial – "I don't have feelings/emotions. I'm a man/tough/strong."
- Numbing – "I avoid difficult emotions through substance or alcohol use or mindless distractions."
- Scapegoating/Projection – "I'm not the emotional one; you are."
- Aggression – "The only acceptable emotion to feel and express is anger or frustration."
- Dumping – "I talk about my emotions constantly, but I don't care about yours."
- Blaming – "My emotions/feelings are everyone else's fault/problem/responsibility."
- Positive Override – "There's no point feeling negative emotions. Don't dwell on the bad."
- Control/Manipulation – "You can't control your own emotions, so the best thing to do is control and manipulate your environment."
- Shaming/Weaponizing – "Emotions are a sign of weakness." "Don't be a crybaby!" "Man up!"
- Gaslighting – "That's not how you really feel."

All those ways of expressing emotion drive disconnection from self and others. They lead to stunted pathways of self-expression as they do not provide the language or the safe space for emotions to be acknowledged. The message in these homes was emotions = pain/shame.

Here are some ways people learned to express their feelings/emotions based on what they saw and experienced growing up in connective and emotionally healthy homes that encouraged self-expression:

- Empathy – "I hear you. I'm here with you."
- Solidarity – "You're not weird for having that emotion. I have felt that too."
- Validation – "Your feelings are valid! It makes sense to me how you feel."
- Curiosity – "Tell me more about how you are feeling."
- Gratitude – "Thank you for sharing your experience with me."
- Support – "Let me know how I can be supportive of you through this experience."
- Not-Solving – "Emotions are not a problem needing to be fixed. It's just information about your experience."
- Acceptance – "Emotions are a part of life. It's okay to be sad/upset/grieve."
- Embracing – "Your emotions are always welcome here."
- Compassion – "I'm sorry you're hurting."

People who grew up in homes where it was okay to connect with their emotions were usually also taught how to express those feelings safely and accurately. They learned the language to express their emotions in homes where it was okay to connect with and explore their feelings. The message in these homes was emotions = information for connection.

Unfortunately, many of us were not raised in homes that welcomed emotions. And this might not just be because your parents didn't want to connect emotionally. Social norms are a big factor that influences how we deal with emotions. Maybe your parents never learned to talk about their feelings in a healthy way either. But either way, many of us were not taught the skills of emotional self-expression or had the chance to practice them growing up.

We all exist in the same world with the same range of emotions, but some people have the tools to talk about them, and others do not. One analogy I like to use is that the people who grew up in disconnective style homes only got the 12-crayon box set of Crayola colors, while those in the connective style homes got the 64-crayon box set of colors.

When you learn new words to describe your emotions, you add a new color to your self-expression box. When you have the language to talk about your emotions accurately and expressively, you become empowered to handle and express them in a safe and healthy way. Accurate self-expression is a skill learned through practice.

GOOD AND BAD EMOTIONS

Our culture tends to embrace "good emotions," i.e., happiness, joy, pride, and hope, and shun "bad emotions," i.e., sadness, grief, anger, and jealousy. When I hear someone tell me they only want to feel positive emotions, that is like saying, "I want to learn to drive with my left eye closed." Can you do it? I mean, sure. But why would you ignore 50 percent of the information you have access to? By doing that, you are putting yourself and your family at risk because closing one eye doesn't make that whole side of the road and its drivers disappear. You are just recklessly ignoring them and hoping for the best.

All emotions are information for connection.

That's it. That's their one and only job. (Have I said this enough times yet?) In relationships, when we only allow ourselves to share "positive emotions" and neglect to acknowledge our "negative" ones, it stunts our ability to form a deep and complete connection. In an emotionally safe relationship, no emotions are off limits.

Of course, there is a reason we have labeled these emotions "good" or "bad." Generally, we like how "good emotions" make us feel, while "bad emotions" are often uncomfortable or painful. Feeling frustrated, sad, angry, or lonely is less pleasant than feeling joy, pride, and gratitude. However, if anything, "negative" or "bad" emotions give us a significantly larger dump of information than a "positive" or "good" emotion.

For instance, anger is an emotion that very frequently gets labeled as "bad"; however, in a healthy relationship, being able to talk about what made you angry is *crucial* to solving the potential underlying issue. What was the trigger for the anger? Is there a recurring theme? Maybe if you start thinking about it, you tend to get angry when your boundaries are crossed, your needs are not being met, or your sense of injustice is activated. If we start with the premise that all emotions are just information for connection, there are no such things as "good" or "bad" emotions. However, when using emotions to share information, *don't let your message get lost in the delivery.* Screaming "I'm *pissed*" at your partner while you trash the house 1) is not safe, 2) doesn't make your partner want to connect with you, and 3) doesn't express any useful information about *why* you are pissed. Your feelings may be valid, but flinging them at your partner like a pie in the face will not get you anywhere.

All emotions are fuel for connection, but like any form of fuel, if they are not handled safely, they can burn your house down. There are *safe* and *unsafe* ways of expressing your emotions. The safe ways are connective—they increase your ability to connect with yourself and others, and the unsafe ways of expression are disconnective—they drive you away from others and others away from you.

Stuffing emotions down, ignoring them, bottling them up, numbing out, or distracting yourself from acknowledging them is a short-term coping strategy, not a long-term solution. If you want a healthy relationship, you must have the tools to accept, connect with, and healthily self-express your emotions. Otherwise, your emotions *will* come out in an unsafe way. A consequence of not having proper tools to deal with difficult emotions healthily is we reach for whatever will distract us from the discomfort of having those emotions. Many addictive and numbing behaviors stem from a desire to avoid feeling difficult emotions.

BUILDING YOUR EMOTIONAL TOOLBOX

When you have the ability to express your emotions safely and accurately, you can maintain and deepen your relational connection with your partner. Accepting, Understanding, and Expressing your emotional experiences are the three main tools for developing the skill of self-expression.

Accept

You must accept your emotions to learn to deal with them healthily. One thing I hear from people is the fear that if they open themselves up to accepting or acknowledging their emotions, they will get stuck there. "If I allow myself to be sad, what if I get depressed?" I hear that. It is a scary thought for sure. However, according to neuroscientist, author, and TED presenter Jill Bolte Taylor, emotions typically last ninety seconds or less.[32] If you don't believe me, think of how not afraid you are of getting stuck in "happy" forever.

When you accept your feelings, you give yourself more opportunities to develop resilience and tolerate the discomfort of emotions. You will become less afraid of them and more confident in dealing with them because you know that they will pass. Practicing riding the wave of an uncomfortable emotion will help you practice distress tolerance and increase your emotional resilience. Emotional fitness happens when you give yourself a chance to work your emotional muscles.

Understand

When we avoid our emotions, we also ignore the message it sends. What Dr. Taylor found was that denial and avoidance of emotion is what actually kept it lingering. An unacknowledged emotion becomes the unread message in the inbox that keeps pinging you to read it. That's what takes up your mental energy! It's not going away until you read it. And ignoring a full emotional mailbox takes more mental energy than you think.

Often "big emotions" that can be disconnective like anger or frustration have another aspect to them that is more vulnerable and connective. See if you can get down past the big stuff to the deeper layer. Try to understand what it is about the situation that is so upsetting to you. Are you angry because you are embarrassed? Because you are hurt? Because you want more connection? What is your history of feeling this way? How far back does this pattern go?

Self-understanding leads to self-mastery. You learn more about yourself when you can understand the message your emotions are trying to tell you. When you know more about who you are and your experiences in the world, the deeper a connection you can form with your partner. Next time you experience an emotion, ask yourself, "Why am I feeling this?" This self-reflection will often give you a trailhead to follow that will unlock a need or a value underneath the emotion.

Express

How many words do you regularly use to talk about your emotions? In his book *I Don't Want to Talk About It: Overcoming the Secret Legacy of Male Depression*, therapist Terry Real notes that a majority of men could be diagnosed with alexithymia,[33] which the Google dictionary defines as "the inability to recognize or describe one's own emotions." If you don't have the language to describe your feelings, connecting with others through a shared experience is going to be more difficult.

Being able to express yourself accurately necessitates having the vocabulary to articulate your feelings. One of the first things I hand clients if they want to work on self-expression is this "emotion wheel." Learning to talk about their emotions is like learning a new language for many people. Most people have the basics: "mad, sad, bad, fine, okay, good." But to have a more complex or deeper emotional conversation that expresses what you are feeling more accurately, you might need to add some more words to your toolbox.

And I get it. Learning a new language is hard. It takes practice, it takes exercising a muscle that may have been neglected for a long time. But even if you start adding one or two new words to your toolbox, you will begin to feel more confident in your ability to express yourself with more clarity. Look at the emotion wheel below for a guide on how to start expanding your emotional vocabulary.

Maybe you notice that your emotional expression tends to stay in the center of the wheel. If that is the case, next time you feel an emotion, try challenging yourself to find a word in one of the outer circles that might be a little more descriptive of what you are feeling.

When working with a couple on their emotional safety and self-expression in a relationship, I break it down like this: Every emotion is a chance to deepen your bond. When you do not accept your feelings, understand or have the language to share your emotions safely, you lose those opportunities for connection. When you have more words to describe your emotions, you can express yourself more accurately. When you can do that, you open the door for a shared experience and deeper connection with yourself and your partner.

**Don't cheat yourself out of a whole experience
by refusing to learn a new language.**

THE FEEL WHEEL

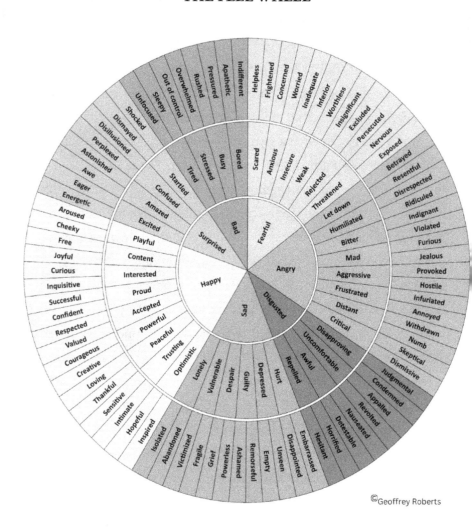

©Geoffrey Roberts

PRACTICE, PRACTICE, PRACTICE

Safe self-expression is a communication *skill.* Like any skill, the more you practice it, the better you will get at it. Give yourself more opportunities to practice your new skill by normalizing expressions of emotion. Normalizing emotional conversations is the biggest hurdle in most relationships. Many couples have assumed that an "emotional conversation" means a challenging or painful conversation. But who said that has to be the case? Emotions color the whole spectrum of human experiences!

Start by establishing a routine with your partner that normalizes emotional conversations. Simply relaying information is not emotionally connecting, but even conversations about logistics *can* lead to emotional discussions if you have the skills to go there. When you have the ability to do that, you can have emotional and connective conversations no matter the subject matter. For instance:

ROB and OLIVIA

PRACTICING EMOTIONAL ACCEPTANCE, UNDERSTANDING, AND EXPRESSION

Rob came to therapy saying that he and his girlfriend Olivia had difficulty when it came to emotional conversations. Through working on the skills for accepting, understanding, and expressing their emotions, they were able to change their communication pattern and connect more effectively.

OLD CONVERSATION PATTERN THEY HAD: AVOIDING EMOTION

Olivia: "How was your day?"

Rob: "Good."

Olivia: "Did you call your mom?"

Rob: "Oh, yup."

Olivia: "How is she?"

Rob: "Oh, not bad."

Olivia: "Great."

Rob: "Yeah."

This pattern left a lot unsaid. The possibility for connection was there, but because they didn't know how to talk about things on a deeper level, their conversations tended to fizzle out.

———

Another type of conversation they had: "Emotional Conversation"—accessing emotion, but not expressing them safely. Just throwing emotion at each other.

Olivia: "How was your day?"

Rob: "Good."

Olivia: "Did you call your mom?"

Rob: "Oh, yup."

Olivia: "How is she?"

Rob: "She's in a nursing home! How do you think she is?"

Olivia: "Well, don't get mad at me."

Rob: I'm not mad. You're the one who asked a stupid question."

Olivia: "Don't call me stupid!"

Rob: "I DIDN'T SAY YOU WERE STUPID. I SAID THE QUESTION WAS STUPID!"

Olivia: "DON'T FUCKING YELL AT ME!"

Fight for the next three hours.

NEW CONVERSATIONS: ACCEPT, UNDERSTAND, EXPRESS

Olivia: "How was your day?"

Rob: "Good."

Olivia: "Did you call your mom?"

Rob: "Oh, yup."

Olivia: "How is she?"

Rob: "Hmmm." (Takes a moment to accept, understand his own emotion before expressing.) "Okay, so I think it's finally hitting me that Mom's getting old. Mom's actually doing really well there, but I'm feeling pretty sad right now. It sucks that we're so far away."

Olivia: "I hear you." (Accepts his emotion.) "I understand it makes you sad to think of your mom getting older especially when we're so far away." (Understands his emotion.) "What do you need right now?" (Expresses support.)

Rob: "Oh, that's it. I mean I'm sad that we're far, but I know Mom is being cared for really well. Let's plan a trip to see her sometime soon."

Olivia: "Sounds good. Do you want a hug?"

Rob: "Yes, please."

And then they can move on to the rest of their day.

In relationships where skills for emotional self-expression are lacking, each person is experiencing their own emotions, but there is no shared experience. There is no ability for a safe emotional connection. To paraphrase a quote by Robin Williams's character in the movie *World's Greatest Dad*, the loneliest feeling in the world is not being alone. It's being surrounded by people and not experiencing connection. If you can express your emotions accurately and safely, it will lead to increased connection, no matter the emotion.

Both Rob and Olivia needed to work on their self-expression skills so they could have emotional conversations safely. When they got better at expressing themselves, they weren't leaving things unsaid or letting emotional conversations spiral out of control. By using tools for healthy self-expression, they changed the way they communicated and connected with each other. This strengthened their relationship by opening up communication channels they previously would have avoided or not known how to handle without damaging their relationship.

When we can accept our emotions, we can use them to connect with others through a shared experience of that emotion. If you cannot connect with and accept your own emotions and talk about your feelings honestly, it makes it almost impossible to fully connect with a partner.

You cannot express what you don't have the words for. You cannot accept emotions in others that you cannot accept in yourself. You cannot understand what you choose not to see.

Emotional connection is the glue of intimate relationships. If you don't have the skills to have a safe emotional connection with a partner, you are entering into your relationships unprepared. Don't show up to the job with an empty toolbox. Set yourself up for success in protecting your family and your marriage from emotional disconnection by making sure you have all the tools you need to be successful.

TL; DR STEPS TO HEALTHY SELF-EXPRESSION

1) BRAIN – Emotions are an essential part of what makes us human. We have a whole *large* part of our brain just dedicated to processing emotions. Everyone has emotions. Even you!

2) SCIENCE – Emotions are measurable brain states like sensations are measurable body states. They are information about how we are experiencing the world. With that said, there are no "good" or "bad" emotions. Some might be more enjoyable than others (like some sensations feel better than others), but they all contain important information about what we are experiencing and what our needs are.

3) PATTERNS – There are safe ways of dealing with emotions that lead to more connection with yourself and others, and there are unsafe ways of dealing with emotions that disconnect you from yourself and others. Most of us learned these patterns of coping with our emotions from the way we were raised and the culture of the families and communities we grew up in.

4) TOOLS – When you can accept your emotions, you can begin to understand what your emotions are telling you. Maybe loneliness is a sign that you need more connection, frustration might be a cry for help, anger may be a warning that a boundary of yours is being crossed. Once you can understand the message of the emotion, you can express it in a safe way that increases connection and deepens intimacy.

SAFETY – A SUMMARY

Safety is at the core of a healthy, STRONG relationship and the first green flag of a STRONG man.

These four skills of safety: Self-Awareness, Stability, Self-Regulation, and Self-Expression help us build resilience by challenging us to find true safety over seeking comfort in one extreme or the other. When we are unsafe in our environments, our bodies, our emotions, and our relationships, we usually run to one of two options: rigidity and over control, or chaos and lack of control. Neither makes for a healthy relationship. Safety is in balance. You cannot control your internal chaos by avoiding, numbing, or maintaining dominance over your environment forever.

The only person you can control is yourself. Get to know yourself more deeply. Seek to understand your triggers and learn how to regulate yourself or walk away from toxic relationships and people. You cannot connect with your partner if you are disconnected from yourself. You cannot find what you don't know you're looking for. When safety is in question, a relationship does not have the ground to build from. You cannot move on to building trust with someone you do not feel safe with.

Getting confident in these four skills will help you feel more confident in your ability to protect and provide Safety in your relationship as a STRONG and safe man and to identify healthy equal partners. The work of change is never easy, and often takes a circular path of learning new skills while dealing with the same issues—I like to use the analogy of a spiral staircase rather than a straight one. We don't get to run away from our issues; however, learning these new skills of Safety will help you have the tools to get above them and deal with them from a new angle.

"A journey of a thousand miles begins with a single step."

– LAO TZU

CHAPTER TWO

TRUST

"It takes two to do the trust tango—the one who risks (the trustor) and the one who is trustworthy (the trustee); each must play their role."

— CHARLES H. GREEN

GREEN FLAG #2

One of the world's leading experts on relationships, Dr. John Gottman, identified trust as *the most desirable quality in a relationship*.[1] Trust is what gives a new relationship security.

Being *trustworthy* is the second green flag of a STRONG man.

Having trust in your partner and knowing they also trust in you is a fundamental building block of a STRONG relationship. Trust is the glue that allows partners to feel secure in their bond. When there is mutual trust in a relationship, it feels like the two people who used to be "me" and "you" are now a "we."

Trust is something that people tend to see as a character quality, but I want to offer a reframe. Rather than seeing trust as something you are innately capable of or not, think of it as something you build with someone. Trust is the bridge between two people. That bridge is holding up your entire relationship. The trust is in the *bond*, the connection between the two of you.

When your partner can trust you to protect the "we," a relationship becomes a true partnership. In a relationship with mutual trust, partners know that they have each other's back and they work together to protect their relationship. When there is no trust, there is no "we." It's every man for himself.

Relationships filled with mistrust lead to partners choosing self-protection and division rather than unity and cooperation. This cycle leads to distrust and cynicism about the trustworthiness of people in general. But how can you prove that you are going to be a trustworthy partner? And how do you decide who to trust?

DEFINE: BELIEF VS. TRUST

Most of us don't have set criteria for deciding who is trustworthy. We say things like, "I just went with my gut." However, without a method of understanding what it would take to gain your trust, it is sometimes difficult to know whether you are placing your trust wisely or foolishly. I mean, if your gut was right 100 percent of the time, wouldn't you have won the lottery by now?

I am a big believer in the power of language. The more specific we can be with defining terms, the easier it will be to communicate effectively. With that said, defining "trust" is a big part of working with relationships. A differentiation of terms started to emerge when defining trust, building trust, and addressing trust issues in my therapy sessions. And it became a crucial difference that I think is important to name.

Believing someone and trusting them are two very different things:

Belief is a gift you choose to give. Trust is earned.

The way I like to explain it is when someone says, "believe me," they ask you to choose to believe them without the obligation of evidence. It is a one-way transaction. You can believe someone on a "gut feeling" or a whim; it doesn't have to be data-based. It is something you decide to do, with or without evidence.

However, so many people use the word *trust* when they really mean *belief*. When someone says, "Trust me," but provides no evidence of their trustworthiness, what they are actually asking is for you to "believe" them. Using the word *trust* when you mean *belief* leads to much hurt and heartbreak in relationships.

When someone says about their partner, "They said they wouldn't cheat on me, and I trusted them," I like to explore that idea by highlighting that if they don't follow through on other promises, you *believed* they wouldn't cheat on you. Because when you look at their actual "trustworthiness," their track record is not impressive.

Here's an example I often use: If a friend asks you for a loan, you have two options: You can choose to give them the money, or not. However, *how* you make the decision is what makes all the difference. Because

A. You can believe the words that they say, or

B. You can evaluate their trustworthiness.

And sure, the outcomes may be the same, but how it *feels* to make the decision is very different.

If you use the belief route (A), you are basing your decision on things like "how generous am I feeling today," "how much do I like this person," and "do I have some extra money to give?" You might still choose to give them money ("Sure, man, I believe you"), but you are doing so without evidence that they are good for paying you back.

However, if you choose to go with choice B) and evaluate their trustworthiness, all the other factors are unimportant. You will make your decision of whether or not to loan this person money based on your past history of lending them things. You will make your choice based on quantitative, not qualitative, data. Trustworthiness is based on evidence of a solid track record.

Your decision-making process will go more like this: "I'm feeling generous today, and I really like this person, but I remember lending them money before and they never paid me back. Also, they tend to forget their promises to follow through with things in general, so no, I don't think I will loan them this money because they are not very trustworthy."

So often, I have seen people choose to believe in someone who is clearly untrustworthy. Then when the untrustworthy person does what untrustworthy people do, they feel like their trust has been broken and violated—which hurts like hell! When you confuse belief with trust, you set yourself up for some serious disappointment.

This difference is also the key to being a trustworthy partner yourself. Do you rely on asking your partners to "believe you," or are you building a track record of being someone who is worthy of being trusted? If you don't know what trusting someone actually looks like or truly means, you may have just been going through relationships believing in your partner or asking them to believe you, but that is different from building trust with each other.

Belief is not interchangeable for trust. Belief is based on hope; trust is based on data. Trust is something that gets built over time. Building trust in a relationship is about consistency. Trust is something that can be gained and lost. Betrayal can break it, and repair can fix it. Confusing belief for trust leads to many people developing "trust issues" in relationships.

TRUST ISSUES

Trust issues are another common presenting problem for people seeking relationship therapy. In general, when trust issues are brought into the room, it boils down to this: either "I do not have enough data about you to trust that you will choose what's best for *us* over what's best for *yourself* when faced with a choice" or "The data says you're untrustworthy, but I want to believe you, so I will ignore it."

<u>LUCA</u>

When Luca came to see me, he told me that he had gotten into a new relationship that he needed some help with. He had met Raye online and hit it off immediately. They shared a love of mountain biking and after chatting a bit, they found they had

many mutual friends in common. Over the past year, they had
spent more and more time together, and even recently traveled
together to Mexico for a ten-day bike race. When they returned,
Raye brought up the topic of moving in together. However,
after she did, Luca began having panic attacks. After a few
uncomfortable and scary experiences, he had decided to seek
therapy.

He told me, "My girlfriend thinks it's because of my trust
issues."

I asked him to elaborate on that, and he continued, "I haven't
lived with anyone since my ex-wife back when I was in my
twenties." As he was in his forties now, I understood the
magnitude of what he was saying.

"Luca," I asked, "who was the last person you trusted?"

He thought for a moment. "I don't trust anyone," he said.

"What must that be like for you" I wondered, "not to be able to
trust anyone?"

"It's great," he laughed. "I never get cheated."

"Okay," I conceded. "You are a very successful businessman
so I can see how being less trusting may be a good strategy in
your work life, but what about in your personal life?"

He scoffed. "People always disappoint me. It's better I don't.
Believe me, I've learned the hard way. When I was a kid, my
dad would promise to come see me and I would wait and wait
for him. One night I stayed out all night on the sidewalk
because that *pendejo* said he would come get me for the
weekend. My grandmother slept with me on the street because
I wouldn't give up. I've had friends and business partners stab
me in the back or try to cheat me and not a single girlfriend I
ever had was faithful for shit. Even my wife freaking stole my
car when she left me."

"But you want to trust your girlfriend now?" I asked.

"I don't know." He paused. "What I mean is," he clarified, "how do I know when to trust?"

Since trust is fundamental to a relationship, people with trust issues will generally struggle to form secure bonds with others, especially in an intimate relationship. Building trust in a relationship is tough if you believe other people are fundamentally untrustworthy. Without a method of understanding what it would take to gain your trust, it is sometimes difficult to know whether or not you are placing your trust in the right person.

Some seek help for their trust or commitment issues, like Luca, while others wear this label as a personal strength until it ruins their relationships. After getting to know Luca a little more, he told me his motto was "You can't get divorced if you don't get married." And, I had to concede, he wasn't wrong. But did that stance protect him against what he was ultimately most afraid of: getting cheated on and having his trust betrayed? It did not.

I can completely understand why people have trust issues. Like Luca illustrated, much of the root cause of trust issues comes from lived personal experiences. Unfortunately, many people have had some experience of being betrayed by friends, siblings, parents, and romantic or business partners. Being deceived by someone you thought you could trust is a painful experience. Depending on the relationship, it can also take a significant toll at the expense of time, energy, and money.

Developing trust issues or deciding not to trust anyone anymore is an attempt to protect yourself from future hurt. After all, one thing we do know is that people are inherently unpredictable. The assumption goes, "If you don't trust anyone, you can't be hurt if they betray you." Although this seems to make sense on the surface, not trusting others does not guarantee protection against hurt or betrayal.

What is predictable, though, is this: Trust issues are a surefire way to ruin an intimate relationship. While it is potentially a savvy way to keep the advantage in business transactions, lack of trust ensures disconnection in your personal and romantic relationships. While distrusting others is one way of attempting to keep yourself safe in a relationship, it only works by maintaining a distance.

One of the biggest obstacles to building trust in a relationship is the inability to open up and allow someone to build trust with you. Of course, if you have been betrayed in the past, it may seem foolish to open back up to someone. It is vulnerable to ask for what we need and hope our partners care enough about us to meet our needs. With that said, you cannot build trust with another person without being able to trust yourself first.

"One of the ways we keep ourselves from being fully alive is through trying to protect ourselves from ever getting hurt again. A key aspect of personal empowerment is making peace with the thought that you will get hurt again, and that it is okay."

– XAVIER DAGBA

TRUSTING YOURSELF

One of the underlying issues around trust arises when someone does not have confidence that they can make good and safe choices for themselves. Take a moment to consider these questions: What is the last good decision you made for yourself? What is your track record of making decisions for yourself that you are proud of?

When men lack trust in themselves, it can lead to a lack of confidence in their relationships because they think, *Well, I am not great at making good choices. Who knows if this is a good choice for me? Better err on the side of caution and choose not to trust.* This pattern was part of Luca's conundrum.

As we worked together, he revealed that his last three relationships had ended because of a betrayal on the other person's part. He was understandably doubtful about his radar for detecting untrustworthy people. He had also made some choices in other areas of his life that he was not proud of. This history had, over time, led to his self-perception as not only someone who was a bad judge of character, but who could not be trusted to make good judgments for himself in general.

Over the course of about six months, Luca worked through therapy to build trust in himself. He worked on his ability to recognize and set boundaries with people who were untrustworthy and to determine his criteria for trustworthiness. He was able to see when he had mistaken belief for trust in the past or when he had ignored his own instincts to meet someone else's needs in a relationship. He also reflected on times in his life when he had his own back and was trustworthy himself.

In one of our last sessions together he said, "Now I know what it means to feel trustworthy in myself. No matter what, I will be able to make good choices in the future. I know I can leave toxic people by setting a boundary, not by being betrayed." You can start trusting others when you know how to trust yourself first.

TRUSTING OTHERS

When it comes to trusting others, like Steven Furtick says, "Look at pattern, not potential." Look at who's asking you to trust them. Trust is built on predictability and consistency. So often, people will say that they trust their partner to do something essential for them, like "I trust that my partner won't cheat on me. I trust that my partner will be there for me when we're old." But, if you cannot trust that your partner will show up on time for a date or follow through on the little things of everyday life, how can you confidently trust them in the more significant things?

> If your relationship is based on "I love you, but I don't trust you," your relationship can only stay at the surface level.

WALSH and BRIANNA

BELIEF VS. TRUST

Walsh and Brianna came to see me for couples counseling. They said they were having a lot of conflict in their relationship, and they wanted to see if there was a way to change that.

Brianna noted, "We love each other so much, but sometimes we make each other crazy."

When I asked them to elaborate, Walsh clarified: "We love hard and we fight hard. Like we will have days where we are just totally in love, but. . ."

Brianna chimed in, "Then like, I'll forget that we had plans or something, and we'll fight about it for days."

In reviewing their relational history, I noticed a pattern: some of the biggest fights they had were after Brianna came home from business trips. Even though the topic of the fight was often something small like weekend plans, I wondered aloud if there was any issue with trust in their relationship. However, each partner swore that they trusted the other implicitly.

Walsh said, "No, I have been cheated on before and my other partner was just one big red flag: drugs, alcohol. I trust Bri not to cheat on me. I just can't trust her to remember things."

Brianna laughed. "Oh, absolutely. We don't have a problem with trusting each other, we are just really bad at remembering our promises. He is even worse than me sometimes!"

I asked them, "Out of all the promises you make to each other, what do you think your track record is for following through?"

They both laughed. "I don't know!!" Walsh exclaimed "Twenty-five percent?"

"Yeah, right! Maybe on a good day," Brianna said.

I said, "Okay, so if the track record is 25 percent follow-through on the little things, what makes you confident that it will be higher in the big things?"

"I'm not sure what you mean," Walsh said.

"How can you say you trust someone 100 percent when they are away if they have only shown themselves to be 25 percent trustworthy when they are home?" I asked gently.

Brianna chimed in, "I don't like what you're insinuating. I would never cheat on him."

"I understand," I said, "but trust in a relationship is built on the little things. You are asking him to trust in you 100 percent when you have only shown yourself to be 25 percent trustworthy. Can you see how that might be difficult?"

Walsh spoke thoughtfully. "That makes sense. I wonder sometimes why it feels like such a big deal when you don't follow through on stuff like calling me back or showing up for a date on time. I don't want to be ridiculous and overreact, but I guess I do wonder if I can really trust you sometimes."

Brianna was incredulous. "Babe, are you serious? You can trust me!"

Walsh spoke quietly. "But that's the problem. Sometimes I don't know if I can. I really want to. I believe that you wouldn't want to hurt me, but I also know that you're pretty bad at following through on your promises. And I'm just as bad."

Brianna thought for a moment. "Now that I think about it, there's something that's made me uneasy at times. I see you do it with your friends like you kinda edit the truth a bit or brush over things you don't want to talk about. Just like little white lies, but I wonder sometimes what you might be not telling me."

"How have you seen that affect your relationship?" I wondered.

Brianna reflected, "I might not bring it up to him if it's not a huge deal, but it definitely affects my mood. I guess it leads to a lack of trust in general."

Walsh agreed, "I mean, that makes sense. I wouldn't trust anyone who had a track record like that either."

I said, "Right now you are both operating on a belief that your partner will be good for their word, but when you evaluate your trustworthiness, it sounds like there are some gaps on both sides. Why don't we start by talking about some ways you can each start to earn your partner's trust and strengthen your bond?"

Reliable, repeated, consistent efforts earn trust. This is where personal accountability shows up as well: people who are trustworthy in other ways are more likely to take relational commitments more seriously. Trust is a fragile thing. Even after years of building, it only takes a moment to break trust. Someone who believes in the importance of being trustworthy will be more aware of that reality and will work harder to prevent breaches of trust.

Learning to trust others starts with seeing who is trustworthy by looking at their pattern of behavior in other aspects of life. Consistency in one area doesn't always translate to consistency in another, but if you are looking at a total stranger, you have to start with what data you have. General markers of trustworthiness are: people who are safe (who have the 4 S's of safety skills under their belt), people who are responsible, dependable, and who have a pattern of maintaining consistent bonds in their life.

Remember that trust in a relationship is in *the bond.* Our bond is trusted because we both help contribute to and protect the security of it. We are attached securely. Trusting someone in a relationship is built on a consistent pattern of call and response.[2] When I need you, you are there for me. When you need me, I am there for you. You have my back. And I have yours.

SHIFT: WHEN THE ME BECOMES THE WE

When it comes to trust in a relationship, this is one of the litmus tests: Do you default to looking out for yourself (the *me*), or can you be trusted to think about the relationship (the *we*)? Can you be trusted to protect the relationship from potential harm? When I need you, will you be there? Whose back do you have? How solid is our bond?

One of the biggest challenges I see in couples is where one person has a default "*me* brain" in which they tend to think of their needs first and foremost, and the other person has a default "*we* brain," where they tend to think of the couple's and family's needs first and foremost. This difference in default is where the impact of birth order, gender, and upbringing often come into play.

People with the "*we* brain" default tend to come from families where they had to take on a lot of responsibility. Maybe their parents were unavailable, unstable, or untrustworthy. Maybe they were the oldest child tasked with looking out for their siblings, or the one labeled "mature." Conversely, people with a default "*me* brain" often grew up in a family in which they didn't have much responsibility for others. More often than not, they only had to think about their own needs.

Another thing to consider is the impact of socialization on the differences between people with *me* brain or *we* brain. It is a relatively accepted idea that girls mature faster and are more responsible than boys. This often leads to parents, teachers, and other adults looking to girls to be accountable for other children. This reinforcement fosters the development of the *we* brain pattern in some girls from a very young age.

On the other hand, often the prevailing idea about boys is that they are not to be trusted to handle anything except themselves—and barely at that. This can lead to the reinforcement of the *me* brain pattern for little boys as the message is "As long as you handle your own needs, you're doing fine."

Unfortunately, this mismatch of the *we* focus vs. the *me* focus in childhood can lead to a lot of frustration in adults. The portrayal of a man looking out for the *me* and the woman looking out for the *we* is a frequent trope on social media, i.e., a reel/TikTok of a mom who is getting the baby ready, the toddler packed, the dog situated, and herself ready for a trip while Dad is sitting there by the door with his shoes on like "I'm ready. What's the holdup?" Even though this is presented as a "funny" scenario on social media, it is much less funny in real life. I often hear from women that real-life scenarios like this contribute to resentment and mistrust regarding whether or not their partner actually cares about her and the family's needs.

Of course, there are men with the *we* brain default and women with the *me* brain default, but this mismatch is something that I frequently see in couples that contributes to trust issues. Being the one who is always looking out for the needs of the family or the couple while the other partner is just looking out for themselves is a common point of frustration that leads to conflict.

Take a moment to consider whether your personal default is the *me* brain or the *we* brain. If your default is to think about your needs first and foremost, you may need to do a little more work to shift your default to looking out for the needs of the *we*. For a relationship to build trust, both people have to be looking out for the *we*. If your partner knows that the *we* brain is not your default, it will be harder for them to trust that you can do it in a pinch. If you haven't trained the muscle, if you haven't practiced, how can they trust you to suddenly show up STRONG?

Strengthening your *we* brain might look like being more proactive in checking in on the needs of your kids, pets, or plants, and ensuring that the couple's and family's needs are met. It also might necessitate checking in more with your partner about the decisions you make. Often, people with the *me* brain default to making decisions based on what's best for themselves and assume that it will translate to what is best for the couple. However, this is not always the case, and it often gets people into a lot of trouble in their relationships. Of course, the opposite is true as well—you cannot make a *we* decision without actually taking both people's perspectives and needs into consideration.

Get ahead of any potential trust issue by bringing the *we* into the forefront of your brain. And remember that learning any new skill takes a lot of time and practice. You're exercising a new muscle. Switching the default of your brain wiring will take a lot of training. If you've ever been in the military, you know how much they have to hammer in the concept of "No man left behind." It takes a lot of training and practice to think of yourself as part of a unit, but you cannot build trust in the team unless *everyone* thinks like a unit. If one guy is only thinking about *me*, the whole mission is in trouble.

ATTACHMENT STYLES AND TRUST

The ability to trust others in a relationship often goes back to our experiences with our parents and our attachment style. Attachment is the crux of the matter when it comes to trust. Because trust develops when you reach out for help, and the help comes. Building trust with someone is a mutual exchange and building of a secure attachment to each other. When there is reliability and consistency, the bond—the attachment between you—becomes stronger.

The security of the bonds you expect from other people typically go back to what you learned to expect from your parental figure growing up. When you cried, who came? When you needed support, who was there? When you asked for help, did you get it? What were your parents like and what did they teach you about the trustworthiness of other people? Maybe in your family it was "every man for himself." Understanding your attachment style can help you understand the impact your childhood had on your ability to trust others in relationships now.

In the 1970s, a researcher named Mary Ainsworth performed a famous experiment called the Strange Situation,[3] which along with other prior research, helped categorize attachment into two distinct styles: **Secure and Insecure.**

Below are very brief and broad strokes of Attachment Theory.

Secure Attachment

People with a secure attachment style grow up with stable and consistent attachment figures. These parents or primary caregivers were emotionally available, attentive to the child's needs, consistently present, and able to soothe the child when upset. These adults provided a stable base for the child to explore their environment and return to when necessary. Children with secure attachment figures grow up to be adults with higher self-esteem, better social skills, and more confidence and trust in their romantic relationships. The patterns they learned in childhood prepared them to enter into relationships knowing what it felt like to be secure in a bond with another person. These people were given the tools, support, and experience needed to become secure bond builders.

Insecure Attachment

Other children grew up in homes where they did not have a secure relationship with their parents or primary caregiver. The parents may have been emotionally or physically absent and unreliable due to substance use disorders, mental health issues, or other obstacles. These parents were inconsistent in meeting their child's emotional needs, leading to the child developing an insecure attachment style.

There are three main ways that insecure attachment gets expressed in relationships.

Type 1) Dismissive: Avoidant – These children realized early on that they could not rely on their parents to be there for them when they needed help or support. From a young age, these children learned to only rely on themselves because they could not trust their parents. As children, they never experienced what it felt like to have a healthy support system. As adults, these individuals tend to be less trusting of others and are quick to leave relationships. Their first instinct is to avoid getting attached to or dependent on others. They might also resist being vulnerable and have trouble being open emotionally. Resisting intimacy is the hallmark of an avoidant attachment style.

Type 2) Preoccupied: Anxious – These children grew up in homes with parents who were also inconsistent, but instead of pushing their parents away, they became desperate to figure out how to get their parents to stay consistent. Anxious children are hyperaware of their parents' moods and become terrified of being abandoned. In adults, this attachment style can look like codependency, people-pleasing, jealousy, lack of healthy boundaries, and clinging to toxic relationships. Fear of being alone and abandoned is the hallmark of an anxious attachment style.

Type 3) Disorganized: Fearful/Avoidant – What happens when the person who is supposed to be the source of safety is a source of danger? As children, our parents are supposed to be our source of safety and comfort. We are biologically hardwired to look to our parents for love and support when we are scared. However, children abused by their parents or primary caregivers get conflicting messages. When your source of love is also a source of pain or fear, it creates a disorganized attachment style. Children who develop a disorganized attachment style often come from homes where they received abuse from those who were supposed to love and care for them. The hallmark of this style is wanting to be loved but expecting, and being terrified of, the pain it may cause.

If you are someone who grew up in a home where there were no loving, stable adults, or you were subjected to any form of child neglect, abuse, or trauma, you may have trouble trusting relationships in your life today. This makes sense! If you grew up in a home where your parents or primary caregiver were the sources of pain, neglect, or danger, you may have developed a protective adaptation. You learned the lesson that "those you love are going to hurt you." People who grew up in homes with insecure attachment bonds to their parents did not receive the tools, support, and experiences needed to trust their attachments to others in their adult relationships today.

Adults with insecure attachment styles can have difficulty trusting in relationships because their brains have learned to equate love with pain. Psychotherapist Deb Dana explains the impact of attachment trauma like this: "Trauma compromises our ability to engage with others by replacing patterns of connection with patterns of protection.[4]" As humans, we are hardwired to avoid pain. It is a healthy adaptation of our brains to protect us from things that can hurt us. Until those neural pathways are healed and separated, people who have an insecure attachment style may struggle to develop the ability to trust others, particularly in intimate relationships.

If you have, or love someone with, a history of childhood emotional neglect, attachment trauma, or abuse, know there is help. Healing from trauma is possible! I see it every day in my practice. Trauma therapy with a trained clinician can help rewire your brain to untangle the experience of love from the expectation of pain.

HEALING OLD WOUNDS

After talking about attachment styles, one of the things I like to point out is that history is not destiny. Those with secure attachment styles may have a head start in the relational trust game, but if you read through those attachment styles and realize that you might tend toward anxious, avoidant, or disorganized attachment, all is not lost.

The point of learning about attachment is not to give yourself a diagnosis or to blame your parents for your relational wiring or your difficulty trusting today. It is to shed some light on how you responded to growing up in an environment that *did not meet your needs* so you can understand your patterns and tendencies in your current relationships.

A common thing I hear from men is the denial that their past impacts them today. I've had clients straight up say to me when I ask them about their childhood or past relationships, "Oh, it didn't affect me, this is just how I am." So, let me address this.

Your past has impacted you. You live through something; it affects you. That's how experience works.

Even if we don't *want* our past to follow us, it just does. Our brains are giant pattern-seeking machines. If your brain learned the pattern that trusting others means pain, it makes sense that it would try to keep you away from that in the future. We bring our entire life history with us into our relationships. If you don't address and acknowledge the impact your past experiences have had on you, you will keep repeating the insecure patterns of your old attachment scripts. Like Winston Churchill said, "Those who fail to learn from history are condemned to repeat it."

And just to clarify, you could have amazing parents who were doing the absolute best they could, or knew how to do, and it still could not have been what you needed as a child. Physically absent parents could have been unavailable for legitimate reasons like having to work two jobs or traveling a lot for work. Emotionally unavailable parents may have focused on providing physical needs and perhaps didn't know how to be emotionally available due to their own childhood experiences. Regardless, your interactions with your primary caregivers in childhood taught you about the trustworthiness of others and the security of creating bonds with them.

However, here is the good news: childhood experiences may have laid the groundwork for your tendencies around trusting others in relationships, but the ability to grow, change, and heal is ever present. Where there is life, there is hope. Brains are malleable. As neuropsychologist Donald Hebb found, and Stanford researcher

Carla Shatz summarized, "neurons that fire together, wire together.[5]" When you choose a new thought, action, or behavior, your brain gets rewired to incorporate that new mental pathway. We learn new information all the time, so our brains change all the time. Your brain is changing *right now* as you read this information.

This is something that I hope gives you hope. Just because your brain did not experience a trusting bond with a secure adult when you were growing up, it does not mean that you can never experience a trusting bond in the future. When you start taking steps toward creating healthy and strong bonds with a trustworthy person, your brain will begin to write a new script for your life and relationships. You can change your brain from one that sees relationships as a source of danger and pain to one that sees relationships as a source of safety and connection.

At the end of the day, your attachment style is your default based on your childhood experiences with your parents. Your attachment style will impact your tendencies toward others in relationships. However, your attachment style can and will change based on the security of your relational bonds. When you acknowledge that your past has impacted you, you can start to take steps to mitigate that impact and ask for what you need to build trust in your relationships now. When you and your partner can work together to foster trust and reassurance, over time, your bond with your partner will become more secure.

UNDERSTANDING THE IMPACT

I see three different types of relationship patterns that relate to trust. These tend to parallel attachment styles and are a way to illustrate what it looks like when you have or don't have a way to build trust in your relationship:

1) Independence – Looks like: less trusting of others

2) Codependence – Looks like: overly trusting of others

3) Interdependence – Looks like: ability to trust self and others

On one side of the relational spectrum is independence. You make decisions based on what's best for yourself and have a lot of trouble settling into a relationship. This tendency might point to an avoidant attachment style. This person's exterior narrative is "I trust me; I don't trust you."

However, in examining the inner narrative of this approach to relationships, one of the things that usually emerges is that, like Luca, these people secretly *don't really trust themselves to make good decisions about others.* Without the ability to discern whether or not they can make good decisions about other people, their default is to reject everyone and avoid situations in which they might be vulnerable.

Independent style relationships often look like two people who are high functioning but do not have much of an emotional connection. When things get tough, they will gravitate away from the relationship rather than working together toward a resolution because they don't know how to build a trusting bond. Although it is healthy to be your own person in a relationship, being totally "independent" and leaning away from your partner in times of crisis is counterproductive to being in a healthy relationship.

When independence is your default, the relationship is the thing that gets thrown under the bus if you ever feel like it is getting in the way of your personal goals. And if your partner cannot trust that you will look out for the relationship when the chips are down, if you always look out for yourself first and foremost, it will be hard for you to earn their trust. You can't build a solid bridge with someone who keeps moving farther away.

On the other end of the relationship spectrum is the opposite type of dysfunctional dynamic in relationships—codependency. This relationship style is prevalent among those who tend toward an anxious attachment style. The external narrative in the codependent style is "I don't trust me, so I will trust you."

However, if we think of the attachment wound that leads to anxious attachment, it came from having inconsistent parents who only intermittently met their emotional needs. So, when we peel back the layers of this type of relationship style, what often emerges in their inner narrative is that these folks secretly *don't really trust that others want to meet their needs.*

People with an anxious attachment style often worry about being rejected or abandoned for being "too much." So, rather than being honest about their needs, which might lead to rejection, they do a lot of work managing their partners and navigating through hoops to passively get their needs met. When you are in a relationship where you don't trust that your partner wants to meet your needs, you must do a complicated mind-reading act to maneuver the other person into giving you what you need. This much emotional guesswork leads to a lot of resentment in these types of relationships.

When a relationship has a codependent dynamic, both partners participate in the cycle of mindreading and emotional guesswork. Both are afraid to acknowledge and articulate their own needs. This prevents them from being confident that they can get their needs met without manipulating the situation or their partner. They don't allow each other opportunities to earn trust, so they stay stuck in the cycle. You can't build a bridge in a bubble.

Interdependence is the healthy balance of relationship systems. This relationship type is the default of most people with a secure attachment style. These folks trust their judgment, and they also give other people opportunities to earn their trust. They have a healthy sense of self and display agency in their relationship. The overarching narrative of this style is: *I trust me, and I can learn to trust you.*

People who are in an interdependent relationship can meet their own needs and ask their partners for help when they need it. They don't test their partners, and they handle rejection well. When their needs are not being met in a relationship, they have the skills to talk about it and try to find a solution. They know their deal breakers and can also acknowledge that a relationship rupture can lead to repair if both people are willing to work on it. They also trust their ability to walk away from an unfulfilling relationship if needed. At the end of the day, they know they can make good decisions for themselves and the relationship.

They avoid the "all or nothing" dynamic that the Anxious/Avoidant folks tend to fall into. They understand that a relationship is made up of two different people with differing needs who are choosing to build a life together. Their default is to relate to each other and find a mutual solution, rather than rejecting or resenting their partners for not meeting their needs. They understand that the relationship will be an ongoing balancing act that will need a lot of opportunities to earn trust in each other. They offer and accept their partner's bids for connection and support. Both partners work together to build a strong bridge of trust between them.

BECOMING SECURE

Something that tends to get a bad rap is the idea of "insecurity." Often this word is used as a weapon against others in relationships: "He's so insecure"; "She's so needy." More than once, I have heard one partner say to the other, "Well, that's just your insecure attachment" or some variation of that. It is a pet peeve of mine because here's the thing—if we look at insecure attachment and its origins, there is not a single person in this world who has an insecure attachment style by choice.

I don't know about you, but most of us don't have a choice over the home we are born into and who our parents are. Our attachment wirings are laid in our brains before we have a conscious say in the matter.

With that said, I like to reframe "being needy or acting insecure" as "seeking reassurance in connection." It is a more accurate reflection of what is behind those urges. So, when your partner is looking to you for reassurance in your connection, rather than shaming them for "being insecure" or pushing it back on them ("Sounds like a you problem"), which is a sign of insecure attachment in itself, why don't you switch to offering reassurance? When you can provide reassurance through consistency and reliability, you build trust in the security of your connection and reaffirm your healthy attachment bond.

Of course, as discussed in the previous chapter on Safety, there is a safe way and an unsafe or controlling way of expressing and getting your attachment needs met. When people are unaware of their patterns and unable to communicate their needs honestly and transparently, it can lead to some untrustworthy and unsafe behavior in relationships. Suppose, after reading about Attachment Theory, you realize that you fall under the insecure attachment umbrella. In that case, it is important to understand how to ask for and get reassurance in healthy ways so as not to damage your relationships.

BECOMING TRUSTWORTHY

There are a lot of great quotes about the importance of truth in a relationship, and for real: *The truth will set you free.* But it might set you free from your relationship if you conceal it. Half-truths and loopholes around honesty and transparency always end up becoming a net that you will eventually find yourself trapped in. Be a man of your word and be brave enough to speak your truth.

Also, a reminder that sometimes being trustworthy means being able to say no. That is actually a really important way to gain trustworthiness: saying what you mean, when you mean it, even if that means saying something the other person might not want to hear. A better way to be trustworthy is not by saying yes all the time, but by being honest and saying no when no is the honest answer.

TIPS FOR TRUST: INSTANT REPLAY

One of the tips that I use in my own marriage and that I've shared with people I work with is this: Give yourself an opportunity for an instant replay.

What that looks like is this. Sometimes you say something, but one second later you realize. . . shoot, I didn't mean that, or I have no intention of doing that.

Example:

Me: "Husband, will you stop by the store on your way home from your doctor's appointment? We're out of coffee."

Husband: "You bet!"

Two minutes later

Husband: "Actually, instant replay. I don't have time to stop by the store. I have to run straight home to change so I can get to work on time."

Me: "Okay, thanks for letting me know. I'll run by later"

The most important thing when it comes to being trustworthy is aligning your words with your actions. Be brave enough to have an instant replay conversation or preemptively have an honest discussion about your intentions, actions, and needs. When you show up with integrity and honesty, you set yourself up for success in building trust in your relationships.

Don't set yourself up to lose trust by saying one thing and doing another. I've worked with so many men who have taken the "what she doesn't know won't hurt her" approach to things, who then are surprised when it blows up in their faces. Friend, *it never works*. It might be a week, month, or years later, but as Shakespeare wrote, "truth will out."

When you have broken trust by not being trustworthy, by going back on your word, or by doing something that caused harm to your partner, it is essential that you immediately start to work on the repair. This will help to establish yourself as a trustworthy person. The sooner you can begin to repair the bond, the easier the healing will be.

If your partner cannot trust that you care about the ruptures you are causing, they will lose faith in your trustworthiness. Being a trustworthy person means caring about your partner's experience in the relationship and making the effort to repair any ruptures you may have caused. If you make no effort to repair, you are lessening trust in favor of belief, and we already talked about where that ends up.

In *The Power of Discord: Why the Ups and Downs of Relationships Are the Secret to Building Intimacy, Resilience, and Trust*, authors Ed Tronick and Claudia Gold explore the strengthening power of disagreements in intimate relationships. Like building muscle, sometimes mini ruptures are crucial in helping the relationship build back stronger. However, you will not get stronger if you repeatedly push your muscles to failure without proper rest and repair. Instead, you will be setting yourself up for injury. The same is true for your relationship. When a relationship suffers too many ruptures without appropriate repair, it becomes less and less stable.

In every relationship, there will be times when you will make a mistake or have a disagreement with your partner. That will happen. You are two different people. You will have differences of opinion and times when you rub each other the wrong way. Conflict and disagreements can be a healthy and valuable part of a relationship, but you must know how to a) have healthy conflict and b) have a healthy repair. We will cover ways to have healthy conflict in the next chapter on Respect, so for now, let's look at the steps to making a healthy repair.

STEPS TO REPAIR

I enjoy acronyms, so I will use the word REPAIR as an easy-to-follow guide for you to use the next time you need to make good with your partner and patch up a rupture in your relationship.

R is for *remorse* – Don't apologize if you are not sorry. Seriously. The word "sorry" is so overused, and if it's not genuine, it can do more harm than good to the relationship. Part of being a trustworthy individual is being a man of your word. If you are not sorry, don't say sorry until you can genuinely express remorse.

Genuine remorse also means that you *stop the behavior*. I cannot tell you how many people I see continue to break their partner's trust by saying sorry and then going back and doing the thing that hurt them in the first place. Apologies acknowledge a relational injury, but they are not a free ticket to repeating damaging behavior. If you are remorseful, you have to show that by stopping the behavior that caused the harm in the first place.

E is for *empathy* – Not explanation. You need to understand the impact of your actions and show empathy for your partner's experience. This is often the uncomfortable part of an apology. You have to assess the wound. You have to understand and acknowledge the pain caused by your actions and sit with that for a bit rather than try to rush to the next stage.

I often see people get tangled up in conflict here because they either try to defend their intent rather than acknowledge the impact of their words/actions/behavior on their partner. Or they say "sorry," but when their partner wants to share specifically how they were hurt, they brush past the details of their partner's pain. Again, a huge part of being trustworthy is caring about your partner's experience. If your partner sees you caring about your defense or "moving on" over their experience, you will lose an opportunity to earn more of their trust.

P is for *perspective-taking* – The next part of repair is understanding the other person's perspective. Getting your partner's perspective on what changes they need to see from you is hugely important as each person is unique, and each person's measure of trustworthiness is different. Asking for an opportunity to hear their perspective and understand what they need from you in the future is another way to establish that you are trustworthy.

In practice, this might sound like, "I am sorry for showing up late to our date. I understand that made you feel disrespected. It sounds like you would have appreciated it if I would have called to let you know that I was running behind so you could adjust your plans I will do that next time."

The saying goes, "well begun is half done." A good REP is an excellent beginning and it is usually enough if there has been a minor rupture, i.e., showing up late to a date, but it won't take you all the way to rebuilding broken trust if there has been a major rupture. If the injury was deep, there are a few more steps to follow. The next part is where repair becomes a mutual process. Remember, building trust necessitates both people who are committed to creating a solid bond. When you have caused a rupture, you have to do the first part, but the second part will require your partner's help.

A note on forgiveness and moving on to the next steps. Just because you crafted a well-done apology and expressed empathy and understanding doesn't mean that the other person is ready to give you another opportunity to earn their trust again. When trust is broken in a relationship, it can be a moment of learning, strengthening, and taking accountability for whatever fallout your actions have caused. It can also be a time to reconsider your needs and values and deepen trust in yourself if you need to make a hard decision about leaving a relationship.

> "It's okay to forgive and move on.
> Forgiveness does not mean. . .
> continued tolerance of unhealthy behaviors."
> **– NEDRA GLOVER TAWWAB**

Pushing for forgiveness to cover up deep relational wounds is like putting carpeting over a crack in the foundation. It covers it with something that feels good but doesn't address the fundamental issue of broken trust. Expecting to "move on" simply because there has been an apology doesn't necessarily allow for true forgiveness or thoughtful repair. The rest of the steps are the hard parts that people often struggle with, but without them, there is no repaired bond and renewed trust.

A is for *accountability* – Accountability is about dealing with the consequences of your actions. An apology without accountability is not going to move you forward. Accountability can look like a lot of different things depending on the type of betrayal. For instance, let's say you took out a loan without your partner's knowledge. Accountability in this area might look like ensuring that financial responsibility is clearly outlined moving forward. This might look like meeting with a financial planner, setting a budget and a plan for repayment, and increasing financial transparency by sharing passwords to bank accounts or keeping finances separate moving forward.

I is for *investigation* – Do we know why this happened? Was the betrayal a dealbreaker? What does the future of this relationship look like? What do we need to do to prevent this from happening again? Investigating the steps of how we got here and what is needed to move forward is crucial. Investigation is especially important when the betrayal is deep or a recurring theme in the relationship. If you notice you continue to break your partner's trust or they continue to break yours, it might be time to take stock of the relationship. Is it stable? Do you share values? Are you actually ready to do the work of being a trustworthy partner? Is your partner willing to work with you by giving you opportunities to earn trust back?

R is for *rinse and repeat* – Repair in a relationship is not something that happens once. Many people believe that apologizing for something once should be enough to "move on." However, repair is like stitches; the deeper the wound, the more stitches you need.

For example, if you ran late to a dinner date, that might be a minor rupture that needs a "Band-Aid" level of repair to get back to good. However, if you financially, emotionally, or sexually betrayed your partner's trust, that's a major violation that causes deep wounds. That might be equivalent to your relationship getting hit by a bus. Relationships can die from these wounds. Healing from that kind of broken trust will take lots of time and require multiple levels of stitching and repair to get that trust back.

Not all injuries are equal. Not all ruptures are equal. Remember that it is not always a "one and done" situation when trying to repair trust in a relationship. If you cheated, lied, betrayed trust, or harmed your relationship in a way that has left a more severe wound, you may need to repeat this repair cycle multiple times for the same injury.

"Trust is built in drops and lost in buckets."

– KEVIN PLANK

MIND THE GAP

Okay, so you got your repair skills down. Your partner has decided to give you another chance. Sweet. Smooth sailing ahead, right? Ummm, don't relax yet. You can be sincerely remorseful, genuinely empathetic, truly understand your partner's perspective, take accountability, and really want to be a trustworthy partner, but. . .

> **Unless you understand the difference between**
> ***wanting to do something*** **and being** ***capable of it*,**
> **you will set yourself up for failure.**

In England, whenever you ride the subway, you will hear the reminder to "mind the gap" over and over. It might seem like an unnecessary announcement; I mean, here is the platform, there is the train. Bring foot from one to the other. But it really emphasizes the need to be mindful when we are taking "obvious" steps. When we fail to realize that the gap between where we are and where we want to be is larger than expected, we may be putting ourselves—or our relationship—in harm's way.

One of the most "obvious" questions I like to ask people who are recovering from a trust issue in a relationship is "How are you going to make this happen?" You are promising your partner that you will never cheat on them again. How? How can you know that you won't do it again? The response I often get is something to the effect of "Because I won't?" Well, that strategy didn't work that great the first time, so how can you be so sure that it will work this time?

This is an area where I see men fail to earn trust back because they fail to acknowledge the gap between *wanting* something and being capable of actually doing it. It is so easy to say, "I will do better next time," but the gap between wanting something to be better and having the skills and capacity to *do* better next time can be massive! And unfortunately, it is a gap that people fall into again and again.

Let's say you've always wanted to be a pilot, so you get a pilot's hat, the little pin-on wings, some sweet aviators, and an American flag patch for your new leather jacket. You look the part. That still doesn't mean you know how to fly a plane. If you have struggled to be trustworthy in the past, just because you have met the person of your dreams does not mean that you are now magically going to delete all your bad habits and become super trustworthy overnight. You can *want* to make a change all day, but you also need to investigate what new skills you need to actually be successful at making the change.

You have to show that you are capable of earning the trust back, not only because you "want to" but because you have the skills and tools to truly hold yourself to a new standard of behavior. You have to acknowledge the gap between who you are: someone who relies on willpower to not gamble, cheat, or forget your anniversary again, and who you want to be: someone who has the support system, self-regulation skills, boundaries, and reminders in his phone to actually accomplish the goals he has set for himself and the relationship.

To be successful, you will require a plan of action. First of all, you need to look at yourself and your patterns of trusting others. Then you can examine what trust means to you and how you define trustworthiness in a partner. From there you can look at ways you allow people to earn your trust and how you handle it when your trust is broken. When you can honestly look at your old wounds and previous attachment injuries you received or caused in previous relationships, you can be empowered to take steps toward healing and change. Becoming trustworthy and earning and repairing trust in a relationship is a lot of work, but it is the underpinning of any true partnership and the glue that holds a relationship together.

TL; DR STEPS TO BUILDING TRUST

1) DEFINE – *Belief* and *trust* are two different things. One is a gift you choose to give without expectation of reciprocity. The other is earned by consistent efforts over time. Trust (not belief) is the glue of a healthy relationship. Trust in a relationship is built through mutual exchange. It takes two.

2) SHIFT – A STRONG relationship needs a commitment to the *we* over the *me*, but when you can't trust yourself, you will have a harder time trusting others. Trust issues can often be traced back to attachment styles. When you heal your attachment wounds, you can shift your perspective from seeing others as fundamentally untrustworthy. Then you can begin to evaluate who is deserving of your trust.

3) GROW – Trust is something that can be broken *and repaired.* When you take the opportunity to make repairs, you are proving that you care about protecting your partner and your relationship.

4) LEARN – There is a difference between wanting something and being capable of making it happen. If you have been untrustworthy in the past, don't just rely on willpower to make a change. Make a plan. Start practicing the skills you need to be trustworthy.

CHAPTER THREE

RESPECT

"Respect for ourselves guides our morals.
Respect for others guides our actions."

— LAURENCE STERNE

GREEN FLAG #3

Most men agree that respect is vital to them. Nobody enjoys being disrespected, and we can all agree that living in a world where we can respect each other leads to greater peace and harmony. Respect is an essential component of a healthy relationship.

Having RESPECT is the third green flag of a STRONG man.

I had a wonderful conversation one morning in a Montana coffee shop. I was in the middle of writing this chapter and had a few mental threads on the topic of respect going. As I waited for my coffee, mulling them over, the logo on the man's shirt in front of me caught my eye. I remarked on it, and he told me his name was

Robert and he was a veteran supporting another veteran's work. After a few minutes of chatting, I asked him, "When you think of the word respect, what comes up for you?"

Thankfully, he wasn't put off by an in-depth question before coffee, and after a thoughtful pause, he began with the social implications of the word respect. "It's about manners," he said. "In a large society, we need to be aware of how our actions impact other people. And having respect for others is about acknowledging differences in lives and backgrounds."

Encouraged, I kept going. "Will you tell me your thoughts on self-respect? And I respect your boundaries if you're done answering!"

He chuckled and considered the question. "Self-respect is about acting in a way that you are proud of," he said. "When you can look at your life and know that you made honest choices and stayed true to your values, that gives you self-respect."

Just then, the barista called out his name, so I thanked him for his time, and Robert grabbed his coffee and walked out into the cold Montana air.

This two-minute conversation encapsulated everything important about respect. In any relationship, whether between two people or in the larger context of our relationship with our communities and society as a whole, we have to start by acknowledging that there are two parts to respect.[1]

For one, no man is an island. Our actions impact other people. To live respectfully, we need to respect the boundaries between ourselves and others, acknowledge our differences, and make space for them. A man who can be relied upon to honor a boundary is a man who demonstrates respect for others. Boundaries are a way to maintain a civil and well-functioning society. Just as every culture will have its own rules of conduct and boundaries for behavior, every person has their own boundaries. Your boundaries will be different from your neighbor's and your partner's boundaries will differ from yours. Honoring other people's boundaries is how we show them respect.

And secondly, we need healthy self-respect. Self-respect is being able to look at your actions and know that you are in alignment with your own values. It is about being accountable and holding yourself to a standard you can be proud of. When we respect and protect the values and boundaries of others, we can develop respect-filled relationships. When we respect ourselves, we live our lives with integrity. These two parts make for respect-filled individuals and respect-filled relationships.

WHAT ARE BOUNDARIES?

There are many excellent resources on boundaries: how to define, maintain, and uphold them. One of my favorites is *Set Boundaries, Find Peace: A Guide to Reclaiming Yourself* by Nedra Tawwab. But there is also a lot of misinformation out there about boundaries. There is often confusion about how boundaries differ from rules, agreements, or barriers. I get it. Language is tricky sometimes, and often words get used in ways that misinterpret their true meaning and purpose.

So, let's start with some definitions for Barriers, Rules, Agreements, and Boundaries.

1) **Barriers** – Google says a barrier is "a fence or other obstacle that *prevents movement or access.*" They are *protective*, but they

are not *connective*. Barriers are designed to keep people out. As we covered in the previous chapter, safety is a core human need. If there is a toxic or unhealthy person who has shown themselves to be uninterested in honoring our boundaries, we might put up a barrier with them. But barriers are not boundaries. They are a protective mechanism and send a clear "stay out" message. On the other hand, if we don't know how to set healthy boundaries and show people how to interact safely with us, we will sometimes overuse barriers to protect ourselves.

2) **Rules** – are about a set code of conduct in a specific area of life. They set a standard to be followed and come with consequences when broken. Rules can have a place in a healthy relationship, but they have to be equally applied to be effective and healthy. Rules differ from boundaries because there is often a power and control aspect to rules, i.e., when parents make rules for their children, or your boss makes a rule about your work attire. Parents and bosses are in a position of power compared to children or employees. When rules are not applied equally in a romantic relationship, i.e., "I can go on a trip with my friends, but you can't," it can lead to resentment, conflict, power struggles, or covert breaking of rules.

3) **Agreements** – These are negotiations of middle ground to suit a mutual need. Healthy agreements respect and consider individual boundaries, but they are not the same as a boundary. Boundaries are personal. Agreements are relational. Agreements are negotiable and can be changed as

the needs of the individuals change, but both people must hold up their end of the bargain for it to continue to work. An example of an agreement could be a couple mutually deciding not to have children until they get married. If the agreement only works by asking you to do away with your personal boundary, it's probably not a healthy agreement. You cannot have a healthy agreement without honoring both people's boundaries.

4) **Boundaries** – Finally! Okay, *boundaries protect you and your values*. That's it. The Google dictionary says they are a "dividing line." The line is where you end and others begin. Your body, your time, your money, your energy, your belongings are yours. Everything inside that boundary is what you have control over. Boundaries are the distinction between "your stuff" and other people's stuff. Some examples of setting boundaries might be saying no to someone's request for your money, time, energy, or access to your body. It can also look like choosing to remove yourself from a situation that is uncomfortable for you or standing up for yourself. Boundaries cannot be used to control other people because they are not about other people. They are about you. Boundaries are personal. And let's get clearing up some myths.

MYTHBUSTERS

Myth #1: Boundaries push people away. – False. Boundaries are not barriers to keep people out, but they do show them where the door is. Your boundaries are how you let others know to connect with you respectfully. Pay attention to people who push your boundaries or punish you for having boundaries.

Punishing someone for having boundaries can happen aggressively, i.e., someone telling you your boundaries are stupid, or it can happen passive-aggressively, i.e., someone sulking when confronted with your boundary.

Respect is honoring other people's boundaries even when you want something that's on the other side of that line.

You protect yourself by setting and maintaining boundaries i.e., "I'm not going to drink tonight because I have work in the morning" and surrounding yourself with people who respect and help protect your boundaries, i.e., people who will not pressure you: "Oh, c'mon, man, just one drink"; punish you: "Oh, I see how it is, Mr. Better than everyone, huh?"; or disrespect your boundaries: "Take the shot, take the shot!"

People who disrespect your boundaries are not people who have your best interests in mind. They want what's best for them ("But I want to climb into your house through the windowwww") over what you tell them is best for you ("Please come through the front door"). The people who want total access to you at all times will be the ones who refuse to use the door and then claim that they are being pushed away.

Myth #2: Boundaries are always just a starting point in a negotiation. Hell to the *no*. However, this very dangerous myth is often perpetuated and encouraged, especially in relationships between men and women. One conspicuous example of this is how men are often encouraged in dating to take a woman's sexual boundary as a challenge, i.e., "She said no, but I think she just needs a little convincing."

Coercion is not consent.

Agreements are negotiable in the context of relationships. Boundaries are not. Pushing boundaries will put both you and the other person in harm's way. Your partner will feel uncomfortable because pushing her boundaries makes you disrespectful at best and dangerous at worst. It will also open you up to being perceived as creepy or predatory, because, let's be honest, it's creepy and predatory behavior.

When it comes to consent, consent is not an "I guess." It's a "Hell, yes!!" Enthusiastic consent is sexy! And you will be doing yourself a favor, and protecting yourself from any possible compromising situations, by thinking of *everything that's not a hell yes as a hell no*. Wait until you get the "Door's open, come on in" rather than sneaking around trying to find an unlocked window. See? Creepy. Don't be that guy. Disrespecting someone's boundaries is showing disrespect for them as a person.

On the flip side, there are women who may try to push past your sexual or personal boundaries. In case no one has ever told you this: You are always allowed to say no. Boundary-pushing behavior is not any less creepy or predatory just because the genders are reversed. Boundaries allow you to let your partner in, but they also allow you a sense of personal agency as to when and where you do so.

Myth #3: "Boundaries" are random and are used as an excuse to get out of responsibilities or obligations. This is a common one that people misuse. For example, let's say your roommate tells you, "I have a boundary about cleaning the toilet." And I get it; it's frustrating because isn't that a personal boundary? I mean, they're talking about themselves and what they will or won't do, right?

And, sure, maybe it's an actual boundary, but not necessarily. Let's look a little closer. Boundaries protect core values, so what's the personal value protected by not cleaning the toilet? You can ask them to clarify their boundary by being curious and seeing if you can come to a mutually respectful agreement that honors both your boundaries. Maybe after being curious, you discover that they have a boundary about not being the *only person* in this house that cleans the toilet because a core value of theirs is equality. Fair. Now, you can discuss a mutually respectful agreement because—well, look at that, you share that value as well!

Values inform boundaries. Some people use the word "boundary" arbitrarily, but when they are true boundaries, they always have a core need or value they are protecting. If you are in a relationship with someone who uses the term "that's a boundary for me" but cannot tell you about the value they are honoring with their boundary, they may be using the wrong term. On your side, if you cannot point to a value behind your boundaries, you might need to do some more self-reflection. Reflecting on and refining your values helps you create better boundaries to protect them.

Of course, no one owes you an explanation of their core value system. All you have to do is respect their boundaries. Still, suppose their boundary impacts your ability to live your life or keep yourself safe and clean, i.e., in the above scenario, maybe the roommate never wants to work toward a respectful agreement with you. In that case, you may have to rethink being in a relationship with someone whose values conflict with yours so negatively. Being a respectful man in a relationship means both honoring others' boundaries and protecting your values.

Myth #4: Boundaries are disrespectful or rude to others. Not at all. If anything, it is the exact opposite. So much resentment and unexpressed anger in relationships happen when someone is unclear about their boundaries. As therapist and author Brené Brown says, "Clear is kind; Unclear is unkind.[2]" Solid values and clearer boundaries to protect them make for better relationships.

For example, let's say your friend says he's having a party. "It's a come-and-go type thing, so just come over whenever," he says. Then let's say you show up at his house around 10 p.m. and he's pissed. "What the hell are you doing here? The party ended after the game was over! Where the hell were you?" And, of course, now you're confused. "Dude, you said to 'come over whenever'! I just got back in town, and I came straight here. How was I supposed to know it was an afternoon thing?"

When you can tell others clearly where your line is, you respect them by giving them clarity about how to treat you. When they know where your boundary is, they can show you respect by not crossing it. If you don't tell others what you might consider disrespectful, you disrespect them by not allowing them the opportunity to get it right. And you disrespect yourself by not honoring and protecting your values.

Myth #5: If I try hard enough, I can just give, give, give forever and not need any boundaries again! So, here's the thing. Do you remember Newton's Third Law says that each action has an equal and opposite reaction? Yeah. That's what happens when people don't respect their own boundaries. I like to use the example of a rubber band that is stretched too far. Eventually it snaps back—hard! People cannot push their own boundaries to accommodate other people's needs indefinitely. The snapback is coming, and it will be ugly. If you are giving, giving, giving all the time, at work, at home, with friends, eventually you're going to stretch yourself too far. This is when resentment in relationships, or burnout at work, starts to show up. Then, the snapback happens and often the ones closest to you are the ones caught right in the middle.

Myth #6: If you truly love someone, you don't need boundaries in your relationship. OH SO FALSE. Boundaries are essential in maintaining respect *and* desire in a healthy romantic relationship. You and your partner are not the same person. Keeping your sense of individuality by respecting each other's boundaries makes for a healthy, interdependent relationship.

Some people neglect themselves as individuals and forsake their boundaries to give to the relationship. This dynamic is limiting and unhealthy as it doesn't allow one to change, grow, or be an individual in any way. It is also deeply unsexy. Psychotherapist, author, and speaker on maintaining desire in a long-term relationship, Esther Perel, talks about the need for individuality in helping maintain a sensual spark in a relationship. In her book, *Mating in Captivity*, she writes, "Love seeks closeness, but desire needs space to thrive."[3] Desire for another requires separateness between two individuals.

Boundaries help foster your identities as separate yet partnered individuals. When you are committed to being your best self, you can support your partner in being their best self, enhancing the relationship as a whole. When you can have your own identity outside of the relationship, have your own friends, hobbies, and goals, it highlights the choice you are making to be in partnership. A STRONG, interdependent relationship doesn't take away from you or your partner as individuals but allows you to be better as a team than you would be on your own.

MUTUAL RESPECT: BROUGHT TO YOU BY BOUNDARIES

If the easiest way to show someone respect is by respecting their boundaries, the easiest way to know someone else's boundaries is to ask them! Now, you might be squirming and thinking, "God, that's so awkward just asking someone about their boundaries. Isn't that weird?" And sure, it might be awkward and uncomfortable at first, but asking directly is a surefire way to get the answer you need.

Asking other people about their boundaries shows them that you respect them and gives you the information you need to protect yourself and maintain your own boundaries. Unfortunately, many people find themselves in situations where they only know where the line is because they have already crossed it. This approach is not only terribly inefficient but can lead to harm and long-term negative consequences.

Can you imagine if we didn't have a code of laws or ethics or conduct, and you would only know when you had committed a crime by trial and error? What a stressful situation to be in! Having clearly defined boundaries keeps you safe from unwittingly crossing other people's boundaries and helps you see who is willing to show you respect by honoring yours.

Boundaries create respect in a relationship. They reiterate that a healthy relationship is a partnership and collaboration between two fully equal and independent people who make a conscious and intentional choice to be together. A STRONG relationship is a choice, not a cage.

THE NEW STANDARD: PLATINUM OVER GOLD

You have probably heard of the "Golden Rule," which is "treat others the way you want to be treated." That one is a pretty basic rule that many people have heard and repeat often. It works okay, but the problem with the Golden Rule is that it assumes that other people want to be treated the same way you do. But the thing is: not everyone is like you!

I much prefer the Platinum Rule, which says, "Treat others the way *they* want to be treated." This is a big difference. Respecting your partner in the way they want to be respected, which is not necessarily the way you want to be respected, is an important distinction. If you treat your partner the way you want to be treated, you might not be honoring their needs at all. Instead, you might be imposing your own wants and needs onto them and calling that respect.

The golden rule is a good place to start when it comes to civility, "don't do things to others you wouldn't want to be done to you," but the real test of respect is the Platinum Rule: doing things for others that *they* want, need, and appreciate, even if it is not something you would like for yourself. This shift from treating others like yourself to treating others as their own person significantly impacts romantic relationships for the better. We have all heard the trope of the guy who gets his wife a saw or new lawn mower for her birthday because that's what *he* would want. Most of those stories are not examples of flaming successes.

Treating others the way they want to be treated and respecting their boundaries and needs, even when they differ from yours, is a way in which you can show respect. When someone treats you the way you want to be treated and respects the boundaries you communicate to them, they show you respect. And mutual respect leads to a higher level of investment and commitment to a relationship.

Switching out gold for the Platinum Rule in relationships will start you off on the path for successful, respectful interactions. It will help you to continue to appreciate all the ways in which your partner is different from you. Together you make a great team, but you are not the same person. Respect in a relationship occurs when partners respect each other's perspectives, needs, and boundaries, even when they differ from their own.

AVOIDING TRAPS: THE ASSUMPTION OF SIMILARITY

Aretha Franklin said it best in her song "Respect." Respect means different things to different people because boundaries are personal. Each person in a relationship will have their own boundaries and ways in which they like to be respected.

One of the biggest pitfalls I see in relationships is what I call the Assumption of Similarity Trap. This trap is the idea that says, "My partner and I are (and should be) the same" using phrases like "I don't need to ask because I already know what he'll say"; "I'm fine with it, so she'll be fine with it"; "It doesn't bother me; why is it bothering you?"; or "I'm not going to tell you; you should just know what I need" are all examples of a couple falling into the trap.

Our society's romantic examples double down on these misguided ideas about what a good relationship looks like. Movies and TV shows are filled with "romantic" moments where a couple says things to each other like, "You always know what I want without me telling you." Or "I know you better than you know yourself." Supposedly, your "true soulmate" will be so in love with you that they can practically read your mind.

Society constantly reinforces this message that you and your partner should be the same and that true love looks like a mind-meld. These on-screen examples of an "ideal" relationship set real-life couples up for disappointment and disconnection because no two people are alike, and humans are terrible mind readers. I once wrote a satirical blog article that laid out how to "Ruin Your Relationship in 5 Easy Steps." Two of the five steps fell under Respect. They were:

1) Stop Being Curious About Your Partner, and

2) Hold Your Partner to Your Standard.

The first one, Stop Being Curious About Your Partner, becomes a problem because when curiosity wanes, respect between partners can begin to wear thin. If you are not actively looking for and respecting the differences between you, you may be inadvertently doing something that the other person considers disrespectful.

When you stop being curious, you stop asking about the other person's needs and boundaries. You stop respecting that your partner is a whole different person! And, if you're not asking about them, you're probably walking into and over their boundaries.

The second one, Hold Your Partner to Your Standard, is another reliable respect dissolver. When couples assume their partner is just like them, they also start holding the other person to their standards: "Well, *I* would have been there on time." "I would have remembered that." "I can't believe you did it that way."

Often, I see men who are frustrated with their partners for doing things that they "would never do." These guys just can't understand why their partner would do something so "out of character." They fail to consider that maybe it is out of character for themselves, but it is totally in character for their partner. Your partner is not you. They are their own separate person with their own ideas, desires, and yes, boundaries.

If you hold your partner to your standard, expect that they will do things the way you would do them, and hope they know how without having to ask, you are 100 percent setting yourself and your relationship up for failure.

ALEX and AVA

THE ASSUMPTION OF SIMILARITY TRAP

Alex and Ava were a couple in their early thirties who had been set up by mutual friends because "y'all like the same things."

When they met, they were impressed by how similar their backgrounds seemed to be. Both were middle children. Both of their moms were schoolteachers, and both sets of parents were still married. They had each had one significant relationship throughout high school and college, and both had gone abroad for their senior year.

As they started dating, they found more evidence of their similarities. Both were into outdoor sports and liked cats more than dogs. With all these similarities going for them, their relationship progressed quickly. After a few months of dating, Alex's lease was up, and Ava offered that they go ahead and move in together. This was when the cracks started to show.

They once got in a two-hour fight about where the broom was supposed to live: Ava said laundry room; Alex said kitchen, and they were off. They fought about what went in the recycling bin, what temperature to set the thermostat at, and more than once ended in a silent standoff over dinner options.

As they progressed in their relationship, they found other ways in which they differed. Finances, the timeline for marriage, and whether or not to have children were new points of contention. After a few months of trying to reconcile their differences, they took a trip together. The hope was that their mutual love of travel would help them remember their similarities. Unfortunately, the trip was a disaster.

Alex's travel motto was "vacations are for relaxing." He imagined enjoying the bars and restaurants at the all-inclusive resort and lying by the pool. The one thing he wanted to do for sure was watch the Cowboys game, which the local pub was planning on showing. Other than that, he really didn't want to make any plans.

On the other hand, Ava had an itinerary for every day of the trip. She had spent weeks researching the local attractions, best sightseeing trips, historical sites, and must-do activities while there. She had a list of things to do bullet-pointed by the hour, which notably did not include spending three of them watching the Cowboys. Her travel motto was "vacations are for expanding your experiences."

They had spent most of their five-day trip in constant conflict and resentment toward each other. The expectation that they would rediscover their similarity had resulted in dashed hopes and disappointment. Now, they were in my office questioning if they even had a future together.

In our first session, Alex was confused. "I don't get it. When we met it seemed like we were the perfect match. Now it seems like we have nothing at all in common."

The beginning of Alex and Ava's relationship did them a disservice by overemphasizing their superficial similarities and downplaying their significant differences. The Assumption of Similarity Trap they fell into left them feeling blindsided by "all the differences that seemed to come out of nowhere."

The Assumption of Similarity Trap is particularly likely for couples who, on the surface, are somewhat similar. Couples who grew up in the same town, went to the same high school or college, worked in the same career field, and ended up getting married often fall into this category. These couples may assume that they are more alike than they are different. While that may be true for some things, the pitfall happens when the couple starts thinking it is true for most things.

On the other hand, when a couple is on the surface very different, there is often more Assumption of Difference from the get-go. With Chen and Fabian, a cross-cultural couple from Taiwan and France respectively, there was an awareness that there would be differences from the day they met. They approached each scenario assuming that "what might be respectful for me in my culture does not necessarily translate to respectful in your culture." They were then able to work together to find an agreement, a middle ground that worked for both of them. Vive la différence!

So much resentment happens in relationships when people forget that their partner is a different person. Sometimes I see people who feel betrayed by these differences; others, like Alex and Ava, even begin to question their compatibility as a couple. "Are we too different?" But here's the thing—even if you grew up next door to someone, you are still two different people. You will have different needs, desires, preferences, values, and personal boundaries. Your partner is not you. Of course, they are going to do things differently.

When you start with a "Couple Blob" and the Assumption of Similarity, often the only way to grow is out. If your relationship is based on the idea that you are the same, any growth you make as a person is threatening to the relationship. When you assume the difference, you can prepare yourself to accept and embrace the difference. This puts you in a curious and collaborative, rather than defensive, mindset. When you start with the Assumption of Difference, you can then move toward finding the middle.

This is where sometimes I hear pushback from people who say, "I don't want to compromise in a relationship. I want to be able to be myself." Okay! I agree; it's not healthy to think of your relationship as a place where compromising yourself is part and parcel of the arrangement. Maybe it's the vagaries of semantics again, but a STRONG relationship is not about finding a compromise.

<hr />

It's about creating collaboration.

<hr />

NEVER SETTLE: SCREW COMPROMISE

Compromising and collaborating are two very different things. One can feel like settling, which can lead to resentment in a relationship. But being able to collaborate is not settling. It is about challenging yourself to be creative to find a unique solution. You create collaboration by respecting your differences and thinking outside the box. One of the phrases I say often to couples in my therapy sessions is "Find the middle."

Mutual respect is about finding a collaborative way to meet the needs of both people in a relationship without one person's needs taking center stage. You win together and you lose together. Collaboration is about being better together. One of the ways I like to illustrate this is when two musical artists from different genres come together to collaborate on a song. The crossover song they collaborate on is something that neither of them would be able to do justice to individually, but together, they create a hit. When you are working in a partnership, the goal is never to win at the other person's expense.

To be collaborative takes an awareness that you are not the only person in the relationship with needs but that you share the relationship with another person who has their own unique set of needs. Collaboration is a skill that ensures both people in a relationship get their needs met. And if you're not willing to collaborate, let's be honest, you're not ready to be in a relationship. A healthy relationship is never going to be just about you.

This is the thing that makes being in a committed relationship hard. People will say they have communication difficulties, conflict issues, scheduling constraints, work stress, personality differences, and other things to explain why they are experiencing problems in their intimate relationships. But ultimately, it all boils down to: Are you willing to accommodate the other person in the relationship? Are you ready to respect their unique needs and work with them to find a collaborative solution that works for both of you, or not? That's it. This is the eternal struggle of relationships.

When you are single, making decisions based on what's best for you is completely acceptable. However, fighting for your self-interest to take precedence in a romantic relationship will put you and your partner on a path of mutual disrespect. This tug-of-war approach sets you up to be in competition and not partnership. When there is a zero-sum game, there's a winner and a loser. And no one wants to be a loser.

SEEK COLLABORATION: FIND THE MIDDLE

Steps to a successful collaboration look like this:

Step 1: RESPECT THE SETTING – Bad timing torpedoes so many relationship conversations. How many conversations have you had go sideways because you didn't have the time, energy, or information ready to have a productive conversation? Take this collaboration seriously. Show respect for yourself and your partner by making an appointment to discuss the issue at hand. Put it on the calendar so you can both come ready and prepared with the right attitude and bandwidth for the conversation.

Step 2: RESPECT YOURSELF – Prepare by understanding your own intention and stating your needs clearly. What do you want out of this conversation? Are you coming into it preparing to dominate your partner or push your agenda? If so, slow down, redirect. Remember, a collaborative agreement is about meeting both people's needs. It is not about pushing someone else's boundaries or feeling pressured to give up your own. It's also not about controlling the outcome of a situation.

In this step, be really clear about three things: 1) What is the thing I want to talk about? 2) How do I feel about it? 3) What do I want to ask for from my partner? Use "I" statements in this stage to fully express what you need without blaming your partner or deflecting from the issue, i.e., "I would like to talk about our credit cards. I feel anxious about the amount of spending we're doing. I'd like to ask that we sit down and come up with a budget for the rest of the year."

You respect yourself by setting this conversation up as an *invitation vs. an accusation*. When you come at your partner with an accusation: "Are you kidding me with this credit card bill?" you put them in a great position to be defensive: "Don't look at me! What have you been buying?" and now you're in conflict. Invite your partner to collaborate with you by starting the message off with an insight into how it is affecting *you*.

Step 3: RESPECT THE MESSAGE – You cannot have a mutually agreeable solution without mutual understanding. Now it's your partner's turn to talk. Listen. Listen. Listen. Simply mishearing someone's point can lead to a lot of miscommunication and unnecessary conflict in relationships. Seek to understand your partner's values and needs as deeply as possible.

One tip for this is to repeat back to your partner what you hear them say to ensure that you are getting the message clearly. I know this is a little clunky, but I promise you it works wonders. Start by saying, "So what I heard you say is _____. Did I get that right?" Don't work too hard. Just repeat back to them what you heard. If you need to ask clarifying questions, now is the time to do so.

Take your time to ensure that you are clear on your partner's position; once they feel heard, you can make sure they are clear on yours. This might sound like asking them for reflection back: "Do you mind repeating my point back to me so I can hear what you heard and clarify if needed?"

Step 4: RESPECT YOUR PARTNER – Sometimes this is where couples get stuck. They think. "Okay, I stated my position, and you stated yours, and now it's a tug-of-war until one of us loses." No sir, no ma'am! We're not doing that anymore. Stay in your windows of tolerance. Stay regulated. Stay respectful. Express your appreciation for your partner's role and the fact that even though there are disagreements, the process can be respectful and collaborative.

And pay attention to those who only care about "winning the problem" in their own favor. If they do not care to respect your needs and boundaries, they are probably not a person who you can have a healthy relationship with.

Step 5: RESPECT THE GOAL – At the end of the day, you are on the same team. Remind yourself that it is the two of you against the problem. Not your needs against theirs. The goal is not *either/or*; it is *both/and*. Remember, collaboration, not compromise. Being part of a successful collaboration and finding the middle is not always easy. But a successful meeting in the middle has an overarching goal:

We are both winners.

Find unique and creative ways to find the middle that will meet both of your needs. Don't forget that when only one of you "wins" in a conflict, the loser is the couple. This is a time for putting your brains together and looking for unique ways to solve the problem so you can both win. Think outside the box. Collaborate to find a mutually acceptable solution that unites you as a stronger, more balanced couple working on the same team toward the same purpose. Think smarter, don't fight harder.

Step 6: RESPECT THE PLAN – You show respect to the plan by upholding your end of the bargain and holding yourself accountable to put the plan into action. The most important part of planning is implementation. Show your respect for the plan by following through on it. A healthy couple requires both partners to commit to its success. Every successful collaboration is one step closer to creating a life that makes both of you feel respected and happy to be in partnership.

SELF-RESPECT: COMMANDING OR DEMANDING?

As I was writing this chapter, actor Will Smith "slapped the shit out of" comedian Chris Rock at the Oscars. Rock was presenting the award for Best Documentary and made a joke about Smith's wife's hair loss (due to a medical condition) before announcing the finalists. Smith walked on stage and slapped the comedian.

After returning to his seat, Smith yelled at Rock to "keep my wife's name out of your f***ing mouth." The interwebs immediately exploded, with some condemning Smith's actions as an immature and violent escalation of a verbal jab. Others defended Smith's actions as a man protecting his wife from disrespect. Some people say they have gained more respect for Smith for his actions, while others say he has lost their respect forever.

To me, this was a perfect example of the difference between commanding and demanding respect. So often, physical violence is used as a way to *demand* that others show respect. However, this approach is based on the ability to physically dominate a situation. Resorting to physical violence to demand that others show you respect is a short-term and often dangerous strategy.

When you choose violence as a way to *demand* respect, you are opening the door for an escalation of conflict, not increased respect.

Although some people claim that Smith's action has increased their respect for him, I would be very surprised if those same people would say the same if a guest slapped them or their spouse at their backyard BBQ for making a joke. They might be chastened, but I doubt they would say, "Wow, I really respect that guy so much more now." No one respects a bully. We might show temporary deference and avoid confrontation with them, but that does not actually translate to genuine respect.

We have probably all encountered people who try to demand respect without doing the internal work to actually have the gravity to *command* it. These people are usually the least respected of all. When people throw their weight around, use physical violence, or scream, "Do you know who I am?" as a feeble attempt to *demand* respect, we instinctively know that these people are not worth respecting.

Conversely, we have also probably met people who might be unassuming and kind, but who are highly respected in their jobs, homes, and communities. What is the difference?

We respect people who are in command of themselves.

When someone is standing in their power, when they are in control of their words and their actions, regardless of triggers or chaos around them, we instinctively feel their power, and we want to show them respect. When you can command respect through standing in your dignity, without resorting to physical violence, you can maintain your frame and hold others accountable when they disrespect you or your loved ones.

If Smith had walked up to the stage and, rather than slapping Rock, would have said, "Chris, your joke was in poor taste. My wife has a medical condition that has resulted in her hair loss. I'd like to take this moment to raise awareness to all those who are suffering from invisible medical conditions and remind us all to be kind. You don't know what others are going through." I think we would be having a very different conversation about Will Smith and respect today.

People who command respect from others do it by being who they are, not by throwing a tantrum or bullying us into giving it to them. When someone can walk into a room and comport themselves with gravity, calm, self-respect, and dignity no matter the instigation, they show us their power. Power over oneself is the most highly respected quality. When you are in command of yourself, you command respect from others. You don't have to demand it.

KNOW THYSELF

Therapist Terry Real talks about the two opposing ways to look at yourself, as "better than" or "less than" other people. It is common for men to look at others and themselves hierarchically, but both of these positions have their issues when it comes to self-image.

The "better than" position makes you arrogant and intolerant of other people and their shortcomings. In a relationship, if you feel that you are "better than" your partner, you better believe your partner can feel your contempt coming their way. Contempt is one of the most destructive elements to a relationship. If your sense of self is based on being "better than" others, you will always be looking for ways to subtly put other people down. No matter how you try to reassure them that the opposite is true, people can feel it, and it probably makes you unpleasant to be around.

The other side of that equation is thinking of yourself as "less than" other people. This is the more obvious "low self-esteem" position that we tend to think of. This "less than" position is not a healthy place either. If you feel you are "less than," you will constantly question your partner's commitment to you. After all, if you're less than them, what's to stop them from eventually realizing they are too good for you and leaving you for someone better? This position leads to a lot of self-questioning and insecurity.

Healthy self-image and self-respect are not based on thinking of yourself as better than or less than others; instead, it is knowing and accepting who you are. Learning healthy self-respect begins with looking at yourself through a new lens: with honesty, compassion, and accountability. It is about getting to know all the parts of yourself—not running away or hiding any of those parts. Self-respect means accepting your shortcomings and weaknesses, and acknowledging and honoring your strengths. Then, you can begin to build toward a sense of self that you accept, love, and have respect for.

CREATE YOUR CHARACTER

– REFLECTION EXERCISE

Questions to ask yourself:

1) If I was writing a book about my life, how would I describe myself?
2) If I asked my friends who I am, what would they say?
3) If I asked my family and partner, what would they say?
4) Are there parts of me I don't show to anyone?
5) Is there a gap between the person I am now and the person I want to be?
6) Do I command or demand respect from others?

ALIGN YOUR ACTIONS WITH YOUR VALUES

One of the starting points of working on your self-respect is to start with your core values. What do you believe is vital to being a man of integrity? What are your values? Take some time to really consider this question. If you are having trouble coming up with your values, think of a man you admire and look up to. Do you have a healthy father figure? A boss, a friend, a mentor? Or is there a fictional character or male public figure who embodies your values? What do his life and relationships look like?

A quick distinction about the word *values*. Values are internal, not external.

Values are about who you want to be,
not what you want to have.

For instance, if you say, "One of my values is a fat bank account," what happens when your bank account takes a hit? If it is something that someone else can take away from you, then it is some*thing* you value; it is not a *core value*.

You can say, "One of my values is thriftiness," or "a good work ethic," which describes a way that you want to be in the world. It is a characteristic—*a trait of your character.* Sure, maybe that will lead to a healthy bank account, but that core value, that way of being, cannot be taken from you and cannot be affected by external circumstances.

Author of *Atomic Habits* James Clear has a Core Values List[4] you can use to get started on examining your core values:

Authenticity	Influence
Achievement	Justice
Adventure	Kindness
Authority	Knowledge
Autonomy	Leadership
Balance	Learning

Beauty	Love
Boldness	Loyalty
Compassion	Openness
Challenge	Optimism
Community	Peace
Competency	Pleasure
Contribution	Popularity
Creativity	Pride
Curiosity	Religion
Determination	Reputation
Fairness	Responsibility
Faith	Security
Fame	Self-Respect
Family	Service
Friendships	Spirituality
Growth	Success
Happiness	Status
Honesty	Wealth
Humor	Wisdom

Take your time to develop a list of five to ten values that truly reflect who you want to be and what is important to you. Now consider why these are your core values. Of all the options you could have picked, why did you choose these ones? Is there a story behind the ones you chose? Was there a defining moment in your life that helped you choose a value to protect?

Take some time to reflect on this list you have created and ask yourself, "Do I really believe these to be *my* core values, or are these values I believe I *should* have?" If there is a value on the list that you cannot articulate why specifically it is important to *you*, then maybe it is not a value you truly hold.

For instance, let's say you chose "adventure" as a value that is important to you. But after further reflection, you realize, "Wait, I don't even really like adventure. I just thought that's one of the ones I should choose because it sounds cool."

One of my favorite sayings as a therapist is one paraphrased from fellow LMFT Clayton Barbeau. It is "Don't *should* on yourself." And the other side of that is "Don't let anyone *should* on you." This world is filled with a lot of "shoulds" when the truth is, *there are no shoulds.* There is only:

"What do I care about and do my actions align with my stated values?"

What? You might be thinking. *So everyone is just allowed to make up their own rules for life and relationships? This sounds like chaos!* Well, here's the thing. Besides actual laws, yes, there is total freedom! The problem is that so many people take this as a free pass to act like assholes. In reality, when you align your behavior with your values, you have a lot more responsibility to be accountable for your own behavior.

Relying on "shoulds" gives you an escape hatch from taking responsibility for your own life. When I hear someone say, "I *should* probably. . ." I ask them to consider if it is *"I want to, I will, or I think I am supposed to?"* When you take ownership for your choices, you take ownership for your life.

The self-respect from living a life that feels honest and truthful to who you are is immensely powerful and irreplaceable. You are the one who is in charge of making sure that your life reflects respect for yourself and others. Taking ownership of your own values, boundaries, and behaviors also means there is no one else to blame for your choices. You are in charge. You are responsible. No one else can choose your actions. No one else is in charge of your life. I tell people in my office often,

**"Don't do things you don't want to do.
If you cannot find an internal value that
motivates you to do the thing, don't do it."**

Contrary to what you might think, this is not giving them a free pass: "Hey, hon, my therapist said I didn't have to do anything I don't want to do." Instead it puts the accountability of their own life right square back in their own lap. If you don't want to do the dishes tonight, what is the core value informing that choice? "Laziness?" Is that a core value for you? No? What's a core value? "Responsibility." Okay. What would you be able to do tonight that would reflect that value? "Probably the dishes." Okay then—but only if you want to. If you can articulate how it reflects your core value, then do the thing. Sometimes you might have to dig a little deeper than you might normally think about something to understand what is really motivating your behavior. Is there a core value behind it? How is this behavior protecting or embodying respect for yourself or others?

So, is your life reflecting your values? If so, who are you? What do people see? What does your life and relationship show about who you truly are? When it comes to family, love, and relationships, many men claim, "My family and my relationships are number one. They are everything to me." Yet, when you look at their life, hmmm, their relationship is like number seven, and their family is struggling to make the top five.

Often the values people claim to have are nowhere in evidence in their life. For instance, if someone says, "Loyalty, honesty, and kindness are my core values," then my question is, "Does your life reflect those values?" If you are cheating on your partner, stealing from your work, and just yelled at someone who bumped into you by accident, I'm going to call bullshit!

Also, do these core values that you hold reflect across your entire life? Or do you have little caveats, i.e., "Courage and honesty* are two important core values I have." (*_Terms and conditions may apply. Courage and honesty are not values I have when it means initiating an uncomfortable conversation with my partner in which I have to let them know an uncomfortable truth about a need I have or a mistake I made._)

A big part of cultivating self-respect is being able to look at your life and feel proud that your values are evident in the life you are living. When you disrespect yourself by not living out your values, you have to convince others of who you are by demanding respect through bluster or intimidation. Your values are either evident in your life and behaviors, or they are not. If your life is sending the opposite message of your held values, you will never be able to command respect because you and everyone else will know that your actions and your values don't align.

You gain self-respect when you can know that you are a man of integrity simply by living a life that reflects your held values. And this is not about seeking perfection. No one is perfect all the time and you will make mistakes and make choices you are not proud of; we all do. However, the more choices you can make that reflect your core values, the closer to your integrity you will be. When you are filled with self-respect and integrity, it will be easier for you to show mutual respect to your partner as well.

To paraphrase a saying often attributed to the Buddha,

**If you truly respected yourself,
you would never disrespect another.**

TL; DR STEPS TO BUILDING RESPECT

1)   BOUNDARIES – Make for good relationships. Boundaries are the way we maintain respectful interactions in society and in relationships. Boundaries protect core values. Respecting other people's boundaries is a way that we show them respect.

2)   AVOID TRAPS – Assuming that you and your partner are more similar than you are different will lead you right into a complacency trap. Complacency breeds contempt. Contempt kills relationships. Avoid the Assumption of Similarity Trap by staying curious about your partner.

3) COLLABORATE – Never compromise. Compromise is lose-lose. Collaboration is win-win. The end product of any collaboration you can think of—a great album, art, sports, etc.— is made better by the unification and collaboration of both talents. Seek to elevate, not devalue. Think outside the box for unique collaborative solutions that work for your needs.

4) SELF-RESPECT – Living by your own values is a way to cultivate self-respect. You disrespect yourself when you fail to align your actions with your values. Look to avoid double standards with the way you apply your values. Mutual respect starts with self-respect. Self-respect starts with personal integrity.

HALFTIME

PAUSE
AND REFLECT

"Well begun is half done."

— ARISTOTLE

So, let's take a pause right here. First of all, congrats on getting to this point in the book. There is a lot of information in the first three chapters, so I want to take a moment and give a little explanation of what's next. The first three chapters: Safety, Trust, and Respect cover essential relationship skills and will help you set a foundation for a healthy relationship to *survive*. The next three chapters: Openness, Nurturing, and Generosity cover the skills needed to help a relationship *thrive*.

Many folks in therapy spend years just working on the 4 S's of Safety: understanding their attachment styles, investigating their values, learning to trust themselves, and learning to set boundaries—because those skills are Relationship 101. The S T R chapters of this book are about basic relationship survival skills. Ensure that you have those skills down solid, and you will probably save yourself about five years of therapy—and be leaps and bounds ahead in the dating game.

The next part of this book is going to deal with the other type of people I see in therapy—couples who are stuck in stagnation. If you start with the first three chapters, you will learn valuable lessons, but the last three, Openness, Nurturing, and Generosity, may be where you find a new spark in an old relationship. If you are in a relationship that is solid but just puttering along, not hitting any significant bumps, but not going anywhere super exciting, give those last three chapters a try. The O N G chapters of this book deal with the skills to help a relationship thrive—getting an existing relationship to that next level of fulfillment.

Or maybe you have a different question: "If I am single, should I keep reading?" I would say one hundred percent *yes*! For you (highly advanced prepper, you), I suggest you read this book from front to back and then figure out where your strengths and growth areas are. What better time to prepare for a STRONG romantic relationship than before you even begin?

CHAPTER FOUR

OPENNESS

"Openness to change is key
to implementing new knowledge."

— ERALDO BANOVAC

GREEN FLAG #4

A crucial skill in life and in relationships is the ability to adapt to new situations and learn new skills. In order to be adaptable, you have to be open to hearing feedback and changing to meet the needs of your environment.

||||||||||||||||||||||||||||||||||||||||||||||||||||||||||||||||||||||||||||||||||||||||||||||||||||||||||||||||||||||||||||||||||||||||||||||||||||||||||||||||||||
Being OPEN is the fourth green flag of a STRONG man.
||||||||||||||||||||||||||||||||||||||||||||||||||||||||||||||||||||||||||||||||||||||||||||||||||||||||||||||||||||||||||||||||||||||||||||||||||||||||||||||||||||

One of the most significant points of resistance I see in some men who come to therapy is an insistence that they are doing nothing "wrong." They have years of well-worn habits that they are loath to reexamine or give up. Some even say that they are "done learning" and embrace their current state as their end-all, be-all state of being. And sure. I always want to validate that there may be nothing "wrong" with what you are doing, but I like to ask, *"If it is no longer working in your relationship,* will you be open to a new way of doing things?" Because if not, if this is "who you are" and you can't (or won't) change, know that your relationship will most likely not survive.

In 2013 the Institute for Divorce Financial Analysts found that a full 43 percent of divorces listed "incompatibility" as the reason for the divorce.[1] Although growth and change are inevitable in a relationship, growing apart doesn't have to be.

GROWING: UP OR OUT?

When I was young, I remember one of the most confusing things I would hear about divorcing couples would be the phrase "they just grew apart." This statement often came coupled with exclamations of surprise or comments like, "We're all so shocked," or "We never saw it coming. They were so good together."

I didn't fully understand this phenomenon, and it worried me. How do married people grow apart? Does it randomly happen? I imagined it happening as a moment in time. Like one day, you would get a knock on the door and a notice saying, "Surprise! Your marriage is over. Hate to break the news, but you somehow grew apart during the night and awoke to the dreaded 'irreconcilable differences' between you. Here's the phone number for a divorce lawyer. Good luck!"

Of course, as an adult now, I understand that much about adult relationships is hidden from children, and for good reason. However, these sudden cracks in what I perceived to be solid families, without a clear explanation of what had gone wrong, definitely impacted me. It made me wonder, "If you see that you are growing apart, can't you stop it before it's too late?"

THE ALEXANDER POINT

Alexander the Great was arguably one of history's most impressive conquerors, and yet, sometime in the 330s BCE, in the words of Hans Gruber, he moaned that there were "no more worlds to conquer."

On a modern map, Alexander's empire spanned from Bulgaria through the Middle East to the Indian border. Sure, it was the largest empire to date, but for goodness' sake! Maybe get on a boat? I mean, America wasn't even on the map yet! Expand those horizons, bro! Aren't you curious about what's on the other side of all that water? Unfortunately, Alexander the Great was not.

I bring this guy up because I see so many relationships that have hit what I call the "Alexander Point." There are no more worlds to conquer in their relationship. Many of the relationships I see in which boredom has set in or where people describe feeling like they have "grown apart" were those in which people had reached this "Alexander Point."

These people come to therapy complaining of feeling disconnected or "like roommates." They had gotten to the point in their relationship where every thought was anticipated, every action routine. The thrill of newness, of discovery, was gone. They had a fixed idea of who their partner was and what they were capable of. No more surprises. It was all downhill from here.

Jay and Marie

"Hello, Kristal?" Jay's gruff voice crackled over the phone. "I was recommended to you by a friend who said that you help couples?" When I affirmed that I did there was a pause. "Marie and I have been together for thirty-eight years," he finally said quietly.

"That's a long time," I noted. "And what's bringing you to seek couples therapy now?"

He heaved a big sigh. "My wife said she's thinking about divorcing me. And I gotta tell you, I really can't tell you why. Nothing is wrong with our marriage. Maybe we're a little boring, but is that a reason to get divorced? I don't understand it. Maybe you can help me."

Jay went on to describe their relationship as "two ships passing in the night." They had no animosity toward each other, they operated smoothly on a day-to-day basis, but he ended the phone call by saying, "She says she feels like we've grown apart and that we no longer have anything in common."

I asked, "And how do you feel?"

"Well," he said, "she's not wrong. We don't do much together anymore. She's got her friends and always wants to do things, and I guess she's tired of me just sitting around the house." He forced a chuckle, "I guess I'm not very exciting." His tone became serious again. "But I love her and would like to see if there's anything left to salvage of our marriage, or if we should just part as friends now."

A study by the Council on Contemporary Families found that between 1990 and 2014, the rate of "Gray Divorces"—divorces among those over age 50—had doubled.[2] In 2021 the US Census Department found that baby boomers (adults between age fifty and seventy) had more than twice the rate of divorce than any other population group.[3] More than 55 percent of these divorces were among couples who had been together over twenty years.[4]

I often see people who have settled into "enduring" their relationships rather than continuing to enjoy them. Often these couples, like Jay and Marie, work pretty well together on the day-to-day stuff; most had no major conflicts or obvious issues that would lead to serious divorce talk. There was no domestic violence, abuse, or infidelity. However, these couples often came in on the brink of divorce without any significant issues other than feeling like their marriage was empty.

Many relationships don't have a dramatic "breakdown," they just putt-putt-putter out when no one is looking. Nothing is sadder than watching a couple with so much raw possibility at their fingertips do the wind-down—and slow burn into oblivion. Boredom and growing apart are often just as lethal to a relationship as an overt betrayal. It may not be as messy as an affair, but like creeping black mold that destroys a house from the inside out, it can bring the identical outcome of destruction in the long run.

"Not daring to rock the boat, we risk sinking with it."

– GABOR MATÉ

DISCOVER POSSIBILITY

When I meet a couple who are in a bit of a slump, the first thing that stands out to me is that they have a great opportunity just waiting to be reactivated. In the beginning stages of a new relationship, nothing is more interesting than hearing your new love interest tell you everything about themselves, their likes, dislikes, childhoods, travels, and even their day-to-day activities, anything and everything! No detail is too small to be considered fascinating.

Couples also do a lot of new things together in the first stage of a relationship, which allows them to learn about who their partner is in different situations and how they behave in the company of friends, family, and even strangers. When a person is in the first throes of falling in love, a stage called "limerence," they want to learn as much as possible about their new romantic interest. All this information helps us decide whether or not to pursue a relationship with this new partner.

As we explored in chapter one of this book, stability is essential in relationship building. Feeling confident in creating a life together necessitates some predictability in knowing who your partner is and how you can expect them to behave. Once people get comfortable feeling like they know their partner pretty well, things can tend to settle into a bit of a routine.

Routines can be comforting and help build stability. But they can also lead to monotony and stagnation in a relationship if there is no opportunity for continued openness, growth, and discovery. One of the core needs in a relationship is to feel like you are truly seen and known by your partner. This gets lost when we forget to see our partner with new eyes. When people stop being curious about their partner, they stop seeing them for *who* they are and instead start to interact with the idea of *how* they are.

THE VILLAIN ON THE COUCH

I often see couples in my office who report some pattern of dysfunction that has been affecting their relationship for years, sometimes even decades. They come into couples therapy wanting things to be different, but when I ask them about their blocks to change, they say the obstacle is their fear that their partner will not be open to change.

They will say things like, "That sounds great in theory, but I don't think she will do that," or "I could ask her, but I can guarantee she's not going to like it" or "I don't think she wants me to change." People will say this to me about their partner—even when their partner is sitting right next to them on the couch saying, "Yes, I'm willing to accept change. I want things to be different too!"

What often happens, particularly in a long-term relationship, is that we have a fixed idea of who our partner is, how they will respond, and what they are capable of. This is adaptive and part of the way our pattern-seeking brain saves energy. If you know your partner likes cream in their coffee, you can go ahead and rely on that information staying consistent morning to morning. If one morning they decided they were going to have tea with lemon instead of coffee, that might take you aback a bit.

When someone starts changing midway through a relationship, we often see that as scary and threatening to our fixed idea of who they are. We often tie sudden changes midway through a relationship to the idea of a "midlife crisis," sign of an affair, or something else threatening. However, the over-reliance on a fixed idea of who our partner is hinders both people's ability to expand and grow.

It also leads to the brittle box idea of a relationship which is the fear that: "I must cut off parts of myself to stay in this little relationship box. If I expand or grow, I will break the box, so there are only two options: stay in the box and be miserable or break the box and shatter the relationship." These are impossible choices.

But I get it; seeing your partner in a new light after so many years together is hard. It may also be hard to believe they will or want to change to help you—which is sad but a genuine fear for many men. However, unless you allow your partner the possibility to be different, you keep yourself stuck in a trap of "I want to change, but I don't think they want me to." There may be a deeply entrenched pattern of behavior that you have come to expect from your partner, sure. However, that often becomes entangled with *who* we now think our partner is and limits what we think they are capable of.

Instead, I like to say, "What if we got rid of the villain on the couch?" The villain on the couch is the idea of your partner as someone who is fixed, rigid, only cares about themselves, doesn't want you to be happy, is committed to making you miserable, and demands that you cut off parts of yourself to stay in the box. What if, instead of predicting their behavior based on this villainous character, you took the chance to act differently and, by doing so, offer them the opportunity to respond differently to your new behavior?

Also, when you do that, it becomes pretty apparent if your partner is an imaginary or real villain. I often tell my clients who have this fear that if you begin to make changes and give them the opportunity to be different, you get the information either way. Either they will prove you right—they are a villain who has no intention of you being happy, which then—maybe it's time to reevaluate if they are a healthy partner for you—or they were an imaginary villain, and all they needed was an opportunity to join you in growth.

One of the ways to defy the "villain on the couch" and see your partner with new eyes is to actively look for times that they acted differently than the script in your mind predicted. We all have a tendency toward confirmation bias,[5] meaning we look for things to confirm what we already think is true. This can be a real problem in couples because once you have decided that your partner is "picky" or "boring" or "rigid," you look for reasons to confirm that belief and dismiss evidence to the contrary.

When you begin to look for the ways in which your partner is acting in opposition to the villain in your mind, you will start to write a new script that will be more reflective of the actual person you are in a relationship with. Being open to changing your view of your partner, and offering them an opportunity to experience you differently, will allow you to break the stifling box of negative and limiting expectations you have of each other. Don't settle for *enduring* your relationship when you could continue to *enjoy* your relationship.

Getting out of your routine and looking for new opportunities to see your partner in a different light is one of the best ways to reignite a dying spark. When we expect change, we can be more open to meeting the new needs that can and will show up in new phases of life and love. These discoveries can continue to breathe new life into your relationship. Openness in a relationship is crucial to ensure that you and your partner continue to grow together instead of apart.

"If you have the impression that you know the other person inside and out, you are wrong. Are you sure that you even know yourself? Every person is a world to explore."

– THICH NHAT HANH

SEIZE OPPORTUNITY

A common block to healthy conflict and communication in a relationship is a lack of openness and willingness to hear the other person's perspective. Creating a culture of open and honest communication is a crucial step in maintaining a STRONG relationship. Some of the hardest conversations that can be had in a relationship are about what is and what is not working. Like with any performance review at work, school, gym, or playing field, you cannot perform to your highest level if you don't know what your blind spots are. You can't improve on things you don't know aren't working. Knowledge is power.

One of the most telling signs of openness in a man is when he is unafraid to open up a hard conversation. This is not a guy looking for conflict, but a STRONG man who is open to hearing about his partner's experience in the relationship. He cares about her experience and has the confidence to open the conversation because he trusts in his skills of adaptability and capacity for growth.

A man who is actively seeking feedback from his partner gathers invaluable information to protect his relationship from unspoken resentments. When you can see your partner's perspective as a valuable addition to the information you already have, rather than a threat to intelligence or knowledge, you are setting yourself up to be in a stronger position to protect your relationship.

Couples often live with long-term dysfunction, dissatisfaction, and resentment in their relationships because they avoid the very thing that they need to do to improve it—openness and honesty in addressing the issues! It takes courage to be open to feedback. It takes bravery to hear what you might not want to hear.

Now, I don't know about you, but the thought of asking a partner "What is being in this relationship like for you?" or "How am I doing as a partner?" or anything that leaves the door open for an answer of "It's hard sometimes" or "Needs improvement" can be daunting.

However, the goal of a STRONG relationship is a thriving partnership. You cannot have a healthy partnership if you are not open to offering your partner the opportunity to share their perspective.

> **"When we avoid difficult conversations, we trade short-term discomfort for long-term dysfunction."**
> **– PETER BROMBERG**

Unfortunately, this relationship pattern is all too familiar in distressed and unhappy couples. People will tiptoe around their particular elephant in the room for *years* rather than having a hard conversation. But, if you have the courage and skills to have an open and honest conversation, you may discover something valuable about yourself and your relationship.

This suggestion on taking the lead to open up a difficult conversation might be where you think back on how communication has gone between you and your partner in the past. If you don't have a great track record, this might feel like a really hard ask. I hear this a lot from men in couples therapy: "I avoid these conversations, not because I'm not open, but because they always get messy and exhausting. We start with feedback and end up in a fight."

So, let's talk communication skills.

POSITION FOR SUCCESS

Let's say your partner is going through a difficult time, emotions are high, it's a little tense in the household, and suddenly it seems like everything you're doing to try to convey kindness and help is just not working. Instead, you notice you're pushing your partner away. Does this feel familiar?

A big reason for this is the way that men and women tend to be socialized to communicate and bond with each other. Men tend to connect and bond by fixing things together—they talk about things to solve a problem. However, women tend to connect and bond by listening and offering support to each other, not solutions. And then you stick these two people into one relationship and expect things to go well? Oh boy. No wonder there's so much confusion.

Many men like to describe themselves as "fixers." When they see someone they love upset, emotionally distraught, or in pain, they want to help take the pain away. And it makes sense—men want to protect their partners from pain and provide solutions to their problems! So they start "fixing." They start offering solutions, thinking, *Hopefully one of these will help and she won't feel so bad anymore.* However, more often than not, these best-intended efforts land wrong.

The short video "It's Not About the Nail"[6] illustrates this common conversation problem perfectly. In the film, the woman is talking about how she is feeling, expecting support and empathy. Instead, she is given a solution by her well-meaning partner. This mismatch leads to frustration on both sides. She is not getting what she is looking for—empathy—which makes her feel like he doesn't understand her. And on the flip side, he is offering some of his best, most thoughtful solutions and feels like his efforts are being ignored or told they are not helpful, which is frustrating to him!

So what's the answer?

Well, when you bring the wrong tool to the job, you're going to struggle. One of the tips I like to share with my clients is to think of *four different positions* you can take when having a conversation with your partner.

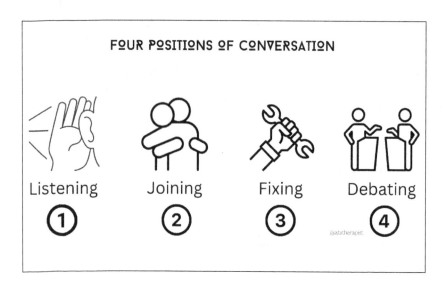

FOUR POSITIONS OF CONVERSATION

Listening ① Joining ② Fixing ③ Debating ④

Each position requires different skills because the goal of each position is different. So many guys get into conflict with their partners by simply playing the wrong position for the conversation they are in. You have to bring the right tool for the job you're trying to accomplish. If you show up to the swim meet in full hockey gear, you will struggle!

The more tools and skills you have, the easier opening and engaging in hard conversations will be. Regardless of how good your solution might be, *unsolicited advice often feels like criticism.* Debating your partner's perspective when they are not looking to debate *will put them on the defensive.*

So, let's go through these four conversation positions.

Position One: Listening

The goal of this position is *paying attention* to your partner. Your role is to say things that indicate attention and openness to hearing more. This conversation is inviting a monologue, not a dialogue. The message you send while in the listening position is *"I hear you, tell me more."*

> WIFE: "Ugh. I need to vent. Today was terrible. I ran out of gas on the way to the office, and when I got there the internet was down again!"

> WRONG TOOL (FIXING): "I told you last night to put gas in the car, remember? Also, we had that conversation months ago about you switching to working from home."

RIGHT TOOL (LISTENING): "You ran out of gas *and* had an internet outage at the office? That sucks! How did you manage?"

This position is a one-sided deal. In this position, you offer a listening ear, a container for your partner to vent in and share whatever they need to say. You are not listening to fix or debate. The main message you are sending in this position is *"tell me more."*

Pro tip for this position is the skill of repeating back what you're hearing them say to let them know you are paying attention.

Position Two: Joining

The goal of this position is *expressing empathy and understanding.* When you join with someone, you let them know they are not alone. The main message you are sending in this position is *"I understand how you feel."*

WIFE: "Yes, and I got tasked with planning the holiday party this year. As if I don't already have enough on my plate!"

WRONG TOOL (DEBATE): "I planned our holiday party last year and it wasn't that bad."

RIGHT TOOL (JOINING): "Wow, on top of everything already on your plate. I can imagine that would feel overwhelming."

In this position you want to let your partner know you can see where they are coming from, *even if you disagree with them!* This is an important distinction and one I often see men struggling with in conversations. To be clear, you *do not have to* agree *with your partner's perspective 100 percent or agree that you would do the same thing.* It's okay to be two different people, remember? But the goal of this position is seeking to understand, empathize with, and *validate your partner's experience.* Put yourself in her shoes. See the world from her perspective.

Resist the urge to fix the problem or debate your partner's position here. If you jump straight to "fixing mode" when your partner is not offering you a "problem to be fixed" or "debate mode" when she's looking for understanding, this is where the friction happens.

If you notice your partner is resisting all the fixes you are offering, or is starting to get a little defensive, realize you might have jumped ahead to a new position and they aren't ready to go there, because either A) they never wanted a fix, B) they aren't in the mood for a debate, or C) they don't feel like you understand them yet, so how can you be offering a solution already? If you are offering a solution, first you have to understand the problem. Stay with the joining until your partner feels understood and validated.

Pro tip: It's almost impossible to argue with someone who is agreeing with you. If you feel things getting a little heated in a conversation, the quickest way to defuse conflict is to start joining and look for points of common understanding.

"Be water, my friend."

– BRUCE LEE

ome phrases you can use to convey empathy and understanding:

EMPATHY BINGO

That would upset me too.	That sounds hard.	My hearts breaks for you.	What do you need right now?	Yes, what has happened makes no sense at all.
That makes sense that you feel that way.	Wow, I'm sorry you experienced that.	That sounds really stressful.	I wish I could have been there to support you.	I've got your back.
I can understand where you are coming from.	Is there anything I can do to support you?		You didn't deserve that.	I can't imagine what you're going through right now.
That sounds scary!	It sucks that this happened to you.	You're not alone.	I'm here for you.	I would be confused too.
I hear you.	Your feelings are valid.	I agree with you.	Thank you for sharing with me.	I can see that.

@eattherapist

Position Three: Fixing

The goal of this position is problem-solving. In this position, you offer your skills of brainstorming and coming up with ways to solve a problem your partner is offering to you.

The message in this position is "*I have some ideas, let's come up with a solution.*"

WIFE: "Yes. I'm exhausted, and I don't know what to do about any of it."

YOU: "I have some thoughts if you're open to hearing them."

WIFE: "Yes, please. I'm open to ideas."

RIGHT TOOL (FIXING): "We've already planned my company party this year. What if you used the same vendors I already have lined up to save some time and make things easier?"

One of the most bonding experiences a couple can have is to solve a problem together. This position can solidify a sense of teamwork. We come together as an "us" against the problem. This is one of the most time-tested ways to form a unified and bonded team. However, asking before jumping in with the "fix" allows your partner to let you know that they are *ready* to shift into open-feedback-ready mode.

Position Four: Debating

The main message you are sending in this position is *"Can I challenge you a bit?"*

Debate, when done well, can be exciting, stimulating, intellectually challenging, and, yes, incredibly bonding. You can learn a lot about a person's philosophy of life and core values when you open up a line of discussion that challenges them. Although debate can be a fun and bonding activity when challenge is the goal, living with someone who jumps to "debate mode" as their default for every conversation is exhausting. It eventually leads to shutting down

rsations, as "everything turns into a fight with you." Talking to
su. eone committed to debating can feel abrasive and confronting
when it is not the goal of the conversation.

Each of these positions is incredibly useful in its own way. Still,
miscommunications and conflict tend to happen when someone
brings the wrong tool to the conversation and insists on using it,
even if it is clearly making the situation worse. In communication,
as in other areas of life, using the right tool for the job is incredibly
important.

If you only have one tool in your toolbox, you are probably
going to be getting it wrong more often than not. It's like the saying,
"To those with a hammer, everything is a nail." Expanding your
conversational toolbox by being open to adding new skills will help
you to have the right tool for whatever the job requires.

I encourage couples to start a conversation by indicating what
you need from your partner, i.e., "Hey, I've had a really bad day. Do
you have time to listen to me vent for a bit?" or "I need some validation
here. Can I get you to join me in this?" or "I've got this concern, and I
want to hear your thoughts," or "I'm trying to workshop this project.
Can you play devil's advocate for a minute?" This will require you to
be honest with yourself and open with your partner about what you
need from them in your conversations. You won't get what you don't
ask for.

One big trap that gets people into trouble is when they believe
the lie that their partner will just be able to read their mind. They
want help, but they don't want to have to *ask* for help. They want their
partner to be a mind reader. They just want to name the problem and
hope their partner will read their mind and figure out what they want

and how to give it to them. For instance, Greg will say, "I don't have enough friends." His partner Gina might respond with empathy: "I'm sorry to hear that; it's tough finding friends as an adult." Greg will agree but low key be frustrated that she hasn't offered a solution, even though he didn't ask for one. The next time Gina goes out with her friends, Greg might be annoyed but unable to articulate why.

However, if Greg would have said, "I don't have enough friends and I'd really like your support and ideas on how I can make new ones," he would have opened the door for Gina to know that he was looking for a solution. Then she would have been able to help to meet his need: "Oh, for sure. I actually saw a thing for a men's group recently." Asking for exactly what you need is vulnerable, but when you don't ask, you take away the opportunity for your partner to offer you the care, support, or solutions you need.

When you can clarify the goal of the conversation, you can eliminate confusion about "what are you doing/what am I doing?" When you and your partner do not have the same goal for the conversation, it can quickly devolve into a situation where both people are frustrated and feel misunderstood.

When you are brave enough to be open and start with your goal clearly stated, i.e., "I need you to help me solve a problem"; "I want you to challenge my perspective on something"; "I just want you to listen to me"; "I need some support and empathy right now," you are taking the lead on setting yourself and your partner up for a successful conversation.

Of course, in a perfect world, we would be able to start conversations like this all the time, but sometimes you might realize halfway through a conversation that "oh, this is not going well at all."

when I encourage you to call a time-out to reassess the strategy. It could be as simple as saying, "Hold on, time-out. What position do you want me to play in this conversation?"

When you openly ask for what you need, you allow your partner the opportunity to meet your needs.

This little reset helps you not to continue trying so hard with something that isn't working, but it also challenges your partner to articulate their needs rather than blaming you for not meeting them. If your partner says, "Why do I have to tell you what I need you to do? Don't you know??" they are probably not someone with whom you can realistically have a STRONG, healthy, and mature relationship. Maybe they are looking for the fantasy of a mind reader. If that's the case, you will be doing a lot of extra work in the relationship. Clarity and openness in communication is a two-way street in a STRONG relationship.

THE HARD TRUTH: IMPACT VS. INTENT

And sometimes, even your best-intended efforts will land wrong. One of the most significant ways you can show growth and openness is by acknowledging the impact of your actions or words over defending your intent. Conflict in relationships always shows up when someone wants to jump to defending themselves before acknowledging their partner's experience. If you choose that route, woo boy, settle in for many fights ahead.

In any relationship, your words and actions have an impact on the people around you. You show openness and willingness to be a better partner by listening to and seeking to understand your impact on others—regardless of your intention. Address the impact before defending your intent always. I often use an analogy to drive this point home.

IMPACT VS. INTENT: MESSAGE VS. DELIVERY

Let's say it's your birthday. You're all dressed up for a nice dinner. Your girlfriend just texted you that she's at the restaurant and your parents are already there. You're about to head out when the doorbell rings. You go to open it, Hey! It's your new friend from work. Wow, you notice he is holding a cake. Aaaaand he shoves it in your face. "Happy birthday!" he yells.

Now, you let the guy know what the impact on you was: "Dude, ouch. Not cool. I've got frosting on my new shirt, crumbs in my eyeballs, and — is my nose bleeding?"

And instead of acknowledging your experience he gets defensive of his intent. "What the hell, man, I didn't mean to hurt you. It was just a bit of fun! Here I am going out of my way to do a nice thing out of the goodness of my heart and all you can focus on is 'oh, my nose is bleeding'? Screw you!" he yells as he storms away.

Understanding the impact of your actions on your partner, regardless of your intent, is one of the most important ways of showing openness in a relationship. If you are genuinely open to acknowledging the impact of your actions on your partner, let their influence you. Be open to their perspective. Acknowledge the of your words and actions on them. Listen to their experience so you can learn from it and let it inform your efforts in the future.

Not being open to hearing how you impact your partner can be a major blind spot that gets men in relationships into trouble. Acknowledging the impact of your actions/words/behavior before defending your intent is one of the *most* essential communication skills you can learn. It is the best way to defuse a conflict and show that you are open to hearing your partner's perspective even when it differs from yours. Again, it goes both ways. A healthy partner will also be able to hear and acknowledge your intent without assuming that the impact of your action was the intent behind it.

ADAPT AND OVERCOME

A telling trait of a strong leader is adaptability—not having total assurance of an easy path ahead but having an inner sense of knowing that you can learn the skills to navigate any new challenge. If you are only confident in yourself and your abilities when you have complete control of any situation, the slightest thing will throw you off-kilter.

Think about it, if you can only survive when the conditions are "just right," you are putting yourself in a precarious state when things inevitably don't go right. True skill and strength are not gained by staying inside your comfort zone, using well-worn tools and tactics, but by being flexible and open to learning the new skills needed to succeed in any given situation.

However, opening the door to new experiences can also bring up some vulnerability. When we open ourselves up to trying something new, we put ourselves in situations we might not entirely be in charge of. Growth is often uncomfortable and can challenge us in ways we haven't been challenged before.

JAY and MARIE

One of the most significant changes in Jay and Marie's relationship, I discovered, happened after her hip surgery a few years ago. As she went through physical therapy, her PT encouraged her to take dancing classes to stay agile and flexible.

"Now she's fully recovered, but she still loves those dance lessons," Jay remarked. "She goes three nights a week."

Marie's face lit up. "Oh, it's so much fun. And I have a great group of friends now, people of all ages who just love to dance. There are parents with their little children, engaged couples preparing for their first dance, and, of course, retired folks like me."

"That does sound fun," I acknowledged. I turned to Jay. "Have you ever been?"

"Pshaw," he exclaimed, "I don't dance!"

"Well," I continued, "is it 'I don't want to?' 'I don't know how?'"

Jay thought for a moment. "I am afraid of looking foolish. And if there's one thing I'm not, it's foolish."

We often stay within the bounds of our comfort zone because it is easy to do what is familiar. Pushing the edges of our comfort zone might highlight skills we need to learn to cope with this new and unfamiliar territory. When we are in our comfort zones, it's easy to be confident that we are competent in how we show up. But sometimes our routines do not allow us to live to our full potential. When you get out of your comfort zone, you find the edges of your capabilities.

Openness and the vulnerability that comes with it is key to learning, growth, and strength.

Vulnerability is often used as a synonym for weakness, but as Brené Brown says, "There is no courage without vulnerability."[7] If you're not feeling vulnerable, you're probably safely in your comfort zone. Safety is a good place to start—courage without safety is recklessness, not vulnerability. However, even when you are in a safe relationship, being open is vulnerable and takes courage, but it is where growth happens.

When you cultivate an inner sense of confidence that you are capable of learning, change may bring challenges, but you will embrace change as an opportunity to learn a new skill or showcase a part of yourself you may otherwise have not shown before. Confidence in your ability to rise to any occasion is more potent than only being confident in winning when the game is rigged in your favor.

If you were a coach, but you only allowed your team to go on the field when you had precisely perfect weather, a 100 percent healthy team, and were absolutely sure you were going to win—maybe you bribed a ref or something—you would have a limited season and a weak team.

On the other hand, suppose you told your team to embrace each new game as an opportunity to learn something new, try fresh tactics, and challenged them to adapt and raise their level of play every time. Your team may not have a perfect winning streak at first. Yet, over time, your team would learn from each match, whether you won or lost, to become a stronger and more flexible, resilient, and adaptable team. No matter the circumstances of the play, your team would gain the confidence that they can adapt, overcome, and win—no matter the circumstances.

> **"It is not the strongest that survives;**
> **but. . . the one that is able best to adapt and adjust**
> **to the changing environment in which it finds itself."**
> **– LEON MEGGINSON**

BEGIN AGAIN

How many men do you know keep themselves small not because they want to live small lives but because they are afraid of doing something that might expose the edges of their knowledge, comfort, or capabilities?

There is a concept in Zen Buddhism known as "the beginner's mind," which is the idea that approaching new experiences like a beginner helps you embrace newness and openness. When you have the beginner's mind, you will not expect perfection from yourself, be hard on yourself, or beat yourself up when you make a mistake. When you have the beginner's mind, you acknowledge every step as the effort it is.

When you can see yourself as a student of life and love, you can see every new step taken toward growth as a gift you are giving to your future self. You don't have to be perfect, but you do have to take that first step toward being open to experiencing something new that can enhance your life and relationship. Stepping outside the bounds of where you feel confident is vulnerable. But there is no opportunity for learning when you do not allow yourself the ability to get it wrong sometimes.

Competence often leads to confidence, but you stifle growth when you stay only within your zone and do not challenge yourself to gain new skills and expand into new areas of growth and discovery. If you shy away from anything that would expose the fact that you don't know something, you will never be in a position to get better at something that might be incredibly useful for you to learn.

It can feel uncomfortable to be a beginner again, mainly if you built your identity as a man around being competent and not beginner-like. Embracing change can be exhausting, and there will be times when you may feel like giving up. But what if you saw setbacks as part of the learning process and being a beginner, not as signs of failure? What if you gave yourself permission to not get it right the first time and instead give yourself credit for trying something new?

> **"The beginner's mind is the mind of compassion.**
> **When our mind is compassionate, it is boundless."**
> **– SHUNRYU SUZUKI**

JAY and MARIE

When Jay realized that the fear of looking foolish was the only thing standing between him and repairing the bond with his wife, he embraced openness. When I saw them for a check-in session six months later, their relationship, and Jay, had completely transformed.

"I've lost forty pounds!" Jay exclaimed. "And we don't feel like roommates anymore, I tell you what."

Marie blushed and squeezed his arm. "I am so proud of him. I could tell how uncomfortable he was the first few times, but he stuck it out. We are having so much fun together. He is actually a very good dancer."

Jay laughed. "Turns out this old dog had a few tricks still left to learn."

I smiled. I had no doubt in my mind at all that Jay would be competent at anything he put his mind to. Due to Jay's willingness to be open, they had gone from a fading marriage to rediscovering the spark that was always there, just waiting to be ignited again.

Be open to the fact that you have an endless capacity for growth and greatness. Be gentle with yourself as you are learning. Learning new skills and attempting new behaviors in your life and relationship will always be challenging. But if you aren't open to new possibilities, you will cut yourself off from new opportunities to learn and grow. If you expect perfection and shy away from imperfection you will stay stuck and stagnant within your comfort zone.

Don't let your fear of trying something new prevent you from reaching your full potential. Don't keep yourself small just to prevent exposing the edges of your competence. When a man is unafraid to be open and can embrace vulnerability as the key to true courage, he is truly unstoppable. Stay open. Stay flexible. Stay full of possibility.

"Fall down seven times. Stand up eight."

– JAPANESE PROVERB

TL; DR STEPS TO BUILDING OPENNESS

1) CHANGE – Is inevitable in any relationship. You have the power to determine whether that change is going to continue to connect you and your partner or lead to eventual growing apart.

2) CURIOSITY – Alexander the Great gave up when he thought there were no more worlds to conquer. Don't make the same mistake. Don't quit discovering your partner halfway through your relationship. Stay curious. Keep exploring each other. Keep giving your relationship opportunities to get to the next level of greatness.

3) COMMUNICATION – Putting yourself out there to open up hard conversations can be tough if you don't have the right tools. Take some time to learn new skills, like the four positions of conversation, that will help you feel confident

opening new lines of communication with your partner. Adaptability is a key trait of a skilled communicator.

4) COURAGE – Opening yourself up to trying new things can sometimes be vulnerable. If, as a man, you have learned to rely on your competence, being a beginner can feel scary and uncomfortable. However, growth happens at the edge of your comfort zone. New frontiers take courage to explore. You cannot be brave without taking a chance. Being a beginner is the first step to becoming great at something new.

CHAPTER FIVE

NURTURING

"The truth is, just as women have always had what it takes to be CEOs, men have always had the power to nurture."

— MICAH TOUB

GREEN FLAG #5

There is a prevailing perception among some people that men are not nurturers and that "nurturing is a woman's job." The idea goes that men cannot be nurturing because they are "wired differently." Have you heard that one?

Well, this may come as a surprise to some, but research shows that men have the same neural pathways in their brains as women do that allow them to have the skills to nurture.[1] Less surprising, hopefully, are the studies that show that men's involvement as nurturers in a family home leads to hugely beneficial outcomes for children.[2]

Being NURTURING is the fifth green flag of a STRONG man.

If you're still convinced that there is something fundamentally different between male and female brains that inhibits a man from being able to be nurturing, I get it. The bias is strong. We have learned in implicit and explicit ways that nurturing is a feminine activity and that "real men" are flat-out ill-equipped for that "gentle stuff."

POTATO-POTAHTO

One of my favorite things to do when I get stuck on something is to break it down to basics. What does it mean to be nurturing? According to the *Cambridge English Dictionary*, to nurture means "to take care of, feed, and protect someone or something...[or] to help a plan or a person to develop and be successful."[3] Okay, so with that definition, nurturing sounds pretty darn close to encompassing both P's of protecting and providing in one fell swoop, doesn't it?

In an interesting twist of semantics, many men who deny any skill in nurturing are happy to claim that they are good at "maintenance." So, what's the difference? Well, the definition of maintenance, again according to the *Cambridge English Dictionary*, is "the work needed to keep something in good condition."[4]

One of the most significant differences I discovered in investigating the difference between "nurturing" and "maintenance" is that one is caring for something alive, and the other is caring for something that is—well, maybe not "dead," but inanimate. Nurturing was used in talking about caring for plants, animals, children, and intangibles like dreams and goals. Men can have those things, right?

Women often have more opportunities to be in nurturing roles, in no small part due to traditional expectations, and thus tend to have more experience, but the *capacity* to nurture has no gender. If that is a hard pill to swallow, think of how many millions of men use their nurturing skills every day as farmers, veterinarians, gardeners, doctors, nurses, teachers, coaches, entrepreneurs, managers, team leaders, social workers, advocates, and therapists (to name just a few professions that require men to be nurturing).

Why do we still have this narrative that men might be capable of nurturing in their professional lives, but when they come home to their families, they lose all ability to nurture their spouse and children? It's like we have just decided that nurturing is not a "guy thing," and by doing so we have not allowed men opportunities to claim things they are doing as "nurturing" when they—by definition—totally are.

Maintaining vs. nurturing is the difference between keeping something *running* vs. keeping something *alive*. To nurture something is to care for it to its highest potential—over and above maintenance levels—to keep it not just alive but thriving.

SURVIVING TO THRIVING

One of the most searched questions about relationships is "how to keep the spark alive." Well, first, you have to realize that a relationship *is* alive. It is a living entity that needs not just regular maintenance but nurturing in real time every day. A house can be maintained. A home needs to be nurtured. A fake plant gets maintained by dusting it once a week; a real plant needs nurturing to stay alive and healthy.

Some people I've worked with have expressed their desire to have an "operating manual" for their relationship. They've said, "Can't you just give us a breakdown of exactly what needs to happen and when so we know how to maintain this relationship?"

OPERATING MANUAL – RELATIONSHIP MAINTENANCE

8:00 a.m. M–F – Tell partner/children "I love you" (if they say it first, respond "Love you too.")

Noon M–F – Ask partner, "How is your day going?" Respond either: "Glad to hear it" or "Sorry to hear it."

4 p.m. M–F – Ask child/ren, "How was school?" Respond either: "That's nice" or "That's too bad."

7 p.m. M–F – Ask partner, "Do you want dishes or homework?" Do chore partner opts out of.

9 p.m. M–T – Hug child/ren goodnight. Hug and kiss partner and say, "Sweet dreams, my love."

9 p.m. Friday – Ask partner, "Would you like to be intimate tonight?" If partner responds "Yes," say, "That's great." If no, say, "That's okay," and follow with regular M–T protocol.

Weekend schedule may vary.

Some of you might be reading that little snapshot and thinking, *Brilliant! I would love that regularity!* And yes, there are maintenance things that every relationship needs that you can put on a schedule, i.e., anniversaries, birthdays, weekly date nights or family dinners, etc. There are lots of great apps and things that can help you remember to do certain home and relationship maintenance duties, but at the end of the day, there is no "set it and forget it" for your relationship.

To nurture your relationship, to have it reach its highest potential, you have to be present, involved, invested, and paying attention to things that enhance or detract from the health of your connection. You can get guidance for the overall broad strokes needed to maintain the structure of a healthy relationship (i.e., this book), but when it comes to the nitty gritty of keeping the spark alive? How to have the best lived experience? That is something that no book can teach you because it is deeply personal.

Any of you who are parents (of pets, children, or plants) know what I mean. It's good to have a basic "care manual" for covering the basics, but if you only played with your pets on a schedule, only fed your children according to preset timers, or ignored any signs of disease in your plants because "I'm doing everything right by the book," your children (of any variety) would not be able to thrive to their full potential. The same is true for your relationship.

Nurturing is the key to keeping a relationship alive and thriving.

Each relationship is unique and has its own unique needs. Some relationships are more challenging than others, but every relationship needs both people to nurture it, or it will die. One person tending to the relationship is not an equal relationship. Two people looking at how they can each shift the bulk of the load of nurturing and tending the relationship to the other person will lead to power struggles and resentment, and the collateral damage will be the relationship.

A relationship is a living thing, not an inanimate one. When a relationship is neglected for too long it doesn't just fall into dusty disrepair, it dies. And sometimes when it dies, no matter how hard you work at the end there, no matter if you rush into couples therapy and decide to give it your best shot, there is no coming back. Sometimes it's just too little, too late.

If we can think of a relationship as its own living thing, we can look at the actions and behaviors of each partner not as "good or bad" but as nurturing or draining to the relationship. Sometimes nurturing your relationship will look like bringing home flowers, and sometimes it is about scheduling the cat's vet appointment or sitting down to talk about holiday plans. A STRONG relationship has to be a partnership with a shared goal: keep this thing alive and healthy.

And the only way you can discover what your relationship and your family need to thrive is by being an active, invested participant. Level up from simply having a relationship survive as the goal to helping your relationship absolutely thrive as your new goal. Why settle for baseline when you could have exceptional?

> "Marriage is not 50–50. Divorce is 50–50. Marriage has to be 100–100. It isn't dividing everything in half, but giving everything you've got!"
>
> **– DAVE WILLIS**

THE THREE P'S

Okay, you might be on board with this idea that your relationship needs nurturing, but what does that look like in real life? Well, one of the easiest ways to help your relationship thrive is to continue to nurture your emotional connection to your partner. Now, this doesn't mean that you have to have a deeply emotional conversation every single day of the week. That might not only be unsustainable but may actually have the opposite effect of raising the stakes in every single conversation you two have, which would be overwhelming.

Instead, one of the suggestions I offer clients who want to nurture their emotional connection and their couple bond but who don't know how to do that without talking about a really high-stakes topic is the 3 P's. Now, at the beginning of this book, I talked about the 3 P's of Protection, Provision, and Procreation as the three ways in which men have traditionally shown up for their relationships, but I'd like to throw out a different set of P's that you can use to begin to provide nurturing to your relationship now.

These new 3 P's that I suggest are Three Points of Connection: **Pride, Pain, and Pleasure.** Let's be honest. In an unhealthy relationship, there is usually an absence of pride, an abundance of pain, and a lack of pleasure. In a healthy relationship, all these things are not only present but acknowledged and used as touchpoints to nurture the emotional connection of the relationship.

Pride is something that needs to be present in a healthy relationship. Feeling proud of something is generally a generator of positive emotions and is something that can give you and your partner an insight into the highlights of your lives. Feeling a sense of pride can also be a measure of personal agency and effectiveness in your personal or work life.

Being in a relationship in which you can openly share what points of pride you experience in your life can also open the door for your partner to validate and cheer for you. Nurturing your relationship as a shared pride point is also something that can give you and your partner a common goal. When you can both look at your relationship with pride, it gives you a sense of mutual accomplishment and shared purpose.

Pain is a tricky one sometimes. Once again, people tend to correlate pain with "bad," but that is not necessarily the case. Like physical pain, emotional pain can be an important indicator that something needs to be addressed. Pain is just a messenger, and an important one! And couples *will* cause each other pain. Even healthy couples will have moments of discord, miscommunication, hurt feelings, and most importantly, shared experiences of pain.

If you are lucky enough to be in a relationship that lasts the rest of your life, you and your partner will experience births, deaths, illnesses, loss, and other painful life experiences together. It is so important that we acknowledge that pain is an integral part of life. Normalizing pain as part of a connective conversation is part of nurturing the long-term success of your healthy relationship. Checking in on your partner's pain points also gives you clear directions on what might need nurturing and care in that moment.

Pleasure is another one that generally brings up positive emotions, but it also allows us insight into what we need to nurture with our partner in the future. Pleasure is something that is deeply personal and being able to share that part of yourself with your partner can reinforce the level of shared intimacy you have. For men, being able to talk about what gave you pleasure in your day or week can expand your ideas of what is allowed to be pleasurable. And, if you check in and neither of you have experienced a moment of pleasure yet that day, that can open a door for the two of you to share a moment of pleasure together: a nice meal, a walk around the block, a relaxing bath, a night out, or yes, sexual pleasure.

So many times when the question of pleasure comes up, the conversation immediately goes to "Are you asking about sex?" And maybe yes, maybe no. But if your idea of pleasure is only linked to sex, you are probably missing out on acknowledging all the other things that can potentially give you pleasure. And vice versa, if you already have a culture of checking in with your partner about their pleasurable experiences that don't have to do with sex, it can make the conversations about sexual pleasure easier to navigate.

There are no limits to the conversations that these Three Points of Connection can open up. And it doesn't take long. Rather than checking in with your partner generically ("How was your day?"), start to check in around these three points of experience. Even if you only have time for a fifteen-minute conversation, picking one of these 3 P's can unlock a deeper connection and avenues for nurturing your relationship. Quantity is great, but when time is scarce, go for quality.

THE 3 P'S IN ACTION: SKILL BUILDING

First – Begin with Presence

One of the casualties of modern life is the ability to be present with a person and have their undivided attention. For this exercise, set a dedicated time and space where you and your partner can be 100 percent present with each other. No phones, no TV, no kids, no distractions.

When you are both ready for connection, you can start by saying, "Tell me about a moment of [Pride/Pain/Pleasure] you experienced today/this week."

When they share a moment of Pride, *validate it*. "Nice work, I'm proud of you too!"

When they share a moment of Pain, *give them care.* "I'm sorry that happened to you. Is there anything I can do to help you feel better?"

When they share a moment of Pleasure, *listen to understand more* about what gives your partner pleasure, "That sounds awesome. What was your favorite part about it?" Or, if they haven't experienced a moment of pleasure yet that day, this could be an opportunity for you to *create a shared pleasurable experience* together.

Use these 3 P's as a way to continue to nurture the emotional connection between you by continuing to be curious, validating, and connected to your partner's inner world and life experiences.

Adapting the 3 P's for dads to use with kids is simple. Just swap out the last P (Pleasure) with Play. Studies show that children bond with fathers primarily through play.[5] If your child hasn't had a moment of play that day or week, take some time to nurture your relationship with them through playtime!

NURTURING DESIRE

Sex is another great way in which the importance of nurturing can show up in a relationship dynamic. Again, one area that men tend to traditionally take pride in is in their sexual prowess, the P of the penis, procreator, etc. However, a common complaint by women is that their partners do not care enough about their *pleasure* in the bedroom. Contrary to some internet opinions, yes, women like sex and have orgasms too. However, women on average compared to men tend to need a little more context to get in the mood and have adequate foreplay in order to reach climax.

Sex therapist and author of the book *She Comes First: The Thinking Man's Guide to Pleasuring a Woman,* Dr. Ian Kerner found—probably not that surprisingly—that regardless of gender, "if any partner is not consistently enjoying sex and orgasm, it can have a big negative impact on a relationship."[6] Another study found that both men and women's *relational satisfaction* was positively correlated to the *female partner's orgasm frequency.*[7]

When working with couples who present with "dead bedroom" or an unsatisfying sex life, one of the main things I look at is the equity of pleasurable sexual experiences up to that point. This encompasses more than just orgasm frequency. We also talk about the difference in Libido, Desire, and Intimacy.

One important thing for men to know is that there are two types of sexual desire: Spontaneous and Responsive. According to Emily Nagoski, author of *Come As You Are: The Surprising New Science That Will Transform Your Sex Life,* up to 75 percent of men identify as the spontaneous type. Their mental arousal—the thought *"I'd like to have sex"* comes first, and then the urge to have sex follows. However, women were more likely to identify as having responsive desire, which means their experience of pleasure has to come first before mental arousal and desire for sex occurs.

Spontaneous Desire – is what we tend to talk about as libido or a "sex drive" (but unlike a true biological drive like hunger, you will not die from no sex). Your libido can be affected by physiological factors like sleep,[8] stress, [9] hormones,[10] physical activity,[11] illness,[12] age,[13] etc. If you are disconnected from your body, you may not notice fluctuations in your libido that much but, just like women, men have sexual cycles too.[14]

This is important to talk about because there is a misconception that men are "always up for it." This myth can be incredibly damaging and cause a lot of problems in a couple. It can lead to shame and performance anxiety for men who believe it, and it can lead to a sense of insecurity or rejection in their partners when men do not initiate sex. However, spontaneous desire is an internal bodily experience that is dependent on your body state and doesn't really have anything to do with a partner.

I usually ask my clients to start noticing: do you have a higher libido at certain times of day or week? Less desire when you're stressed or lacking sleep? When you start to track your baseline, you can start to see how your body's cycle matches or differs from your partners, i.e., maybe your libido is higher in the morning and hers tends to be higher in the afternoon. Maybe both your libidos are lower after a big meal and higher after the gym or on the weekend. It is important to have the language to talk about your fluctuations in your libidos and how that affects spontaneous desire so you can start finding a pattern of intimate connection that works for you both.

Responsive Desire – This is the "pleasure first" model of desire. As Emily Nagoski writes, "Instead of emerging *in anticipation* of sexual pleasure, like spontaneous desire, responsive desire emerges *in response* to sexual pleasure."[15] Context and arousal are important for stimulating this form of desire. For instance, if you're not really hungry but someone starts cooking you a homemade meal—they set some music on, pour you a glass of wine, and begin filling the kitchen with mouthwatering smells—then they place a perfectly reverse-seared, brown butter basted ribeye in front of you, well, your hunger might start to kick in. If they just opened a can of beans and put a spoon in it, it wouldn't do the same thing for you.

Much of our societal attitudes and expectations around what a "healthy" sex life looks like elevates spontaneous desire as the ideal. This leads to a lot of frustration in men: "She's never in the mood!" However, when your partner tends toward responsive desire, they need more stimulation and activation of pleasure in order to have a sense of desire. The desire might be there, but for many women it needs help to be activated.[16] The brain is the largest sex organ![17] Don't neglect it.

Nurturing a satisfying sexual connection in a relationship is not just relying on both of you being hungry at the same time, which I often ask couples to reflect on how miserable and frustrated they would be if they only ate when they were hungry for the same thing at the same time. Stimulating responsive desire necessitates listening to and understanding what turns your partner on. What's her sexual high-end steak scenario? What activates her arousal?

In the same way that libido can be affected by physical factors like stress or lack of sleep, responsive desire also changes with experience and exploration. The more you discover what you like and don't like, the more your desire, arousal points, and experiences of pleasure evolve. Desire can be affected by a variety of factors and can be generated in response to a multitude of scenarios and motivations. It is an interactive experience between your body, your imagination, your environment, and the stimuli. In his book *Tell Me What You Want: The Science of Sexual Desire and How It Can Help You Improve Your Sex Life*, social psychologist Justin Lehmiller notes that exploring your desires and sharing your fantasies together can also be a way to create sexual intimacy.

Intimacy – Sexual intimacy is the whole connected experience. It is not only the "I'm hungry" or "I could be tempted by a steak dinner" but it's the "with *you*" part of the equation. Sharing sexual intimacy with another person can encompass mental, emotional, relational, energetic, and even spiritual aspects. Not all sex is intimate. However, in an intimately connected romantic relationship, sex can take on a whole new role. It can be an expression of love or reassurance, a tender and comforting connection, a passionate affirmation of attraction, a moment of emotional vulnerability, an exploration of yourself and your partner, and even spiritual bonding.

Sexual satisfaction and pleasure come in a lot of different forms, but when cultivating intimacy, you open a dialogue that expresses care about your partner's needs, not just yours. When you continually look for ways to nurture desire and intimacy between the two of you, you cultivate a pleasure-filled connection. Create a relationship filled with experiences where pleasure is the focus, not just orgasm. Invite your partner into an environment where both of your pleasure needs are honored, explored, and enjoyed on a variety of levels. Nurturing a pleasure and intimacy focus in a relationship benefits all involved and leads to a more satisfying and fulfilling sex life.[18]

> **"The focus shouldn't be about your destination
> (i.e., your own orgasm); it should be about
> the pleasurable journey together."**
>
> **– ZACHARY ZANE**

LEGACY: WHAT LIVES ON

A poll conducted in 2013 found that men placed a higher emphasis on procreating to carry on a family line or pass on family traditions than actually wanting to, you know, parent. However, the same poll found that nearly 80 percent of men wanted to be fathers![19] This disconnect between the idea of fatherhood vs. the reality of the actual raising and nurturing of the children—a task still largely relegated to women—is a stark contrast.

**To leave a legacy that is living and alive,
you have to be involved in its care and nurturing.**

In hunter-gatherer societies, fathers were integral in passing down the skills and traditions of surviving and thriving in the natural world to their children. The role of parenting was not only shared between the biological mother and father, but by members of a tribe as a whole[20]. Both women and men were actively involved in raising the children of the tribe to be successful and contributing members of their society. A successful legacy was the survival of the tribe.

Prior to the Industrial Revolution, most families worked together to survive and thrive. Although there were gender-based chores and roles, the duties of parenting were shared more equally between the mothers and fathers. In his book *Fatherhood in America: A History*, Robert Griswold notes that most parenting manuals in the eighteenth and nineteenth century were written for fathers, not mothers.

So, what happened? Well, some theorists say that the Industrial Revolution is when society began to restrict men to a singular role: that of sole financial provider. Author and historian Ralph Larossa notes, "Before the Industrial Revolution, women and children, as well as men, were thought to be major contributors to a family's finances."[21] Professor Gabriel Rosenberg describes the reality of life on the American family farm like this: "Flexibility was the watchword of the day. With survival at stake, everyone worked—gendered ideals be damned—even if it meant women contributed field labor during harvest and men mended their own socks."[22]

However, the rise of factory jobs primarily required male parents to leave their homes to work. This is where we begin to see the rise in messaging around the woman's place being in the home and the man's place being at the office.[23] Unfortunately, this meant that whether they still wanted to be involved or not, many men were restricted from spending a lot of time in a nurturing role with their children due to the burden of being the primary breadwinner.

With the new definition of a successful father as not one who was actively involved in the caretaking and upbringing of his children but as one who brought home the biggest paycheck, many men transitioned to see their work and careers as their primary contribution to their families. Over time, the idea of "leaving a legacy" meant amassing a large amount of wealth or business capital that you could hopefully leave to your children one day.

This shift has driven more and more men to see their careers and financial success as the marker of their identities, their worth, and ultimately, their legacies. With men being removed from the multifaceted role of equally involved parent and relegated to the one of sole financial provider, it not only saddled women with the entire responsibility of nurturing, it has led to men feeling less connected at home and in their communities.

This entanglement of a man's financial status, career success, and paycheck with his worth to his family puts him in a precarious position.[24] Finding his identity in being the financial provider has led to some men feeling stressed by the idea of a partner who out-earns them.[25] This may lead to men supporting their partner's career but discouraging them from pursuing promotions, even though a bigger paycheck for her would mean a better lifestyle for them both.

Although the perception of men as primary financial providers is still strong, a study by the Pew Research Foundation found that "the importance of being the financial provider ranks behind being caring and compassionate when it comes to being a good spouse or partner."[26] However, due to societal, familial, or relational expectations and fear of being judged harshly by their male peers, some men may flat-out refuse to take on a nurturing role even if that's what they want, and their partner can support the family financially.[27]

When society decided that men were only objects of production, not sources of warmth, love, care, and comfort, we stripped an entire gender of their humanity and ability to contribute to living legacies. The restriction of men from taking on a nurturing role has done a huge disservice to men, women, relationships, families, and society. And all of us are paying the price.

"No one died wishing they had spent more time at the office."

– JO IDA HANSEN

HOW THE MYTH OF THE NON-NURTURING MAN
CAUSES HARM

This idea that men are not wired to be nurturing is not only untrue but ultimately hurts men, their partners, and their families in a variety of ways. One of the biggest impacts we see is in the realm of parenting. Many men are looked on as "babysitters" when they are watching their own children. This comes from the assumption that the children's mother is the primary parent and that when dad watches the kids, it is something way out of his comfort and/or skills zone. Dads are often seen as "helping" rather than parenting.[28]

This view is not only harmful to men in two-parent homes, but it is doubly harmful to men who are divorced or single parents. It may be shocking to discover (it was for me) that only in 2018 did a US state (Kentucky) establish that 50–50 custody between parents was to be sought as the national standard.[29] For partnered men, this idea that men cannot be equal parents leads not only to the dismissal and exclusion of dads as equally involved parents, but also to a massively increased load on moms.

All of this comes back to the assumption that men are not "wired" to be caretakers and nurturers and that women are by default the nurturer, the home manager, the planner, the better parent. And this is not just men thinking they're not good at this stuff. Women engage in and perpetuate the myth of the non-nurturing man as well.

Unfortunately, research shows that the more a mother believes in traditional gender roles, the more likely she is to engage in gatekeeping behavior between a father and his children.[30] This gatekeeping behavior positions the woman with the children as a unit with the father on the outside. Women who believe in the "women are more nurturing by nature" ideology are more likely to micromanage a man's parenting and by doing so affect his perception of and ability to improve his own parenting skills.[31] She is also more likely to limit his time and minimize his involvement with the children. Men who believed in traditional gender roles also reported feeling less influential in the decision-making for their children.[32]

On the other hand, when a man is involved in the decision to have children, prenatal care, and education process before the baby arrives, he feels more satisfied and less stressed as a new dad.[33] A man's level of confidence in his parenting skills also leads to more closeness between the couple in the parenting process. [34] The better a couples' relationship as co-parents, the better the outcomes for the children as well.[35]

Overall, men who can be nurturing have higher levels of self-confidence, better relationships, and more often play pivotal roles in their communities[36]. However, there are lots of people who still seem to think that men are not capable of this nurturing thing. Again, back to stereotypical gender roles, we are told the man is the "provider and protector," not the nurturer.

DADS THAT D'OH

Media portrayals of fathers in the last few decades have also played a major role in helping to perpetuate this myth. Many sitcoms of this genre (*Malcolm in the Middle, Everybody Loves Raymond, Married with Children, The Simpsons, Family Guy*) follow the trope of a nuclear family in which the mother is a hyperfunctioning superhuman who is somehow CEO of a major company, president of the PTA, chair of some committee, and primary caretaker/parent. At the same time, the dad is a lovable but buffoonish character who brings home a paycheck, but otherwise continuously makes the woman's life harder by screwing up in some way.

Some of the descriptions of these TV shows read literally like, "A lovable middle-class family that follows a bumbling idiot (Dad), his permanently exasperated wife (Mom) and her attempts to keep him, and her other children, in line." The kids roll their eyes at him, and his wife treats him like her "other child." So often, life imitates art, and expectations of gender roles around nurturing and caretaking are no exception.

In actuality, the modern American dad is much more involved in his children's daily life than dads in previous generations. Modern dads have expressed that parenthood was central to their identity at a higher percentage rate than women do (58 percent to 57 percent).[37] The 2021 dad spent triple the amount of time the 1965 dad spent with his kids, but nearly 50 percent of dads still feel like they are not spending the amount of time they would like to spend with their children.[38]

Science supports not only the capability of men to be nurturers but also the importance of men taking on a nurturing role in their homes and children's lives. The National Fatherhood Initiative reported:

"Positive forms of father involvement (involvement in child-related activities, engagement in multiple forms of involvement and developing a positive father-child relationship) were associated with children's social and emotional well-being as well as behavioral adjustment and academic achievement."[39]

Some of the more interesting tidbits of research I have found are the studies showing that fathers, more than mothers, impact infants' and toddlers' verbal and communication skills.[40] When dads read to and talk to their children, their children have increased vocabularies, more advanced emotional and language skills, and are better prepared when entering school.[41] Dads who are warm, nurturing, and engage with their children positively impact their children's lives in significant ways.[42]

Although men are gaining equal footing in the parenting arena, the role of nurturing the home in other ways is still typically falling to the female partner. Maybe we've come to accept that men can keep their children housed, but the question remains: can men create a home?

LEARNED HELPLESSNESS / WEAPONIZED INCOMPETENCE

There are two concepts that have crept in and damaged men's ability to be seen as nurturers and equally capable partners. One is learned helplessness and the other is weaponized incompetence.

In learned helplessness, a person is shown or told over and over that they are helpless or powerless in some way. Eventually they believe it.

THE ELEPHANT AND THE ROPE:
A LESSON IN LEARNED HELPLESSNESS[43]

"I was walking one day when I happened upon an elephant tied with a thin rope to a small tree. It seemed evident to me that the rope was not sturdy enough to hold the elephant, and yet the animal made no attempt to break free from this feeble hold. When the animal's trainer returned, I remarked at the fact that such a large animal would be held by such a thin rope.

"The trainer replied, 'He has been conditioned to believe that he cannot escape. From infancy, he is tied with the same rope. When he is young, the rope is strong enough to hold him fast. He struggles against it, but eventually learns that he is not stronger than the rope. As he grows older, his strength increases, but his mind has already decided that the rope is stronger. He will no longer test his strength and so this simple rope is enough to hold him.'"

At its core, learned helplessness is the idea, reinforced over time by external factors, that you are powerless to effect change on your environment. It is exhausting to fight against what you believe to be an inevitability, so eventually you stop trying. Learned helplessness can manifest itself in many areas of a person's life, but in the realm of relationships and nurturing, the message being sent to men is often that they "are not wired that way" and that they "are no good at that stuff."[44] Traditional expectations for men often discourage the display of empathetic, compassionate, or caring traits.[45]

Peggy Orenstein, author of *Boys and Sex: Young Men on Hookups, Love, Porn, Consent, and Navigating the New Masculinity*, found in her research that "there is no difference between boys' and girls' need for connection, nor neurologically in their capacity for empathy.[46] And yet I wonder how many men and boys have internalized the false message that they are not nurturing or capable caretakers. Like the elephant, they are limited by a faulty belief about what they are and are not capable of.

The other damaging behavior though is less about helplessness and not being given the opportunity to be nurturing in the relationship or childcare, but an active *avoidance* of stepping into the caretaking and nurturing role. This is called weaponized incompetence. There are many examples of men who weaponize their "incompetence" in the house/childcare arena in order to shift the majority of the household load onto their partner.

When it comes to advocating for men as equally capable parents and partners, sometimes this inherent bias against men as "non-nurturers" gets bolstered by the reality of the gender gap still evident in the homecare sphere. Mothers are still saddled with more of the "busy work" of homemaking. Only 38 percent of women feel satisfied with the way household chores are divided.[47] Women, on average, handle 71 percent of this aspect of nurturing and family care, particularly when it comes to meal prepping and grocery shopping.[48]

Weaponized incompetence is where we see men act like they've never loaded a dishwasher in their life, are incapable of folding laundry, can't remember their children's teachers' names, forget everything but beer when they go to the grocery store, or act like a date night or child's birthday party is the hardest thing they've ever been asked to plan in the history of ever.

This is an actively harmful version of the "bumbling idiot" dad from the sitcoms, because unlike Homer Simpson, who is a fictional character, these men actually do know better and they are choosing not to participate as equal partners in the caretaking and nurturing of their homes and relationships.

This idea that men can't recognize when something is dirty or empty or when a child's diaper needs changing or when an anniversary is coming up is ridiculous. I mean really. How are men running companies and construction projects, flying planes, and being president if—according to some of their wives—they would leave their head at home if it wasn't screwed on their body? Women need to stop infantilizing men, but also, men, stop infantilizing yourselves.

DADS THAT DO

Another common point of conflict between parents is the polarization of the "fun parent" and the "duty parent." These roles often get divided along gender lines, with dad grabbing the role of fun parent, leaving mom with the less fun role of duty parent. The fun parent gets to be the one who shows up for playtime and movie nights, while the duty parent is the one making doctor appointments, attending parent-teacher conferences, and planning play dates.

This imbalance leads to a significant amount of resentment among moms, and I often see this frustration be part of the discussion about divorce. If Dad has custody of his children 50 percent of the time, surely *then* he will figure out how to be an equal parent? As Audrey Cade expressed in her blog "Divorce Made My Ex a Better Father," "Although I will always feel bad for my kids because they are children of divorce, I am pleased for them that they finally have a father who is more attentive to their needs, involved in their lives, and carrying his share of our family's load."[49]

There are hundreds of books, blogs, and articles on the frustration and confusion that women experience when their previously equal *partner* suddenly becomes a backseat *parent*. Being in a "partnership" with someone who is not an active and involved partner will lead to resentment and frustration long-term. It also very often contributes to an environment of contempt and criticism, which is toxic to any relationship. You can't expect something to thrive in a toxic environment. My plea to you is: Don't take the hard way to learn that lesson.

Trey and Katy

THE FOLLOW-THROUGH

I opened my email on November 1 to read this booking request: "I'd like to book a session for myself and my husband Trey," Katy wrote. "I have asked, begged, and pleaded for him to step up with the kids. We both work full-time, but I feel like a single mother. I am at the end of my rope and this Halloween was the last straw. I don't want to get divorced, but I don't know what else to do."

I met with Trey and Katy and began to explore what had brought them to this point.

Me: "What happened on Halloween this year?"

Katy: "I got held up at work, so I got home later than expected. I was supposed to get off at 5:00, but someone else didn't come in so I got held over until 7:00."

Trey: "We planned to be at the pumpkin patch at seven."

Katy: "I realize I got off late, but I said that I would meet you and the kids there. He couldn't even get it together to get the kids there by himself. So I get home, the kids are all a mess, crying and melting down because "Daddy promised" and now I'm the bad guy and I'm just sick of it!"

Me: "Trey, what happened on your end?"

Trey: "We have three kids, seven, five, and two, and they all have costumes and—"

Katy: "Which I got ready for them this morning. I have taken the kids trick or treating by myself the last two years! Going to the pumpkin patch was your idea."

Me: "Trey, what would you have needed to have this situation turn out differently?"

Trey: "I just want things to be better. Our relationship was great before, but since the kids it's like. . . I'll want to go camping for the summer like I did as a kid, or take them to the beach, or do something cool, hell, even have a barbecue, and she will just shut it down. Maybe our values are just different as parents."

Katy: "No, Trey. I want our kids to have an amazing childhood too. I'm just exhausted. I'm the one who gets stuck doing all the planning and prepping and cleaning and driving and everything! When you say you want to have a barbecue, what you mean is you want me to do all the shopping, send out all the invites, clean the house, prepare all the food, get the kids ready, so you can stand by the grill and drink beer for three hours and then I get to clean up afterward. It's not that I don't want to have a barbecue; I don't want to do all the work that comes with it by myself. It's the same with your beach trips and camping ideas. I'm not trying to kill your dreams, I just hate your follow-through."

Trey was quiet. After a few moments of silence, I checked in with him to ask what he was thinking.

Trey: "I'm thinking about golf."

Katy looked at me incredulously and began grabbing her purse to leave.

Trey: "Katy, please, hold on. I think it finally clicked. So," he explained , "I played golf in college. I wanted to go pro, but I was never quite good enough. In golf it's the tiniest thing that makes the difference between someone who makes it and someone who doesn't. To the untrained eye, you could watch footage of a pro versus an amateur and not really tell the difference, but the difference is always in the follow-through."

Me: "I'm not a golfer, but I think I'm getting what you're saying. Will you keep going?"

Trey: "Yes, so my idea is the ball. I tee it up—I get the kids excited about it—and it's right there ready to be hit. But I have poor set up, bad takeaway, weak grip so I have a shitty swing—excuse my language—and the execution goes flat." He turned to his wife. "Unfortunately, you're the caddy, and you're the one who has to go get the ball from the weeds, the water trap, god knows where."

Katy: "Yeah, my job sucks."

Me: "If I am remembering what I know about golf, you have to begin with the end, right?"

Trey: "Exactly. The best way to fix your follow-through is work backward from the finish position."

Me: "Can you bring that metaphor home to the Halloween incident?"

Trey: "Absolutely. If I wanted to get the kids to the pumpkin patch, it's not good enough to just tee up the ball, I needed to think about the ending. The goal was having a fun family memory and having all of us there at 7:00. I could have started getting the kids ready earlier in the day too, regardless of Katy being late at work or not. I was home with them all day and I didn't even think about getting them ready. I just figured since Katy bought the costumes that she would know how they went on and stuff. But how hard can it be?" He turned to his wife. "Babe, I'm so sorry, I'm realizing how much I leave up to you. I'm the shittiest golfer ever."

Katy: "I mean if we're running with this metaphor, yeah, I guess so."

Me: "Again, not knowing a ton about golf, but to fix the follow-through, it's just about practice, practice, practice, right? I'm remembering Malcolm Gladwell's 10,000 hours rule."[50]

Trey: "Yeah, so what's that like. . . a year and a few months?"

Katy: "That's assuming you're spending twenty-four hours a day."

Trey: "Well, I mean it would take even longer if I get divorced and only have half custody—which I don't want. Katy, I might not get 10,000 hours in, but will you give me a year to fix my follow-through?"

Being a fully engaged dad who can be counted on for the care as well as the fun is rewarding on so many levels and has multiple positive impacts on dads, children, and marriages. All it takes is a little dedication to the follow-through. Katy agreed to give Trey a year to work on his follow-through. They continued to attend therapy together, and one session Trey showed me a picture of what he had made for their anniversary. It was a plaque that read: "Dream your dreams; Plan your dreams; Work your plan; Live your dreams."

"This is our new family motto," he said. "I've hung it on the living room wall. We call it our Family Follow-Through."

Katy chimed in, "We also took your advice and when Trey has an idea but hasn't got a plan yet, he will say, 'Dream with me,' and I will know that he doesn't expect me to make it happen. It really helps me not to feel stressed when he starts talking about his ideas."

Trey continued, "And it helps me to hear my ideas out loud sometimes so I can really think about what kind of work it would take to do the follow-through." Thanks to Trey's dedication to doing the work and Katy's patience, they were able to give their children the childhood they had always hoped for, and they continue to be married to this day.

PUTTING SKIN IN THE GAME

Marriage counselor Corinn Voeller created a TikTok that went viral last year. In it, she talks about the difference between taking active and passive responsibility in a marriage.[51] These terms came originally from the business world, and they describe the different ways that organizations can be set up. If you are an "active partner," you actively make decisions for the direction of the company and are deeply invested in the venture's success. As a "passive partner," you take on the role of observer and wait to be told when your help is needed.

Emma C. writes about the tendency for men to "offer help" to their wives when it comes to parenting or household duties in her comic book *The Mental Load*. Although this seems like a nice thing to do ("Oh, look, he wants to help!"), it subtly positions the women as the "owners" of those chores and managers of home responsibilities and the men as the "helpers." This sets up a dynamic in which the nurturing and care of your home and family is your partner's responsibility, and you are just along for the ride waiting to be told what to do. She is the active driver; you are the passive passenger.

The over functioning woman/under functioning man dynamic also damages sex lives. A study by the *Archives of Sexual Behavior* found that the "casting of women into a caregiver-mother role to men partners contributes to the women's lower desire."[52] As Michael Fray says in his viral post "She Divorced Me Because I Left Dishes by the Sink," "The sexiest thing a man can say to his partner is 'I got this,' and then take care of whatever needs taken care of."[53]

In an equal relationship, there is no room for a passive partner. A STRONG relationship is a mutual venture. An equal relationship needs both partners to be equally invested in the nurturing and cultivation of a thriving partnership. You can't row a boat with one oar.

Taking ownership and becoming an active participant in nurturing your relationship means being deeply invested in its success. When you shift your perspective to being an equally active participant in your relationship, home management, and parenting, you will look for opportunities rather than wait to be directed. This approach helps position you and your partner as equal investors toward the same goal: keeping this relationship (and family) nurtured and thriving to its highest absolute potential.

"If the grass is greener somewhere else, start watering your own lawn!"

– MICHAEL BECKWITH

NURTURING WHAT MATTERS

A 2020 study found that nearly one in four Americans had at least one family estrangement, with children being more likely than parents to initiate the cutoff.[54] When a child moves out of the family home, if healthy emotional connection has not been nurtured among the family members, the relationship ends when the function does. Divorce contributes to the increased risk of estrangement, with fathers more likely to lose connection with their children than mothers.[55]

However, these losses can be a source of deep regret, pain, and sadness.[56] Karl Pillemer, director of the Cornell Legacy Project and author of *Fault Lines: Fractured Families and how to Mend Them* writes, "I learned that people who are estranged from a family member feel deep sadness, long for reconnection and wish that they could turn back the clock and act differently to prevent the rift."[57]

Maintaining relationships is not just important, it is lifesaving. In a longitudinal study by Harvard that has tracked a group of 754 men since 1938 (and is still going with the over 2000 children of these men), they found that the biggest predictor of health and happiness was the quality of the men's relationships.[58] In a TEDx Talk on this study presented by Robert Waldinger in 2015, he noted that seventy-five years into the study, the most significant findings of the study were threefold:

"The first is that social connections are really good for us, and that loneliness kills. . . the second big lesson that we learned is that it's not just the number of friends you have, [or] whether or not you're in a committed relationship, but it's the quality of your close relationships that matters. . . [a]

nd the third big lesson that we learned about relationships and our health is that good relationships don't just protect our bodies, they protect our brains [from cognitive decline and memory loss]."[59]

There is an epidemic of loneliness, and most of its victims are men. A 2021 report by the Survey Center on American Life found that one in five single American men reported having *no* close friends.[60] Men also report having less intimacy in their close friendships as compared to women.[61] It is crucial that we change the narrative about men's needs and abilities in this area. One of the biggest myths perpetuated against men is the idea that men—"true" men anyway—do not have the emotional and relational needs that women do. They don't nurture others and they *definitely* don't need nurturing themselves.

This is absolute garbage first of all, and second of all, this message is dangerous because it not only kills relationships, but it reinforces men into patterns of isolation and disconnection. The physical impact of loneliness can be measured in higher rates of stroke,[62] heart disease,[63] Alzheimer's,[64] depression,[65] and suicide[66] in men who are disconnected from loving, nurturing relationships in their lives. People who are socially isolated consistently have the highest death rate.[67]

Social isolation was correlated with higher rates of death among men during the Chicago heat wave in 1995 where, despite more elderly women living alone, men were twice as likely to die as women. Eric Klinenberg, author of *Heat Wave: A Social Autopsy of Disaster in Chicago* notes, "To understand this we have to look at the social relationships that elderly women retain but that elderly men tend to lose."[68] Having solid relationships with others is a determining factor in a long and healthy life and a protective factor against early death.[69]

The way our society has traditionally been set up, men do not get as much practice, opportunities, or encouragement to be vulnerable and nurturing, but the limitation of that approach is starting to become clear. It is crucial that we change the narrative about men's abilities in this area. We all, regardless of gender, seek genuine and authentic human connection. So many men I talk to these days describe feeling like they are emotionally starving. However, these men are often surrounded by "buddies" who they spend casual time with, but who they fail to connect with on a deeper, more vulnerable level.[70] The lack of depth in many men's friendships lead to all of them suffering in silence.[71]

This suffering often leads men to become overly dependent on finding a partner who they imagine will be the source of love and support they are searching for. This not only places an undue burden on women,[72] but it also leads to anger, frustration, and rage against women who refuse to play that role.[73] Men who depend on their female partners for their relational needs often find themselves losing not only their partner but their entire social network, if and when the relationship comes to an end.

We need to break the stigma that men's friendships cannot provide intimacy and that women are the only sources of and conduits for nurturing, intimacy, and care.[74] When men show up vulnerably and embrace authenticity in their friendships,[75] their connections can be deep, intimate, satisfying, and lifesaving.[76] Men, you are equally capable of providing nurturing in your friendships, families, and personal relationships. You can nurture your own ability to be nurturing by learning new skills, seeking support, and deepening your connections with your friends and family members.[77]

<u>TL; DR STEPS TO BUILDING NURTURING</u>

1) WIRING – Men are equally capable nurturers. Up until the Industrial Revolution, men were heavily involved in parenting. Providing and Protecting a living legacy requires more than just putting in time at the office. It requires men to be active members of the home and equally involved parents.

2) MAINTAINING – Is about keeping something running. If you can maintain something, that's a good first step, but the next level of skill is keeping something alive. Nurturing is maintenance 2.0 because it takes active investment, awareness, and ongoing participation. There is no "set it and forget it" mode for your relationships.

3) PRACTICE – Checking in with your partner on the 3 P's is an easy way to maintain an emotional connection. When you can see and talk about what needs to be nurtured, you give yourself opportunities to practice your nurturing skills. Nurturing is key to long-term relationships.

4) MESSAGING – We perpetuate the myth that men are no good at nurturing to the detriment of men and their relationships. When we tell men over and over that they are no good at nurturing, we remove the opportunities for them

to get equal as fathers and husbands. Men are dying from loneliness and diseases related to social isolation. Healthy relationships are crucial to mental and physical health. Let's break the stigma of men as non-nurturers and instead encourage men to be invested, present leaders in nurturing their relationships.

CHAPTER SIX

GENEROSITY

"Generosity is the beginning of everything."

-WALEEPORN GUNAN

GREEN FLAG #6

I n intake sessions with new clients who are presenting for couples therapy, I sometimes ask, "If I had a magic wand and could wave it right now, what would change in your relationship?"

Overarchingly the theme of most of the wishes I hear are a desire to have a kinder relationship. STRONK didn't quite have the right ring to it, so I looked for another word to describe this state of being that couples wished they would be able to exist in more often.

The sixth green flag of a STRONG man is Generosity.

According to the *Cambridge English Dictionary*, *generosity* is "a willingness to give help or support, especially more than is usual or expected."[1]

When some people hear the phrase "generosity in relationships" they immediately think about financial generosity—gifts like jewelry, handbags, or something expensive. Now, you may be thinking, *Aha, here it is, the same old message. I knew it. Women always want more, more, more.* Well, let me explain what *generosity* means in this book.

In a STRONG relationship, generosity is the willingness to give the other person the benefit of the doubt, to offer kindness, compassion, and understanding. It is about showing up fully. It does not mean giving more than you are willing or able to give. It is also not about letting yourself be taken advantage of.

THE SECRET INGREDIENT

In considering this final ingredient of a STRONG man and a healthy relationship, I went back to thinking about the red flags/green flags and had a realization. In working with people with relational trauma, I have heard hundreds of stories: stories of people who were abandoned by or suffered neglect at the hand of a parent. Stories of people who were betrayed by a friend. Stories of people who were cheated on, lied to, or neglected by a spouse. Most of the people who hurt others in relationships are not evil or malicious people. It would be much easier if they were. No, what I saw as an overarching theme in all these stories really boiled down to one thing. It was almost too simple. It was *selfishness*. Selfishness is at the root of many of the attachment injuries inflicted in relationships.

Selfishness hurts people in relationships far more often than maliciousness. Often when I bring this idea up, that selfishness is at the core of most relational injuries, people are quick to reject it. "No, I'm not selfish, I'm a good person" or "I'm not selfish, I'm just busy." And it makes sense that people would reject the categorization of "selfish." From a young age, most of us were taught not to be selfish. We are told that "sharing is caring" and being selfish means you're a terrible person. Look at Scrooge. We are taught in movies, books, and experiences in school that selfish people are bad people, and we don't want to be bad people.

SPECTRUM OF SELF

I like to use a spectrum to talk about selfishness with selfishness at one end and self-neglect at the other. Both extremes are unhealthy in relationships. In the middle is self-mastery, the healthy balance between both extremes. This is where healthy generosity comes from.

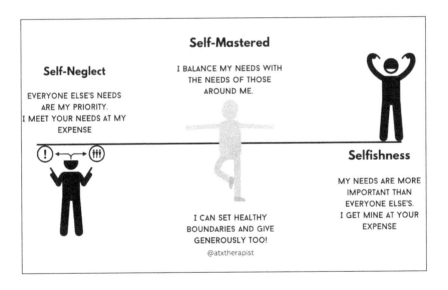

When I use the term selfish or selfishness from here on, I'm talking about "looking out for your own self-interest *at the expense of others.*" It is the position of "my needs are the most important." When someone has that mindset, they don't hesitate to take advantage of others to get their own needs met. Being selfish doesn't automatically mean that you are a bad person, but it will make you very bad at being in relationships.

On the opposing end from selfishness is sometimes what people might think of as "selflessness." We like to idealize the type of person who is giving, giving, giving all the time. Sometimes this is held up as what generosity looks like—but it's not. Unfortunately, this ideal of selflessness can actually be self-neglect in reality. Many of the people who operate on this end of the spectrum end up neglecting their own boundaries and meeting other people's needs to their own detriment.

Realizing that you have been selfish in the past and have maybe dominated relationships by being aggressive in getting your own needs met to the detriment of others is a good first step of awareness. However, deciding to slide to the other end and "never need anything again" keeps you in a dysfunctional dynamic. Just to be clear, the other end of dysfunction is still dysfunction.

I see so many men who hear the dictum "don't be selfish, be generous" who immediately slide to the self-neglect end of the spectrum. They then embrace the "happy wife, happy life" mentality and start to neglect their own needs in their relationships. Self-neglect looks like consistently neglecting your own boundaries and disrespecting your own needs to satisfy someone else's. You have needs too. Just choosing to shove them down and ignore them never leads to a positive and healthy outcome.

The middle is the goal: finding balance in self-mastery. Existing here looks like being able to set healthy boundaries, and to acknowledge and advocate for your own needs without taking advantage of others. You help take care of others, but you know not to cross the line into self-neglect. When you are full, you can give generously to others.

SURVIVAL AND SELFISHNESS

Some people believe that humans are inherently selfish and that only social conditioning forces us to act in a "polite" manner. Otherwise, we'd all be rampant greedy, selfish monsters. Well, good news, it's not that grim! In my research for this book, I found a fascinating fact: Humans are actually the most generous of all primates.[2]

Many animals will exhibit "sharing" behavior, but there is usually some form of payoff or exchange of resources. This is reciprocal altruism (you scratch my back, I'll scratch yours), which is not true generosity. Humans are consistently generous in times where there is no measurable payoff—and even at times where it would be costly to the giver.

Being generous is part and parcel of what makes us human.

We humans love being generous. This confuses computer simulation models trying to predict human behavior based on the idea that humans are solely motivated by self-interest. Humans are complicated, and one of the reasons is our penchant for generosity. We are generous even when it makes no sense to be.

Our closest ape relatives, the chimpanzees and the bonobos, share a little bit, but they will usually look for one thing to hold back. Bonobos won't share their tools, but they'll share food; chimps won't share their food (unless they are being pestered, which makes it reciprocal), but they will share their tools with the other chimps.

Humans, on the other hand, will willingly share not only food and tools but time and resources with other humans with no foreseen benefit to themselves. Examples of non-reciprocal human generosity might look like:

- Pulling over on the side of the road to help a stranger with a flat tire
- Donating to a charity that has no personal impact or connection
- Giving money or food to a homeless person
- Leaving a generous tip when there is no "social reward" to be gained
- Holding a door open or offering to put away a shopping cart for a stranger
- Allowing someone to cut in line in front of you

This flies in the face of some commonly repeated myths about human nature that paints all humans as inherently selfish and out for their own gain. We're not! The science shows that humans are actually the sharing-est of all the species![3] Ironically, this little quirk of our human nature may have actually helped us gain an evolutionary advantage[4] and contributed to our status as the dominant species.

The Human Generosity Project is a non-profit coalition of anthropologists, psychologists, and computer scientists dedicated to studying the effect of generosity on human evolution and social development. Since 2014, they have conducted a ton of really cool and interesting studies (seriously—check them out).[5]

The top finding that emerged from all their research was that communities and relational systems that were generous and giving were stronger than those that operated on a "tit for tat" basis. The giving cultures were wealthier, had enhanced survival chances, and had higher risk mediation across the system. What they found was: Generosity beat Reciprocity every time.[6]

"In short, human generosity, far from being a thin veneer of cultural conditioning atop a Machiavellian core, may be a bedrock feature of human nature."[7]

But here's the thing. The dueling needs of self-preservation and preservation of the relationships needed to maintain community are part of our evolutionary heritage. When we are in survival mode and feeling scared and insecure, we will take care of our own needs first and foremost. Everything is a zero-sum game to the lizard brain. This part of the brain is hardwired to look out for our own best interest. And if we have to screw someone else over to get what we need to survive? So be it. It's survival.

Before we had the capacity to think about what others need, we developed to consider what *we* need. Our brains still start from there. Even the limbic brain, which we share with our ape relatives, still wants to look for the one thing to hold back for ourselves. Only our rational prefrontal cortex has developed to the point where we can understand that sharing and generosity are better for us than being selfish.

With the old primitive parts of our brain working against us sometimes, it's hard *not* to be selfish. To be generous requires a shift toward looking out for our relationships, rather than just ourselves, as the number one goal." Most people are not evil or malicious.

However, we all have the *capacity* to cause harm when we choose selfishness over generosity in our intimate relationships.

SHAME, GUILT, AND SELF-COMPASSION

Maybe, after reading about selfishness, you are feeling some kind of way about your past behavior in relationships. Maybe you realize you have been selfish, gotten your needs met at the expense of others, and caused harm to your partner or loved ones by doing so. It doesn't often feel great to look back on our past behavior, especially if we know we wouldn't make the same choice now. We might experience some feelings of remorse, regret, shame, or guilt. These feelings aren't always comfortable, but are they healthy?

Well, let's talk about the difference between *shame* and *guilt*. We often use these two words interchangeably, but there is a difference. I really find it so important to distinguish between these two words because the way they work and feel are very different. One is healthy. One is not.

Let's start with the healthy one: *guilt*. Guilt is healthy because it is an appropriate response to a harmful behavior. If you have done something that hurt someone or damaged something, it is appropriate that you feel guilty. Guilt is adaptive because it often leads to feelings of remorse and attempts to make a reparative action. It helps you to learn from and moderate or change your behaviors to avoid causing future harm.

For example, if you hit a parked car and drive away, you may start to feel guilty. Which is good! First of all, it shows that you have a working conscience. You regret that you made the choice you did that caused harm to somebody. That shows empathy. Maybe you imagine the person who owns the car—now they can't get home or it's going to cost them money they don't have to try to repair the damage you caused. Thinking about that, you feel remorseful. You realize you made a bad decision that goes against your values. Which leads to the healthy part of guilt because you now have another choice. You can make it right.

You can drive back to the scene of the accident and make amends. You can also reflect on the remorse you feel and make a different choice in the future. Feelings of guilt are focused on your behavior. Guilt says, "You *did* a bad thing." It holds you accountable for what you have done, but there is the possibility that you can make it right or make amends. Guilt helps us learn from our actions so we can modify our future behavior. Behavior can change.

However, the other option: *Shame* is about personhood. Shame says, "*You* are bad." Not just you did a bad thing, no. You are a bad person. This is why shame is corrosive and unhealthy. Because if this is who you are, bad, what are your options from there? If you hit the parked car and ran away because that's just the kind of person you are: just a crappy, selfish, reckless, bad person, then there's nothing you can do to make it right.

Shame is not healthy because, compared to guilt, it does not lead to reparative action or moves to making things right or learning to act differently in the future. Instead, it leads to trying to hide the evidence of your actions. When you feel like there is a possibility to make something right, even though guilt is not a great feeling, there is some hope. However, with shame, there is no hope. There is no possibility of change because shame makes you feel like: *this is who you are, and this is how you'll always be. Bad.*

So, instead it leads to feelings of worthlessness, powerlessness, increased anger at the situation and more of a tendency to blame others rather than show empathy for them. *That was a dumb place to park anyway—stupid person. It's their fault I hit them.* Shame gives no option for redemption. It instead leads to a shame spiral which continues to bring you further and further down. You start with shame, beat yourself up with more criticism and negative self-talk, and end up with self-loathing.

The antidote to shame is self-compassion.

One of the most amazing things I have discovered in my time as a therapist is the power of self-compassion. Having self-compassion has been shown to be more important than "healthy self-esteem" when it comes to mental health. As Dr. Kristen Neff, author of *Self-Compassion: The Proven Power of Being Kind to Yourself*, explains, "Self-compassion gives you a stable self-worth whereas self-esteem goes up and down depending on how your day is going. Your sense of self gets rocked every time you have a little setback."[8]

Self-compassion is also linked to a higher sense of self-efficacy. Researchers Juliana Breines and Serena Chen found that "paradoxically, taking an accepting approach to personal failure may make people more motivated to improve themselves."[9] On the other hand, "Increased levels of self-criticism and a lack of self-compassion have been associated with the development and maintenance of a range of psychological disorders."[10]

If someone was compassionate with themselves, they avoided spending time and energy on self-punishment or criticism, and they exhibited higher levels of learning and resilience after making a mistake. Shaming, criticizing, and being hard on yourself in the name of "self-improvement" never works. You can't hate yourself into being a better version of you. You have to love yourself into change.

When you cultivate self-compassion, it leads to generosity in a relationship. When you can be compassionate with yourself, you can accept imperfection in yourself and your partner. People who are less self-compassionate tend to be highly self-critical and this tendency often blends into the way they interact with and see others in their relationships.

When you accept the reality that you will both mess up at some point or another, but that doesn't make either of you bad people or mean that the relationship is doomed, you will be more willing to own, talk about, and learn from your mistakes. Dr. Neff notes, "The research is really overwhelming at this point, showing that when life gets tough, you want to be self-compassionate. It's going to make you stronger."[11]

Everyone makes mistakes. However, when there is no generosity in a relationship, there is no grace, no room for understanding, and no room for learning from those mistakes. As Tara Brach says, "Feeling compassion for ourselves in no way releases us from responsibility for our actions. Rather, it releases us from the self-hatred that prevents us from responding to our life with clarity and balance."[12]

Showing yourself compassion and acting with generosity toward yourself will help you to be the person you want to be in your life and in your relationship. When you begin with self-compassion rather than shame, you can distinguish between who you are and your behavior. You can then start to choose new behaviors that will lead to a better, kinder, more generous stance toward yourself and your partner. Feeling empowered to make change, and doing so from a compassionate place, will lead to higher personal and relational satisfaction.

> **"Our sorrows and wounds are healed only when we touch them with compassion."**
>
> **– JACK KORNFIELD**

CHOOSING GENEROSITY

In his relationship research, Dr. John Gottman found that there is a defining quality that differentiates relationships that work from those that don't. Tracking this data point allowed him to divide couples into what he called "masters" and "disasters" and predict with 94 percent accuracy whether or not that couple would eventually get divorced if nothing changed. The data point? It was the number of positive to negative interactions between a couple[13].

He found the couples he labeled "disasters" operated on a 1:1 basis: one positive interaction to one negative one. Technically their relationship was "fair," but turns out that doesn't feel very good. The "master" couples? Turns out they had a whopping interaction ratio of 20:1! Twenty positive interactions to one negative one. Now, that might be the gold standard to shoot for, but what if that feels a long way away from where you and your partner are right now?

Well, Dr. Gottman found that even slightly increasing the number of positive to negative interactions in a couple can keep them from becoming a "disaster" statistic.

Turns out the "magic ratio" is 5:1.

When a couple had at least a 5:1 ratio of positive to negative interactions, it increased their sense of connectedness, generosity, and well-being. They felt more positively about their relationship and had more fondness, admiration, and respect for one another. Having a generous "goodwill buffer" also helped get them through tough times. Couples with high positive to negative ratios in their relationship were more likely to give each other the benefit of the doubt in times of disagreement or conflict.

The most important thing a couple could do to increase their levels from 1:1 to 5:1 or higher was so simple. It was turning *toward* your partner when they made a bid for connection rather than turning *away from them*.[14] When one partner said, "Hey, babe, come look at this," the other partner was faced with a choice. They could either respond antagonistically: "No, I'm busy"; not respond at all—which is also a negative because it's leaving your partner hanging. Or, they could respond positively to their partner and connect with them: "Ooh, what'd you find?"

This is the epitome of what generosity looks like in a relationship. Taking that one extra moment to pause and choose to give your partner a point to connect to rather than turning away to attend to your own desires. Connection is the life blood of a STRONG relationship, and it will often require choosing Generosity over Selfishness. Make that connection.

PRESENCE OVER PRESENTS

Providing compliments, attention, care, consideration, manners, kindness, affection, interest, and thoughtfulness cost nothing besides the commitment to being present and generous in your relationship. The realization that your marriage and the success or failure of it can hinge on these tiny sliding door moments can be a powerful tool for self-empowerment. When you come to a choice point, do you turn toward your partner with your time, attention, energy, warmth, understanding, and patience? Or do you turn away?

This could be the difference between a marriage that lasts a lifetime and one that ends up as another statistic. Sometimes I like to say the only truly hard thing about being married or in a committed partnership is protecting the needs of the couple when our own needs are fighting for dominance. When we are single, our time, energy, and money are spent toward the things that we want and need and the things that will make us happy. We are our only priority.

But to be in a fully committed relationship requires a *fundamental shift in priorities*.

Some of the saddest conversations I have seen happen on my couch is when one partner is begging the other to just show some genuine care. If your "give a shit" meter is only set to things that impact or affect you, and you see your family and partner as simply a well of support for you to dip into when you need, you're doing it wrong. I saw a T-shirt one time when I was traveling in Japan that said *"There for you when I need you."* I remember thinking, "hmmm, that's not as romantic as they probably intended it to be."

For the relationship to survive, it needs to have both people generously choosing to protect and provide for the relationship rather than choosing their own self-interest at the expense of the relationship. We know where that ends up. True generosity in a relationship shows up as a state of being. It is looking for ways to be thoughtful and think of ways to make your relationship better as a default, not an exception. It's giving to the relationship because you want to, not because you have to.

LOVE LANGUAGES

Love Languages are a really easy way to make a tangible step toward embodying generosity in your relationship. The Five Love Languages are from a book by Gary Chapman,[15] and they describe the ways in which people like to give and receive love.

Knowing your Love Language can be a really important way to understand yourself and to let your partner know how you like to be loved. Discovering your partner's Love Language is a simple way to be more efficient and effective in giving your partner love in the way they like to receive it. Here is the overview of each type. See if you can find yours and recognize your partner's.

Words of Affirmation

If you are a words of affirmation person, you enjoy hearing verbal affirmation of your partner's love. You need to hear loving words from your partner to hear how your partner notices and admires you. If you aren't getting words of affirmation but are getting words of criticism, it can cut doubly deep.

If your partner's Love Language is words of affirmation, but words are not your strong suit, one tool I offer is what I call **Walking Down the Trail**. It goes like this. Rather than simply stopping at "You look nice," use it as a "trailhead" to go deeper into some specifics about the person you are talking to. Maybe the next stop on the trail is "That color looks great on you" and the next one is "It really brings out your eyes." "Walking down the Trail" helps to make a general compliment more personal.

Acts of Service

If you like acts of service, you are the opposite of the words of affirmation person. To you, actions speak louder than words. You might not need to hear lots of "I love yous" because you want proof of love in action. You, more than most, enjoy when someone anticipates and takes care of a need you have without having to be asked. This might also show up in the way you show love. You like to show, rather than tell, your partner how much you love them by doing things for them.

If acts are your thing, one suggestion I offer is called **Highlighting.** First of all, let your partner know that acts of service are the way you show them love. Then, when you do an act of service that is specifically an act of love, let your partner know by highlighting it. "I put gas in your car so you'll have a full tank in the morning." When you highlight the act, it sends the message "I love you." The reason I say let them know about your Love Language first is because if you don't, they may think you're keeping score or highlighting where they are *not* doing something. That would have the opposite effect as the one intended.

Important caveats: Household chores are not always acts of service *for your partner*. You both live there, remember? See if you can find acts that are specific to making them feel loved and cared for as a person.

Quality Time

Not to be confused with "quantity time." Quality time is one-on-one connection between the couple that is *about the couple*. Couples can get a little frustrated when one partner has Quality Time as their Love Language and the other feels confused when they have "hung out" all weekend, but their partner still feels neglected. Quantity—spending time in a group, doing other activities, or simply existing in the same space together—does not necessarily mean that the time together was Quality.

One very simple way to honor this need is to **Block off Time** on your calendar. Life gets busy quick. One way to ensure that you and your partner are getting your Quality Time needs met is to get a shared calendar and block off time weekly to share with each other. Schedule a date! Don't take each other for granted. Sometimes I ask couples to reflect on "if we weren't living together, how much time in our lives would we actually be planning to spend together?" If you are relying on catching the crumbs of your days, your Quality Time needs are probably not being met.

Gifts

This is one of those Love Languages that gets a bad rap. If someone's Love Language is gifts, sometimes the stereotype is that they are superficial or materialistic, ("money is my Love Language,") but that is not the truth. If your Love Language is gifts, what you might be responding to is the thoughtfulness behind the gift.

If your partner's Love Language is gifts, **Think Outside the Box**. A gift can be freely obtained, made, or bought. The most important thing if you or your partner's Love Language is gifts is not the dollar amount of the gift, but the personal resonance of the gift because that is what shows thoughtfulness. Knowing that your partner thought of you, remembered something that you said you liked or wanted, and the effort it took to bring it home to you is what makes you feel loved. When it's not about the dollar amount, the possibilities for gift-giving are endless!

Physical Touch

This is another one that gets conflated with "sex is my Love Language" all the time. And once again, that's not it. It is easier sometimes for men to initiate or ask for sex rather than asking for a more comforting or vulnerable form of touch. But if physical touch is your Love Language, you want to give and receive touch to feel connected with, soothed by, and intimate with your partner in all sorts of tactile ways.

One of the biggest complaints I hear from women is "he only touches me when he wants sex." This can be frustrating to men who have physical touch as their Love Language. If you have physical touch as your Love Language, it's so important to communicate verbally that physical touch represents love, presence, tenderness, and not just a prelude to sex. Let your partner know you would appreciate a hand hold, a back, shoulder, or foot rub, a kiss on the cheek, a head scratch, or a hug and all the other ways physical interaction can be soothing, reassuring, and not necessarily sexual.

Giving yourself a cheat sheet to successfully embody generosity in your relationship is one of the reasons I encourage you to take the Love Languages Quiz[16] (and hey, do a refresher if you haven't done it in a while). Encourage your partner to take it as well. Words of Affirmation, Acts of Service, Quality Time, many Gifts, and Physical Touch are free and available to be given at any point in your relationship to boost the generosity quotient.

It can be super discouraging in a relationship when partners' Love Languages are mismatched and they don't have the language to discuss it. When I see couples who don't know what their Love Languages are, it often becomes apparent that they are both trying hard to show love to their partner in the way they like to receive it and they are silently hoping that their partner will reciprocate in kind. Unfortunately, they never do, because they have a whole different Love Language!

What I say is *stop working so hard unless you know it's working.* If you search for weeks finding the perfect gift for your partner, order it engraved and personalized, stay up late wrapping it just so, and then when your partner gets it, they're like, "Oh, okay," it can be a real gut punch. However, if you know that your partner's Love Language is not gifts at all, but Quality Time, then you can spend the time you would have spent on the gift just hanging out with them — for free — and be appreciated more for it!

And if your partner knows that your Love Language is gifts, well, then instead of hanging around you while you're trying to get work done—as they might like—they can instead spend that time finding you a nice gift so you feel the love the way you want to feel loved. Some couples have a lot of overlap and similarity and that's great, but for many couples there might be a little bit of grace required to stretch outside of your comfort zone to give your partner love in their language, not yours. It's the generous and kind thing to do, but it's also the more effective thing to do.

Learning just a few "words" in your partner's Love Language will help you communicate your love more effectively to them. As we know, yelling at someone louder in your own language doesn't make them understand you more, it just makes you both frustrated (and kind of makes you an asshole). Learning their language is the generous choice. Sharing your language with them allows them to be generous in return.

"There is no love; there are only proofs of love. Whatever love I may feel in my heart, others will see only my actions"

— PIERRE REVERDY

FLIP IT AND REVERSE IT

You cannot give what you have not received. If I asked you to teach someone to fly a plane, it would be super useful for you to have been on the receiving end of instruction at some point yourself, right? So this is where I will end by saying. . . Generosity begins with you.

That's the "flip it and reverse it" I want to encourage here. There is a saying that I learned while in therapy school: "You cannot pour from an empty cup." Another one you might be more familiar with is: "Make sure you secure your own mask before helping others." You cannot give generously to others without taking care of your own needs first.

"What the heck, lady! You just said not to be selfish—now you say take care of yourself first? Which one is it?" Well, it's both! You have to take care of yourself first, but self-care doesn't have to be self-*ish*. To truly be generous, you must give from a place of abundance. And it is really difficult to be generous when you are starving.

If you are going to be providing the stability and balance of your family, you have to start by giving that to yourself first. So, let me go existential if I can for a minute. We are all organisms. We are part of nature. Nature has a fundamental urge toward homeostasis. Maybe you remember from Biology 101, homeostasis is "the tendency toward a relatively stable equilibrium between interdependent elements, especially as maintained by physiological processes"[17] or basically a fancy word for *balance*.

On a fundamental level, we are all seeking to lead balanced lives. When our bodies become unbalanced, we become ill. When our lives are unbalanced, our relationships suffer. Wellness and balance go hand in hand. However, sometimes our busy lives, our coping mechanisms, our adaptations for survival get in the way of optimal health.

STRONG SELF-CARE

Getting back to balance will require self-care. Now what is self-care? I mean it's right there in the name—taking care of yourself. Wow. I know. Big revelation. But really. Breaking it down, self-care is about taking care of yourself in the same way you would care for someone you love. It is about giving yourself what you need and not denying yourself the love you need to thrive. This love can come in many different forms as the care you need will look different depending on the circumstance.

Self-care has become one of those buzzwords that I have noticed tends to dis-include men. Depictions of "self care" on Instagram, articles, or blogs sometimes over-focus on superficial "self-care" behaviors that tend toward incredibly female audiences. But self-care is not a gendered activity. Self-care is absolutely essential for everyone. It is the ultimate in self-sustainability. Self-care can look like a bath, a cup of tea, or a pedicure, sure. But self-care can also look like a run, time spent on a passion project, or a chat with a friend.

So where do you start? In my research for this book and in my therapy practice over the years, I have found a few different studies on the principles of wellness, the essential areas of healthy lifestyles, and the elements of balance.

These varied slightly but mostly covered the same areas, so I have gone ahead and combined them all into the biggest pizza. This is the Pizza of Wellness. A hefty eight slices of balance. If you think of this lovely pizza as something that needs equal distribution in order to be well balanced, you can see how skipping the toppings on one slice can imbalance the whole thing.

Pizza Of Wellness

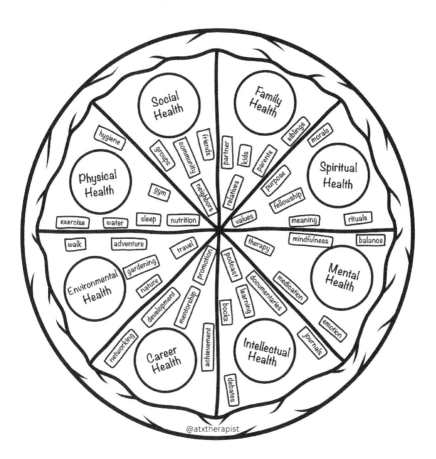

@atxtherapist

Let's start breaking this pie down:

Physical Health – physical health is a *huge* component of a healthy life. Exercise, good nutrition, and getting enough sleep and water are fundamental ways in which you can keep this slice nice and full. Another thing is getting any medical needs taken care of. There is a stereotype that men don't like to go to the doctor. This might come from a place of fear of what you might find out, it might come from putting yourself last and not taking your needs seriously, it might come from feeling embarrassed about the need to seek help, but neglecting your physical health takes a huge toll on your wellness and well-being. Take care of yourself. You will feel better and live longer.

Taking self-care in the physical realm can look like a variety of things, not just pedicures or going to the gym, but it definitely covers both! Sometimes this will look like going to the gym, other times it will look like taking a nap, other times maybe it's about taking the extra effort to home cook a meal rather than getting takeout. Diversify your options and learn what makes you feel good physically. This slice is about focusing on what you need to be a healthy human being in your body so you can feel and be your best in other ways.

Social Health – Do you have friends, support systems, community engagement? As we saw earlier in this book, loneliness is an epidemic in men. One of the biggest findings in the research on men's relationships is that they tend to neglect their friendships and lack support systems. They then often over-rely on their female partners for their social and community needs.

However, it is crucial to your own health and wellness that you feel connected to your own friends outside of your "couple friends." Do you have friends from school, college, military service, or former jobs that you have neglected? Are there groups or clubs that you can look at joining? Getting connected socially is a major protective factor and an essential part of wellness. Keeping social connections and strong friendship ties are a part of providing yourself with a safety net and context in the world.

Family Health – Are you taking care of your core relational needs? This is slightly different from your social health slice because this slice focuses on your needs for tending to your core family connections. Not everyone has a family of origin that is healthy to reconnect with, so setting clearer boundaries with them might be a part of tending to this part of health.

Your intimate and family connections are really what are going to impact your functioning on an ongoing, daily basis. So much stress can be alleviated by ensuring that this slice is not neglected. Giving attention to what your partner and your family needs can look like Quality Time with the kids, planning a date night, or reaching out to your siblings to plan the next family reunion.

Spiritual Health – What gives you a sense of purpose and meaning in life? For some people it may be a sense of a higher purpose or a dedication to a religious higher power, but for others, spirituality can be an investigation into your sense of values and morals. What does this look like for you? Do you spend any time reading or listening to faith leaders (if this is important to you)? If you are non-religious, there are still lots of ways to take care of your "spirit."

Listening to motivational podcasts, philosophers, thinkers, and leaders who encourage a sense of internal mastery can be other ways to fill this slice of health and wellness. A purpose-filled life is an essential and motivating part of life. Research shows that having a sense of purpose and meaning in life is protective against depression and low self-esteem.[18] Viktor Frankl, Holocaust survivor and author of the book *Man's Search for Meaning*, wrote, "Life is never made unbearable by circumstance, but only by lack of meaning and purpose."[19]

Mental Health – Men's mental health is another often overlooked and neglected slice of the wellness pie. In his book *I Don't Want to Talk About It: Overcoming the Secret Legacy of Male Depression*, therapist Terry Real writes, "We tend not to recognize depression in men because the disorder itself is seen as unmanly. . . [but] hidden depression drives several of the problems we think of as typically male: physical illness, alcohol and drug abuse, domestic violence, failures in intimacy, self-sabotage in careers."[20] There is still a lot of stigma around men reaching out for mental health help.

Many men worry that admitting they need help will be seen as a weakness or a failing. However, mental illness is like any other illness (which again, men are less likely to seek help for, unfortunately), but depression and anxiety are highly treatable! I hope to see a shift in men's acknowledgment of mental health as an integral part of wellness as a whole.

Just as we normalized going to the gym over the past fifty years, I hope that having a therapist will be eventually as accepted as having a trainer. Mental health is part of health. If you are suffering from depression, anxiety, or unaddressed trauma, it is like walking on a broken ankle. You're not performing at your best, and if anything, you might be permanently damaging yourself. Get the help you need to be your best self, mind and body.

Intellectual Health – Stimulating your intellectual curiosity and continuing to expand your learning is not only good for you as an individual, but it will also bring you into contact with others who are seeking to learn as well. The saying "If you're the smartest guy in the room, find a new room" is a good maxim to apply in this slice.

Intellectual challenges can look like getting outside of your comfort bubble and engaging with someone who has a different opinion from you, reading about a culture totally foreign to you, or learning about a specialty that you know little to nothing about. There are a variety of ways that you can learn new things and expand your intellectual prowess: documentaries, books, podcasts, scientific journals, new experiences, debates—I mean the list is really endless. And information is power. The more you know, the more accurately informed your decisions and actions will be.

Career Health – Having a sense of ownership and impact in your career is another important aspect of wellness. Knowing that your job and your career have the potential to bring you security and advancement can be an integral part of a man's self-esteem and sense of power in his ability to provide. However, this slice is one that I see men *over*identify with and overfill many, many times.

Your career cannot be your entire sense of self or the whole of your identity. It is one part of what makes your entire life feel stable and whole, but you cannot only exist in this one-eighth of the wellness pizza. The dangers of overidentification with career as identity can be manifold, but one of the biggest risks is when your sense of self-worth is attached to your career, your sense of self is based on something outside of your control.

After a sudden job loss, men who have placed their sense of identity in their careers are at a higher risk of depression and suicide than men who have not.[21] You are more than your job. Your job and what you do can be an important way you find meaning, belonging, and make an impact on the world, but it cannot be all that you are, or it will lead to an unhealthy, unbalanced psyche.

Environmental Health – Seeking balance is happening on a global, environmental scale. We are all a part of nature, and we neglect nature to our own detriment. Also, there are proven benefits to getting out into nature and letting our bodies interact with the natural environment.[22] Interacting with nature is also a way to cultivate a sense of resilience and adventure. As Sebastian Junger writes, "An adventure is a situation where the outcome is not entirely within your control."[23] When you allow yourself to experience a release of control, you also find the reach of your possibility. Being in nature soothes our nervous system, activates our sense of calm, renews our sense of wonder, and reminds us of our oneness with and dependence on our environment.

Michael Easter, author of the book *The Comfort Crisis: Embrace Discomfort to Reclaim Your Wild, Happy, Healthy Self,* created the 20:5:3 rule which you can use in this slice if you'd like. The rule is: Twenty minutes outside three times a week, five hours in nature once a month, and three days of "wilding" once a year. Getting out into nature for twenty minutes three times a week can be as simple as a walk in the neighborhood (as long as your neighborhood has nature). Five hours a month allows for more extended periods of enjoyment, i.e., visiting your local trails or lake on a weekend. Three days a year allows for a fully immersive nature experience, i.e., a camping trip to a state park or an off-grid hunting or fishing trip.

Whew, after eating that whole pie, you might be feeling a little overwhelmed or like "Jeez, how can you fit all this stuff in a day?" And the answer is—you can't. However, if you make an effort to give something to each sector on a regular basis, you will eventually find that you are more balanced and feeling more fulfilled and whole in the entirety of your life. It's little steps often that makes the difference.

Sometimes I see guys who are like "Great, I will live in this sector in my twenties, this sector in my thirties, and then devote time to these things later on in life."

Unfortunately, that's like saying, "Eating a balanced diet sounds like a lot, so I will eat only carbs for a month, only protein for another, only fats for another," and you see how unbalanced that kind of life would eventually be. You don't have to be perfect in allocating every minute of every day to be perfectly balanced, but take some time to glance at this wheel and assess each sector. Are you overfull in one area? Lacking in another?

It is very common for people to have one or two areas that get all their attention and energy, and other areas that are completely neglected. Just notice what might need a little attention moving forward and start to set yourself up for success by making your health a priority. Generosity begins at home—with you giving yourself permission to take care of you!

FINAL P'S

Earlier in this book we talked about 3 P's of masculinity, then we talked about the 3 P's of nurturing emotional connection, but now I want to talk about 3 P's in the context of simplifying and structuring self-care. I like to talk about this as the **Parts of Self**. When a client comes into my office and doesn't know where to start, I often ask them to check in with how they are doing as: a Person, a Professional, and as a Partner (sometimes I add Parent if that applies).

Where are you feeling good? Where are you needing a little more care or support? What's going well? What feels challenging? This practice can help you to remember that you are not just one thing all the time. You are a complex human being with complex needs and you can be doing amazing and feel really confident in one area, but need a little more care, support, and generosity in another.

At the end of the day, checking in with yourself as a Person, a Partner, a Professional, and a Parent will help you remember that health is in balance. A healthy you will be the major contributing factor to the overall health of your relationship. You cannot give what you do not have.

When you take care of your needs, you will not feel the need to keep score in your relationship. When you give to yourself generously, you can provide care and support to others from a place of abundance. Being generous with yourself by starting to balance your wheel will help you be generous in your relationships.

"There is only one way to eat an elephant: a bite at a time."

– DESMOND TUTU

TL; DR STEPS TO BUILDING GENEROSITY

1) TRIBE – Generosity is an essential part of being human. We are stronger together than alone. Generously tending to the needs of the relationship benefits everyone involved. Generosity is a quality that is a lot like unselfishness, but it doesn't veer into self-neglect.

2) MASTERY – You cannot give what you don't have. You can't be generous if you are starving. Taking care of your own

needs is not selfish, it's self-mastery. The importance of self-compassion outweighs self-esteem every time. You cannot hate yourself healthy. You have to love yourself enough to want to be a better person. As the psychotherapist Carl Rogers put it, "The curious paradox is that when I accept myself just as I am, then I can change."

3) PRESENCE – over presents. Connection is the key to a relationship that survives and one that doesn't. Giving generously of your time, energy, attention, and keeping a 5:1 positive to negative interaction ratio keeps the magic alive. Learning your partner's Love Language is a way to increase the opportunities for generosity in a relationship.

4) PIZZA – Wellness is balance. It's not about perfection every day, but it is about giving yourself a well-rounded, balanced life. Taking care of your physical, social, family, spiritual, mental, intellectual, career, and environmental health needs will help lead you closer to balance and a STRONG self-care routine.

SNACKS

"If you have built castles in the air,
your work need not be lost; that is where they should be.
Now put the foundations under them."

-HENRY DAVID THOREAU

This field guide to relationships is not the be all and end all. I was describing this book as a field guide to a friend, and you know, a field guide has some key pointers, things to look out for, things to try, things to avoid. It gives basic broad strokes information, but at the end of the day, the quality and experience of the journey is really up to you. How much did you plan? How much did you learn? How much did you take ownership of the experience?

There is no one "right way" to do a trip, but if you're going into a specific region or area (i.e., Equal, Healthy Relationship Park) then you might benefit from a field guide to that specific spot. However, if you are into other regions or want something completely different, there are lots of books and resources out there for you to find. Some of my favorite resources on sex, relationships, masculinity, and mental health are referenced throughout this book and in the bibliography. I have a running database of resources on my website: www.strong.

love/resources where I share new materials and resources for men as they continue to be created and I continue to discover them.

Also, as Dr. Alexandra Solomon says: "Go to couples therapy with your partner the first time they ask you to go."[1] On average, people think about divorce for one to three years before pulling the trigger.[2] Seriously, therapists are here to help if we can. But, if you wait too long, it may be too little too late. Studies have found that up to 26 percent of men had *no idea* there was a problem in their relationship until the woman brought up divorce.[3] Prevention is always better than cure.

> As every therapist will tell you, healing involves discomfort,
> but so does refusing to heal. And over time,
> refusing to heal is always more painful."
> – RESMAA MENAKEM

Do the work of becoming a STRONG man and give yourself a life full of STRONG relationships. Do the work, even if it's hard, even if you are the only man you know who is dedicated to doing something different. The biggest obstacle to growth is often the "crabs in the pot" mentality. However, every great endeavor in history started with a brave man (or woman) who was not afraid to stand outside the pack, to be the man in the arena, rather than a spectator on the sidelines of their own life.

You have endless and unlimited potential. No one else can unlock that potential. Not a job, not a woman, not a therapist. You have to be the one to show up. You have to be the one to do the work.

And no matter how you cut it, a STRONG relationship is work. This work is not for everyone, it is the harder path. But in the end, being Safe, Trustworthy, Respectful, Open, Nurturing, and Generous will make all the difference in your life and your relationships.

You are the master of your own destiny. Make your choices and make them honestly. If your life does not reflect your values, if you claim to hold values that are not reflected in your surroundings, interactions, or relationship with yourself, then embrace the challenge to change. Don't hold onto a life that's not yours for the fear of letting go into the unknown of possibility.

At the end of the day, change happens when you look at your life, relationships, and behaviors and realize that you are capable of so much more—*and* you want to do something about it. It happens when you hold yourself accountable to your own goals. All you have to do is start by giving yourself the chance to live the life and travel the road that will lead you to the most authentic and fulfilled version of yourself.

And just in case you haven't heard this in a while:

"You are braver than you believe, stronger than you seem, smarter than you think, and loved more than you'll ever know."

– A.A. MILNE

ACKNOWLEDGMENTS

This book would not be in the world without the support of my amazing friends, colleagues, and supporters. Thank you to all of you who have listened, given feedback, supported, and shared your wisdom with me.

Tiffany Berry and Lauren Little, thank you for dedicating your time, energy, and indefatigable minds to this project. Your perspectives, research, and teamwork have been instrumental in making this book a reality.

Johanna, thank you for your love, sisterhood, research, and support. I hope this book helps make the world a better place for Gunnar.

Husband, I would not be the person I am today without you. You are everything I never knew I always wanted. Thank you for being my rock and giving me unconditional love and encouragement.

Chey, thank you for being my family.

RESOURCES

FOR IMMEDIATE HELP:
The Lifeline: Text 988
1-800-273-TALK (8255)
https://988lifeline.org/

The Domestic Violence helpline:
1–800–799–SAFE (7233)
https://www.thehotline.org/

TO FIND A THERAPIST IN YOUR AREA:
Therapy Den: https://www.therapyden.com
Good Therapy: https://www.goodtherapy.org
The Inclusive Therapists' Directory: https://www.inclusivetherapists.com
US VETS: https://www.usvets.org
The Compassion Alliance: https://compassion-alliance.org/
SAMHSA: Substance Use Disorder help directory: https://www.samhsa.gov
NAMI: National Association for Mental Illness: https://nami.org
The National Center for PTSD: https://www.ptsd.va.gov/gethelp/find_therapist.asp
American Association of Sexuality Educators, Counselors, and Therapists: https://www.aasect.org
American Association of Marriage and Family Therapists: https://www.therapistlocator.net

FOR BOOK RECOMMENDATIONS AND OTHER RESOURCES:

FOR BIBLIOGRAPHY:

ENDNOTES

PREGAME: THOUGHTS ON A THEME

1   "Women More Likely than Men to Initiate Divorces, but Not Non-Marital Breakups," American Sociological Association, August 22, 2015 https://www.asanet.org/women-more-likely-men-initiate-divorces-not-non-marital-breakups/.

2   "The 3 P's Of Manhood: A Review," The Art Of Manliness, last modifie March 31, 2014, https://www.artofmanliness.com/character/behavior/th 3-ps-of-manhood-a-review/.

3   Esha Sarai, "Gun Ownership Steadily Increasing Among US Women," Voice of America, July 3, 2021, https://www.voanews.com/a/usa_gun-ownership-steadily-increasing-among-us-women/6207787.html.

4   "The Cut: Exploring Financial Wellness Within Diverse Populations," The Prudential Insurance Company of America, 2018, https://news.prudential.com/content/1209/files/PrudentialTheCutExploringFinancialWellnessWithinDiversePopulation pdf.

5   National Women's Business Council Annual Report, 2020, https://cdn.www.nwbc.gov/wp-content/uploads/2020/12/21113833/pdf/NWBC-2020-Annual-Report-Final.pdf.

6   Jess Cockerill, "More Adults Are Choosing to Live Childfree and They Probably Won't Change Their Minds," *Science Alert*, August 2, 2022, https://www.sciencealert.com/more-adults-are-choosing-to-live-child-fre and-no-they-probably-won-t-change-their-minds.

7   James Findlay, "Why Aren't Straight Women Having as Many Orgasms as Men?", Australian Broadcasting Corporation, September 20, 2017, https://www.abc.net.au/triplej/programs/the-hook-up/closing-the-orgas gap:-why-arent-straight-women-having-as-man/8963526.

8   David A. Frederick et al., "Differences in Orgasm Frequency Among Gay, Lesbian, Bisexual, and Heterosexual Men and Women in a U.S.

National Sample," *Archives of Sexual Behavior* 47 (2018), https://doi.org/10.1007/s10508-017-0939-z.

9   Andreas Walther et al., "Status Loss Due to COVID-19, Traditional Masculinity, and Their Association with Recent Suicide Attempts and Suicidal Ideation," *Psychology of Men & Masculinities* (2022), https://doi.org/10.1037/men0000408.

10   Jennifer Wright, "Millennial Men Want 1950s Housewives after They Have Kids," *New York Post*, May 7, 2022, https://nypost.com/2022/05/07/millennial-men-want-1950s-housewives-after-they-have-kids/.

11   Wendy Wang and Paul Taylor, "For Millennials, Parenthood Trumps Marriage," Pew Research Center, March 9, 2011, https://www.pewresearch.org/social-trends/2011/03/09/iii-millennials-attitudes-about-marriage/.

12   Cady Lang, "Singles Are Starting to Care Less about Looks. Here's What They Want Instead," *TIME*, November 9, 2021, https://time.com/6115383/match-singles-in-america-study-2021/.

CHAPTER ONE: SAFETY

1   "The Sexes' Sense of Safety," Farah & Farah, https://farahandfarah.com/studies/sexes-sense-of-safety/.

2   Steven Crabtree and Faith Nsubuga, "Women Feel Less Safe than Men in Many Developed Countries," Gallup, Inc., July 6, 2012, https://news.gallup.com/poll/155402/women-feel-less-safe-men-developed-countries.aspx.

3   Amanda Barroso, "Key Takeaways on Americans' Views of and Experiences with Dating and Relationships," Pew Research Center, August 20, 2020, https://www.pewresearch.org/fact-tank/2020/08/20/key-takeaways-on-americans-views-of-and-experiences-with-dating-and-relationships/.

4   "Marriage and Divorce," Centers for Disease Control and Prevention, 2019, https://www.cdc.gov/nchs/fastats/marriage-divorce.htm.

5   Beth Bailey, "The Marriage Crisis," review of *Marriage, a History: How Love Conquered Marriage* by Stephanie Coontz, May 14, 2005, https://www.chicagotribune.com/news/ct-xpm-2005-05-15-0505140051-story.html.

6   W. Bradford Wilcox, "The Evolution of Divorce," *National Affairs*,
       September 2009, https://www.nationalaffairs.com/publications/
       detail/the-evolution-of-divorce.

7   Brené Brown, *Braving the Wilderness: The Quest for True Belonging
       and the Courage to Stand Alone* (New York: Random House, 2019).

8   Joe Luft and Harry Ingham, "The Johari window, a graphic model
       of interpersonal awareness," proceedings of the Western Training
       Laboratory in Group Development, Los Angeles: UCLA, 1995.

9   John Mordechai Gottman and Nan Silver, *The Seven Principles to
       Making Marriage Work* (New York: Crown Publishers, 1999).

10   Brian G. Ogolsky, Renée Peltz Dennison, and James Kale Monk,
       "The Role of Couple Discrepancies in Cognitive and Behavioral
       Egalitarianism in Marital Quality," *Sex Roles* 70, 7-8 (2014): 329–
       342, https://doi.org/10.1007/s11199-014-0365-9.

11   Carly Marie, ed., "Having a Clean House Is Preferable to Sex,
       according to New Study," *The Versed*, May 20, 2019, https://www.
       theversed.com/96356/having-a-clean-house-is-preferable-to-sex-
       according-to-newstudy/#.4x0iOiY1ix.

12   Matthew D. Johnson, Nancy L. Galambos, and Jared R. Anderson,
       "Skip the Dishes? Not so Fast! Sex and Housework Revisited,"
       Journal of Family Psychology 30 (2): 203–13, https://doi.org/10.1037/
       fam0000161.

13   Stephen W. Porges, "Polyvagal Theory: A Science of Safety," *Frontiers
       in Integrative Neuroscience* 16 (May 2022), https://doi.org/10.3389/
       fnint.2022.871227

14   [26] University of Colorado at Boulder, "Your brain on imagination:
       It's a lot like reality, study shows," *ScienceDaily*, https://www.
       sciencedaily.com/releases/2018/12/181210144943.htm (accessed
       November 13, 2022).

15   Jean-Philippe Gouin, "Chronic Stress, Immune Dysregulation, and
       Health." *American Journal of Lifestyle Medicine* 5, 6 (2011): 476–85,
       https://doi.org/10.1177/1559827610395467.

16   Daniel J. Siegel, *The Mindful Therapist: A Clinician's Guide to
       Mindsight and Neural Integration* (New York: W.W. Norton & Co.,
       2010).

17 "It's so Much More than Just Fight or Flight," (blog), PTSDUK, 2022, https://www.ptsduk.org/its-so-much-more-than-just-fight-or-flight/.

18 Pete Walker, *Complex PTSD: From Surviving to Thriving: A Guide and Map for Recovering from Childhood Trauma*, (Lafayette, CA: Azure Coyote, 2013).

19 Hyoun K. Kim et al., "Emotion Dysregulation in the Intergenerational Transmission of Romantic Relationship Conflict," *Journal of Family Psychology* 23, 4 (2009): 585–95, https://doi.org/10.1037/a0015935.

20 Vincent J. Felitti et al., "Relationship of Childhood Abuse and Household Dysfunction to Many of the Leading Causes of Death in Adults," *American Journal of Preventive Medicine* 14, 4 (1998): 245–58, https://doi.org/10.1016/s0749-3797(98)00017-8.

21 A. Ma et al., "The mutual constitution of culture and psyche: The bidirectional relationship between individuals' perceived control and cultural tightness–looseness," *Journal of Personality and Social Psychology*, 2022, https://doi.org/10.1037/pspa0000327.

22 "Partner controlling behaviors appear to be associated with relationship violence," ScienceDaily, accessed November 14, 2022, https://www.sciencedaily.com/releases/2011/04/110404161708.htm.

23 Thomas Scheff, "Repression of Emotion: A Danger to Modern Societies?", *Emotions in Politics* (London Borough of Camden: Palgrave Macmillan, 2013) 84–92, https://doi.org/10.1057/9781137025661_5.

24 Jennifer S. Lerner et al., "Emotion and Decision Making," *Annual Review of Psychology* 66 (January 2015): 799-823, https://www.annualreviews.org/doi/10.1146/annurev-psych-010213-115043.

25 Rupa Gupta et al., "The Amygdala and Decision-Making," *Neuropsychologia* 49, 4 (2011): 760–66, https://doi.org/10.1016/j.neuropsychologia.2010.09.029.

26 Travis Bradberry, "Emotional Intelligence – EQ," *Forbes*, January 9, 2014, https://www.forbes.com/sites/travisbradberry/2014/01/09/emotional-intelligence/.

27 Frans de Waal, "The Surprising Science of Alpha Males," July 9, 2018, TED, video, 15:54, https://www.youtube.com/watch?v=BPsSKKL8N0s.

28   Jared S. Allen et al., "What Matters More for Entrepreneurship Success? A Meta-Analysis Comparing General Mental Ability and Emotional Intelligence in Entrepreneurial Settings," *Strategic Entrepreneurship Journal* 15, 3 (September 2021): 352-76, https://doi.org/10.1002/sej.1377.

29   Jainish Patel and Prittesh Patel, "Consequences of Repression of Emotion: Physical Health, Mental Health and General Well Being," International Journal of Psychotherapy Practice and Research 1, 3 (February 12, 2019): 16–21, https://doi.org/10.14302/issn.2574-612x.ijpr-18-2564.

30   Benjamin P. Chapman et al., "Emotion Suppression and Mortality Risk over a 12-Year Follow-Up," *Journal of Psychosomatic Research* 75, 4 (2013): 381–85, https://doi.org/10.1016/j.jpsychores.2013.07.014.

31   Gabor Maté, *When the Body Says No: The Cost of Hidden Stress*, (London: Vermilion 2019), 38.

32   Jill Bolte Taylor, *Whole Brain Living* (London: Hay House, 2021).

33   Terrence Real, *I Don't Want to Talk about It: Overcoming the Secret Legacy of Male Depression*, (New York: Fireside 2003), 146.

CHAPTER TWO: TRUST

1   John M. Gottman, *The Science of Trust: Emotional Attunement for Couples* (New York: W.W. Norton & Company, 2011).

2   "Serve and Return," Center on the Developing Child, Harvard University, 2021, https://developingchild.harvard.edu/science/key-concepts/serve-and-return/.

3   Mary D. Salter Ainsworth and S. M. Bell, "Attachment, Exploration, and Separation: Illustrated by the Behavior of One-Year-Olds in a Strange Situation," *Child Development* 41, 1 (March 1970): 49–67, https://www.jstor.org/stable/1127388.

4   Deb A. Dana, *The Polyvagal Theory in Therapy: Engaging the Rhythm of Regulation* (New York: W. W. Norton & Company 2018).

5   Carla J. Schatz "The developing brain," *Scientific American* 267, 3 (1992): 60-67.

CHAPTER THREE: RESPECT

1   David De Cremer and Laetitia B. Mulder, "A Passion for Respect: On Understanding the Role of Human Needs and Morality," *Gruppe. Interaktion. Organisation. Zeitschrift Für Angewandte Organisationspsychologie (GIO)* 38, no. 4 (December 1, 2007): 439–49, https://link.springer.com/article/10.1007/s11612-007-0036-1.

2   Brené Brown, "Clear Is Kind. Unclear Is Unkind," Brené Brown, October 28, 2021, https://brenebrown.com/articles/2018/10/15/clear-is-kind-unclear-is-unkind/.

3   Esther Perel, *Mating in Captivity: Reconciling the Erotic + the Domestic* (New York: HarperCollins 2006).

4   James Clear, "Core Values List," James Clear, June 12, 2018, https://jamesclear.com/core-values.

CHAPTER FOUR: OPENNESS

1   "Survey: Certified Divorce Financial Analyst® (CDFA®) Professionals Reveal the Leading Causes of Divorce," Institute for Divorce Financial Analysis, August 2013, https://institutedfa.com/Leading-Causes-Divorce/.

2   Susan L. Brown and I-Fen Lin, "Gray Divorce: A Growing Risk Regardless of Class or Education," Council on Contemporary Families, n.d., https://sites.utexas.edu/contemporaryfamilies/2014/10/08/growing-risk-brief-report/.

3   Benjamin Gurrentz and Yeris Mayol-Garcia, "Marriage, Divorce, Widowhood Remain Prevalent among Older Populations," United States Census Bureau, April 21, 2021, https://www.census.gov/library/stories/2021/04/love-and-loss-among-older-adults.html.

4   Renee Stepler, "Led by Baby Boomers, Divorce Rates Climb for America's 50+ Population," Pew Research Center, March 9, 2017, https://www.pewresearch.org/fact-tank/2017/03/09/led-by-baby-boomers-divorce-rates-climb-for-americas-50-population/.

5   P. C. Wason, "On the Failure to Eliminate Hypotheses in a Conceptual Task," *Quarterly Journal of Experimental Psychology* 12, 3 (1960): 129–40, https://doi.org/10.1080/17470216008416717.

6   Jason Headley, "It's Not About the Nail," May 22, 2013, video, 1:41, https://www.youtube.com/watch?v=-4EDhdAHrOg.
7   Brené Brown, *The Call to Courage*, Netflix, 2019, https://www.netflix.com/title/81010166.

CHAPTER FIVE: NURTURING

1   Lesley-Anne Johannes, "It's in the Brain, Dads are Wired to be as Nurturing as Mothers," News 24, September 20, 2018, https://www.news24.com/parent/Family/Parenting/its-in-the-brain-dads-are-wired-to-be-as-nurturing-as-mothers-20180920.
2   Marc Grau Grau, Mireia las Heras Maestro, and Hannah Bowles, *Engaged Fatherhood for Men, Families and Gender Equality: Healthcare, Social Policy, and Work Perspectives*, (New York: Springer Publishing 2021).
3   *Cambridge English Dictionary*, s.v. "Nurture," (n.d.), https://dictionary.cambridge.org/us/dictionary/english/nurture.
4   *Cambridge English Dictionary*, s.v. "Maintenance," (n.d.), https://dictionary.cambridge.org/us/dictionary/english/maintenance
5   Annabel Amodia-Bidakowska, Ciara Laverty, and Paul G. Ramchandani, "Father-Child Play: A Systematic Review of Its Frequency, Characteristics and Potential Impact on Children's Development," *Developmental Review* 57 (September 2020): 100924, https://doi.org/10.1016/j.dr.2020.100924.
6   Julie Vadnal, "Women Aren't Having Orgasms. Men Don't Know Why. Let's Talk About It," *Men's Health*, November 16, 2018, https://www.menshealth.com/sex-women/a25164827/women-orgasm-gap/.
7   Nathan D. Leonhardt et al., "The Significance of the Female Orgasm: A Nationally Representative, Dyadic Study of Newlyweds' Orgasm Experience," *The Journal of Sexual Medicine* 15, 8 (2018): 1140–48, https://doi.org/10.1016/j.jsxm.2018.05.018.
8   Jun Kyu Mun et al., "Sleep and Libido in Men with Obstructive Sleep Apnea Syndrome," *Sleep Medicine* 52 (December): 158–62, https://doi.org/10.1016/j.sleep.2018.07.016.
9   John L. Arnett, John A. Toews, and Harry Prosen, "Loss of Libido Due to Stress," *Medical Aspects of Human Sexuality* 20 (1): 140–48, https://psycnet.apa.org/record/1987-22551-001.

10   Victoria Holloway and Kevan Wylie, "Sex Drive and Sexual Desire," *Current Opinion in Psychiatry* 28 (6): 424–29, https://doi.org/10.1097/yco.0000000000000199.

11   Anthony C. Hackney et al., "Endurance Training and Male Sexual Libido. Edited by American College of Sports Medicine," *Medicine & Science in Sports & Exercise*, February 2017, https://www.researchgate.net/profile/Anthony-Hackney/publication/313740861_Endurance_Exercise_Training_and_Male_Sexual_Libido/links/5a65d3eca6fdccb61c58dfc3/Endurance-Exercise-Training-and-Male-Sexual-Libido.pdf.

12   Kenneth A.Hirsch, "Sexual Dysfunction in Male Operation Enduring Freedom/Operation Iraqi Freedom Patients with Severe Post-Traumatic Stress Disorder," *Military Medicine* 174, 5 (2009): 520–22, https://doi.org/10.7205/milmed-d-03-3508

13   Harvey Sternbach, "Age-Associated Testosterone Decline in Men: Clinical Issues for Psychiatry," *American Journal of Psychiatry* 155, 10 (1998): 1310–18, https://doi.org/10.1176/ajp.155.10.1310

14   James G. Pfaus and Lisa A. Scepkowski, "The Biologic Basis for Libido," *Current Sexual Health Reports* 2, 2 (2005): 95–100, https://doi.org/10.1007/s11930-005-0010-2.

15   Emily Nagoski, "Pleasure Is the Measure," *Medium*, August 19, 2015, https://enagoski.medium.com/pleasure-is-the-measure-d8c5a2dff33f.

16   Osmo Kontula, and Anneli Miettinen, "Determinants of Female Sexual Orgasms," *Socioaffective Neuroscience & Psychology* 6 (1): 31624, https://doi.org/10.3402/snp.v6.31624.

17   K. McKenna, "SSI Grand Master Lecture 3 'the Brain Is the Master Organ in Sexual Function: Central Nervous System Control of Male and Female Sexual Function,'" *International Journal of Impotence Research* 11 (S1): S48–55, https://doi.org/10.1038/sj.ijir.3900484.

18   Robin Chester, "Intimacy Domains in Men as a Predictor of Their Relational Satisfaction" (Master's thesis, Tennessee State University, 2011), https://www.proquest.com/openview/437d4261d27cfa5003b73f10c7834807/1?pq-origsite=gscholar&cbl=18750.

19   Associated Press-WE tv "Poll: Most Men Aspire to Be Dads." 2013. KnowlegePanel https://www.usatoday.com/story/news/nation/2013/06/15/poll-most-men-aspire-to-be-dads/2427123.

20   Karen L. Kramer and Amanda Veile, "Infant Allocare in Traditional Societies," *Physiology & Behavior* 193 (Pt A): 117–126, https://doi.org/10.1016/j.physbeh.2018.02.054.

21   Ralph LaRossa, "The Culture and Conduct of Fatherhood in America, 1800 to 1960," *Kazoku Syakaigaku Kenkyu* 19, 2 (2007): 87-98, https://doi.org/10.4234/jjoffamilysociology.19.2_87.

22   Gabriel Rosenberg, "Fetishizing Family Farms," *The Boston Globe*, April 10, 2016, https://www.bostonglobe.com/ideas/2016/04/09/fetishizing-family-farms/NJszoKdCSQWaq2XBw7kvIL/story.html.

23   Ralph LaRossa, *The Modernization of Fatherhood: A Social and Political History* (Chicago: University of Chicago Press 1997) 1-21.

24   Michael S Kimmel, "What Do Men Want?", *Harvard Business Review* (November-December 1993), https://hbr.org/1993/11/what-do-men-want.

25   Joanna Syrda, "Spousal Relative Income and Male Psychological Distress," *Personality and Social Psychology Bulletin* 46, 6 (October 2019), https://doi.org/10.1177/0146167219883611.

26   Kim Parker and Renee Stapler, "Americans See Men as the Financial Providers, Even as Women's Contributions Grow," Pew Research Center, https://www.pewresearch.org/fact-tank/2017/09/20/americans-see-men-as-the-financial-providers-even-as-womens-contributions-grow/.

27   Rachel Melton Chavarria, "Stay-At-Home-Fathers and the Absence of Masculine Identity," (Master's thesis, Texas Tech University, 2011), https://ttu-ir.tdl.org/bitstream/handle/2346/ETD-TTU-2011-08-1425/MELTON-CHAVARRIA-THESIS.pdf.

28   Barbara J. Risman and Pepper Schwartz, *Gender in Intimate Relationships: A Microstructural Approach*, (Belmont: Wadsworth 1989) 138-54.

29   Matt Hancock, "Kentucky Takes a Leading Role with the Nation's Best Joint-Custody Law," The Courier-Journal, accessed November 20, 2022.

30   B. J. Zvara, Sarah J. Schoppe-Sullivan, and Claire M. Kamp Dush, "Fathers' Involvement in Child Health Care: Associations with Prenatal Involvement, Parents' Beliefs, and Maternal Gatekeeping," *Family Relations* 62, 4 (2013): 649–61, https://doi.org/10.1111/fare.12023.

31   Elizabeth A. Cannon et al., "Parent Characteristics as Antecedents of Maternal Gatekeeping and Fathering Behavior," *Family*

Process 47, 4 (2008): 501–19, https://doi.org/10.1111/j.1545-5300.2008.00268.x.

32   Zvara, "Fathers' Involvement."

33   Sarah J. Schoppe-Sullivan et al., "The Best and Worst of Times: Predictors of New Fathers' Parenting Satisfaction and Stress," *Adversity and Resilience Science* 2, 2 (2021): 71–83, https://doi.org/10.1007/s42844-021-00032-y.

34   Anna L. Olsavsky et al., "New Fathers' Perceptions of Dyadic Adjustment: The Roles of Maternal Gatekeeping and Coparenting Closeness," *Family Process* (April 2019), https://doi.org/10.1111/famp.12451.

35   Wonjung Oh, Seowon Song, and Sylvia Niehuis, "Processes Linking Mothers' Perceptions of Relationship Satisfaction with Their Partner, Coparenting, and Parenting to Children's Competence and Behavior Problems," *Family Science Review* 25, 1 (2021), https://doi.org/10.26536/rhst4996.

36   Gretchen Livingston and Kim Parker, "8 Facts about American Dads," Pew Research Center (Pew Research Center, June 12, 2019), https://www.pewresearch.org/fact-tank/2019/06/12/fathers-day-facts/.

37   "Parenting in America," Pew Research Center's Social and Demographic Trends Project (December 17, 2015), https://www.pewresearch.org/social-trends/2015/12/17/parenting-in-america/.

38   Paul Taylor, "A Tale of Two Fathers More Are Active, but More Are Absent Social & Demographic Trends," 2011, https://www.pewresearch.org/wp-content/uploads/sites/3/2011/06/fathers-FINAL-report.pdf.

39   Kari Adamsons and Sara K. Johnson, "An Updated and Expanded Meta-Analysis of Nonresident Fathering and Child Well-Being," *Journal of Family Psychology* 27, 4 (2013): 589-599, https://doi.org/10.1037/a0033786.

40   Nadya Pancsofar and Lynne Vernon-Feagans, "Fathers' Early Contributions to Children's Language Development in Families from Low-Income Rural Communities," *Early Childhood Research Quarterly* 25, 4 (2010): 450–63, https://doi.org/10.1016/j.ecresq.2010.02.001.

41 Kevin Shafer, "Nurturing Dads Raise Emotionally Intelligent
    Kids – Helping Make Society More Respectful and Equitable," *The
    Conversation,* June 16, 2021, https://theconversation.com/nurturing-
    dads-raise-emotionally-intelligent-kids-helping-make-society-more-
    respectful-and-equitable-161395.

42 Sarah Allen and Kerry Daly, "The Effects of Father Involvement: An
    Updated Research Summary of the Evidence.," Father Involvement
    Research Alliance, (May 2007), https://fatherhood.gov/research-
    and-resources/effects-father-involvement-updated-researchsummary-
    evidence.

43 "The Elephant Rope," Motivational Stories (blog), AcademicTips,
    accessed November 20, 2022, https://academictips.org/blogs/the-
    elephant-rope/.

44 Pelin Gul and Ayse K. Uskul, "Men's Perceptions and Emotional
    Responses to Becoming a Caregiver Father: The Role of Individual
    Differences in Masculine Honor Ideals and Reputation Concerns,"
    Frontiers in Psychology (June 2019), https://www.frontiersin.org/
    articles/10.3389/fpsyg.2019.01442/full.

45 Kristi Walker, Kristen Blallk, and Patrick van Kessel, "Strong Men,
    Caring Women," Pew Research Study: Social Trends, July 2018,
    https://www.pewresearch.org/social-trends/interactives/strong-men-
    caring-women/.

46 Peggy Orenstein, *Boys & Sex Young Men on Hookups, Love, Porn,
    Consent, and Navigating the New Masculinity* (New York: Harper
    2020).

47 Amanda Barroso, "For American Couples, Gender Gaps in Sharing
    Household Responsibilities Persist amid Pandemic," Pew Research
    Center (January 25, 2021), https://www.pewresearch.org/fact-
    tank/2021/01/25/for-american-couples-gender-gaps-in-sharing-
    household-responsibilities-persist-amid-pandemic/.

48 Katherine Schaeffer, "Among U.S. Couples, Women Do More
    Cooking and Grocery Shopping than Men," Pew Research
    Center, September 24, 2019, https://www.pewresearch.org/fact-
    tank/2019/09/24/among-u-s-couples-women-do-more-cooking-and-
    grocery-shopping-than-men/.

49   Audrey Cade, "Divorce Made My Ex a Better Father," *Divorced Moms*, November 27, 2017, https://divorcedmoms.com/blogs/divorce-warrior/divorce-made-ex-better-father.

50   Malcolm Gladwell, *Outliers: The Story of Success*, San Francisco: Little, Brown and Company 2008).

51   Corinn Voeller, Passive Responsibility vs Active Responsibility #Relationships #Therapy #ThatCloseMessenger #Marriage #IDeserveTuitionContest, TikTok, https://www.tiktok.com/@corrinthecounselor/video/7010078014914563334.

52   Sari M. van Anders et al., "The Heteronormativity Theory of Low Sexual Desire in Women Partnered with Men." *Archives of Sexual Behavior*, August 2021, https://doi.org/10.1007/s10508-021-02100-x.

53   Matthew Fray, "She Divorced Me Because I Left Dishes by the Sink," January 14, 2016, https://matthewfray.com/2016/01/14/she-divorced-me-because-i-left-dishes-by-the-sink/.

54   Tamara Markard, "When the Ties That Bind Are Cut: The Silent Epidemic of Parental Estrangement," *Greeley Tribune*, June 19, 2022, https://www.greeleytribune.com/2022/06/11/cp/.

55   Rin Rezeck, Lawrence Stacey, and Mieke Beth Thomeer, "Parent–Adult Child Estrangement in the United States by Gender, Race/Ethnicity, and Sexuality," *Journal of Marriage and Family*, December 2022, https://doi.org/10.1111/jomf.12898.

56   Kylie Agllias, "Missing Family: The Adult Child's Experience of Parental Estrangement," *Journal of Social Work Practice* 32, 1 (May 11, 2017): 59–72, https://doi.org/10.1080/02650533.2017.1326471.

57   James Dean, "Pillemer: Family Estrangement a Problem 'Hiding in Plain Sight,'" *Cornell Chronicle*, September 10, 2020, https://news.cornell.edu/stories/2020/09/pillemer-family-estrangement-problem-hiding-plain-sight.

58   Anahad O'Connor, "The Secrets to a Happy Life, from a Harvard Study," *Well*, March 23, 2016, https://archive.nytimes.com/well.blogs.nytimes.com/2016/03/23/the-secrets-to-a-happy-life-from-a-harvard-study/?_r=0.

59   Robert Waldinger, "What makes a good life? Lessons from the
     longest study on happiness," filmed January 25, 2016, video, 12:46,
     https://www.ted.com/talks/robert_waldinger_what_makes_a_good_
     life_lessons_from_the_longest_study_on_happiness.

60   Daniel A. Cox, Brent Orrell, and Karlyn Bowman, "The State of
     American Friendship: Change, Challenges, and Loss," Survey Center
     on American Life, April 7, 2022, https://www.americansurveycenter.
     org/research/the-state-of-american-friendship-change-challenges-and-
     loss/.

61   Brant R. Burleson, "A Different Voice on Different Cultures:
     Illusion and Reality in the Study of Sex Differences in Personal
     Relationships," *Personal Relationships* 4, 3 (1997): 229-241, https://
     doi.org/10.1111/j.1475-6811.1997.tb00142.x.

62   Christian Hakulinen et al., "Social isolation and loneliness as risk
     factors for myocardial infarction, stroke and mortality: UK Biobank
     cohort study of 479 054 men and women," *Heart (British Cardiac
     Society)* 104, 18 (September 2018): 1536-1542, https://heart.bmj.
     com/content/104/18/1536.

63   Javier Yanguas, Sacramento Pinazo-Henandis, and Francisco José
     Tarazona-Santabalbina, "The Complexity of Loneliness," *Acta
     Bio Medica: Atenei Parmensis* 89, 2 (2018): 302–14, https://doi.
     org/10.23750/abm.v89i2.7404.

64   Samia Akhter-Khan et al., "Associations of Loneliness with Risk of
     Alzheimer's Disease Dementia in the Framingham Heart Study,"
     Alzheimer's & Dementia (March 2021), https://doi.org/10.1002/
     alz.12327.

65   Stephen Neville et al., "Loneliness in Men 60 Years and Over: The
     Association with Purpose in Life," *American Journal of Men's Health*
     12, 4 (2018): 730–39, https://doi.org/10.1177/1557988318758807.

66   Richard J. Shaw et al., "Living Alone, Loneliness and Lack of
     Emotional Support as Predictors of Suicide and Self-Harm: A Nine-
     Year Follow up of the UK Biobank Cohort," *Journal of Affective
     Disorders* 279 (January 2021): 316–23, https://doi.org/10.1016/j.
     jad.2020.10.026.

67   Carin Lennartsson, Johan Rehnberg, and Lena Dahlberg, "The
     Association between Loneliness, Social Isolation and All-Cause

Mortality in a Nationally Representative Sample of Older Women and Men," *Aging & Mental Health* 26, 9 (September 22, 2021): 1–8, https://doi.org/10.1080/13607863.2021.1976723.

68   "Dying Alone: An Interview with Eric Klinenberg," University of Chicago Press, 2002, https://press.uchicago.edu/Misc/Chicago/443213in.html.

69   William J. Chopik, "Associations among Relational Values, Support, Health, and Well-Being across the Adult Lifespan," *Personal Relationships* 24, no. 2 (April 19, 2017): 408-422, https://doi.org/10.1111/pere.12187.

70   Mark Greene, "Why Men's Friendships Can Feel so EMPTY," *Medium*, May 3, 2018, https://remakingmanhood.medium.com/why-mens-friendships-can-feel-so-empty-5fd0f5dbfbdf.

71   Brian Keum et al., "Distress Disclosure and Psychological Distress among Men: The Role of Feeling Understood and Loneliness," *Current Psychology* (August 2021), https://doi.org/10.1007/s12144-021-02163-y.

72   Melanie Hamlett, "Men Have No Friends and Women Bear the Burden," *Harper's BAZAAR*, May 2, 2019, https://www.harpersbazaar.com/culture/features/a27259689/toxic-masculinity-male-friendships-emotional-labor-men-rely-on-women/.

73   Lauren Menzie, "Stacys, Beckys, and Chads: The Construction of Femininity and Hegemonic Masculinity within Incel Rhetoric," *Psychology & Sexuality* 13, 1 (2020), https://doi.org/10.1080/19419899.2020.1806915.

74   Lauren Larson, "The Men Who Have Mostly Female Friends," *GQ*, May 9, 2019, https://www.gq.com/story/men-with-mostly-female-friends.

75   Randi Mazzella, "Bromance: The Truth about Male Friendships Right Now," PSYCOM, October 28, 2022, https://www.psycom.net/relationships/bromance-guy-relationships.

76   Stefan Robinson, Adam White, and Eric Anderson, "Privileging the Bromance," *Men and Masculinities* (October 2017), 1097184X1773038, https://doi.org/10.1177/1097184x17730386.

77   Julia Furlan, "Men Can Have Better Friendships. Here's How," NPR, August 23, 2019, https://www.npr.org/2019/08/19/752412752/men-can-have-better-friendships-heres-how.

1   *Cambridge Dictionary*, s.v., "generosity," https://dictionary.cambridge.
    org/us/dictionary/english/generosity.

CHAPTER SIX: GENEROSITY

2   Andrew W. Delton et al., "Evolution of Direct Reciprocity
    Under Uncertainty Can Explain Human Generosity in One-Shot
    Encounters," *Proceedings of the National Academy of Sciences* 108, 32
    (2011): 13335–40, https://doi.org/10.1073/pnas.1102131108.
3   Summer Allan, "The Science of Generosity," Greater Good Science
    Center at University of Berkeley, May 2018, https://ggsc.berkeley.
    edu/images/uploads/GGSC-JTF_White_Paper-Generosity-FINAL.
    pdf.
4   Katherine Unger Baillie, "Penn Biologists Show That Generosity
    Leads to Evolutionary Success," *Penn Today*, September 3, 2013,
    https://penntoday.upenn.edu/news/penn-biologists-show-generosity-
    leads-evolutionary-success.
5   "Computational Modeling," The Human Generosity Project,
    accessed November 19, 2022, http://www.humangenerosity.org/
    computational-modeling/.
6   Leah Shaffer, "Human Generosity Study Shows Altruistic Societies
    Better Survive Hard Times," *Discover Magazine*, February 25, 2019,
    https://www.discovermagazine.com/planet-earth/human-generosity-
    study-shows-altruistic-societies-better-survive-hard-times.
7   Delton, "Evolution."
8   Jennifer Tzeses, "Why Self-Compassion Is More Important than
    Self-Esteem," PSYCOM, June 1, 2020, https://www.psycom.net/self-
    compassion.
9   Juliana G. Breines and Serena Chen, "Self-Compassion
    Increases Self-Improvement Motivation," *Personality and
    Social Psychology Bulletin* 38, 9 (2012): 1133–43, https://doi.
    org/10.1177/0146167212445599.
10 T. Krieger et al., "An Internet-Based Compassion-Focused
    Intervention for Increased Self-Criticism: A Randomized Controlled
    Trial," *Behavior Therapy* 50, 2 (2019): 430–445, https://doi.
    org/10.1016/j.beth.2018.08.003
11 David Robson, "Why Self-Compassion – Not Self-Esteem – Leads
    to Success," BBC, January 13, 2021, https://www.bbc.com/worklife/

article/20210111-why-self-compassion-not-self-esteem-leads-to-success.

12   Tara Brach, "Reaching out for Compassion," April 22, 2014, https://www.tarabrach.com/reaching-out-for-compassion/.

13   K. T. Buehlman, J. M. Gottman, and L. F. Katz, "How a couple views their past predicts their future: Predicting divorce from an oral history interview," *Journal of Family Psychology*, 5, 3-4, (1992): 295–318, https://doi.org/10.1037/0893-3200.5.3-4.295.

14   "Overview – Research," The Gottman Institute, 2015, https://www.gottman.com/about/research/couples.

15   Gary D. Chapman and Jocelyn Green, *The 5 Love Languages: The Secret to Love That Lasts*, (Chicago: Northfield Publishing 2017).

16   "The Love Language Quiz," 5 Love Languages, 2022, https://5lovelanguages.com/quizzes/love-language.

17   A. Hobson, *The Oxford Dictionary of Difficult Words* (1st ed.), (Oxford: Oxford University Press 2004).

18   Kristin D. Neff and Roos Vonk, "Self-Compassion Versus Global Self-Esteem: Two Different Ways of Relating to Oneself," *Journal of Personality* 77, 1 (February 2009): 23–50, https://doi.org/10.1111/j.1467-6494.2008.00537.x.

19   Viktor E. Frankl, Harold S. Kushner, and William J. Winslade, *Man's Search for Meaning*, (Boston: Beacon Press 2006).

20   Real, *I Don't Want to Talk about It.*

21   Walther et al., "Status loss due to COVID-19."

22   Colin A. Capaldi, Raelyne L. Dopko, and John M. Zelenski, "The Relationship Between Nature Connectedness and Happiness: A Meta-Analysis," *Frontiers in Psychology* 5 (September 8, 2014), https://doi.org/10.3389/fpsyg.2014.00976.

23   Sebastian Junger, *Fire* (New York: W.W. Norton 2001) 150.

POST GAME: SNACKS

1   Alexandra Solomon, "Three Fights That Mean It's Time for Couples Therapy," Dr. Alexandra Solomon, November 30, 2015, https://dralexandrasolomon.com/common-fights/.

2   The National Divorce Decision-Making Project, "What Are They
    Thinking? A National Survey of Married Individuals Who Are
    Thinking About Divorce," 2015, Provo, UT: Family Studies Center,
    Brigham Young University.
3   Xenia P. Montenegro, "The Divorce Experience: A Study of Divorce
    at Midlife and Beyond," Washington, DC: AARP Research, May
    2004.

Printed in the USA
CPSIA information can be obtained
at www.ICGtesting.com
LVHW051522221223
767218LV00071B/2352